The
HARDEST SERMONS
You'll Ever Have to
PREACH

Help from Trusted Preachers
for Tragic Times

THE
HARDEST SERMONS
YOU'LL EVER HAVE TO
PREACH

CONTRIBUTORS:
Tim Keller, John Piper,
Michael Horton, Jerram Barrs,
Dan Doriani, Robert S. Rayburn,
Mike Khandjian, Wilson Benton,
Bob Flayhart, Jack Collins,
George Robertson

BRYAN CHAPELL

ZONDERVAN®

ZONDERVAN.com/
AUTHORTRACKER
follow your favorite authors

ZONDERVAN

The Hardest Sermons You'll Ever Have to Preach
Copyright © 2011 by Bryan Chapell

This title is also available as a Zondervan ebook. Visit www.zondervan.com/ebooks.

Requests for information should be addressed to:
Zondervan, *Grand Rapids, Michigan 49530*

Library of Congress Cataloging-in-Publication Data

Chapell, Bryan.
  The hardest sermons you'll ever have to preach : help from trusted preachers for tragic
times / [compiled by] Bryan Chapell.
    p. cm.
  ISBN 978-0-310-331216 (softcover)
  1. Suffering — Religious aspects — Christianity — Sermons. 2. Consolation — Sermons. 3.
Sermons, American. I. Chapell, Bryan.
BV4909.H364 2011
252'.56 — dc22   2011001500

Cover design: Jeff Gifford
Interior design: Ben Fetterley & Matthew Van Zomeren

Printed in the United States of America

12 13 14 15 16 /DCI/ 23 22 21 20 19 18 17 16 15 14 13 12 11 10 9 8 7 6 5 4

To
faithful pastors
I have had the privilege of teaching
and encouraging for more than three decades.

By your lives and ministries
God's people have known
the love, comfort, and strength of Jesus Christ
in times of tragedy.

Your ministry as Christ's ambassadors
amidst affliction and pain
is victory beyond words, treasure beyond measure,
and grace most precious.

Hope still blooms in darkness
because you were there with the light of the gospel.

I thank God upon every remembrance of you.
Though the world despises your office or discounts your care,
your loyalty to your calling and devotion to your Savior
is recorded in heaven and honored by all who dwell there.

You have made an eternal difference
by anchoring souls to unshakable truth in their worst storms.

No word of Scripture you have spoken
has been without God's intended effect.

No loving deed has been too obscure to escape his notice.

No grief you have borne has been futile.

Your labor is not in vain.

He who began a good work in you
will carry it on to completion
until the day
of Christ Jesus.

CONTENTS

Editor's Note 9
Introduction: The Message of the Cross for the Mystery of Tragedy. 11

Part One
PREACHING IN RESPONSE TO TRAGEDY

Chapter One: ABORTION 19
   Bryan Chapell

Chapter Two: CHILD ABUSE 37
   Dan Doriani

Chapter Three: COMMUNITY TRAGEDY 57
   Tim Keller

Chapter Four: NATIONAL TRAGEDY. 71
   Bryan Chapell

Part Two
PREACHING AFTER THE LOSS OF A CHILD

Chapter Five: SPECIAL NEEDS CHILD. 89
   Bryan Chapell

Chapter Six: MISCARRIAGE OF AN EARLY-TERM INFANT . . .97
   Dan Doriani

Chapter Seven: MISCARRIAGE OF A LATE-TERM INFANT . . .109
   George Robertson

Chapter Eight: NEWBORN LOSS 119
   John Piper

Chapter Nine: CRIB DEATH 127
   Wilson Benton

Chapter Ten: YOUNG CHILD 137
   Robert S. Rayburn

Chapter Eleven: CONJOINED TWINS 145
   Bob Flayhart

Part Three
PREACHING FUNERALS WITH ESPECIALLY DIFFICULT CAUSES OR CIRCUMSTANCES

Chapter Twelve: "LIFESTYLE" CONSEQUENCES. 159
Bryan Chapell

Chapter Thirteen: DRUNKEN DRIVER. 167
Bryan Chapell

Chapter Fourteen: CANCER: LONG-SUFFERING. 175
Bryan Chapell

Chapter Fifteen: MURDER 183
Bryan Chapell

Chapter Sixteen: ACCIDENTAL DEATH 189
Robert S. Rayburn

Chapter Seventeen: NEW PARENT 197
Bryan Chapell

Chapter Eighteen: SPECIAL NEEDS ADULT 203
C. John "Jack" Collins

Part Four
PREACHING FUNERALS FOR PUBLIC FIGURES

Chapter Nineteen: NATIONAL BUSINESS LEADER: CANCER. 211
Bryan Chapell

Chapter Twenty: CELEBRITY: UNEXPLAINED CAUSES. 219
Mike Khandjian

Part Five
PREACHING AFTER SUICIDE

Chapter Twenty-One: SUICIDE OF A PASTOR. 227
Bryan Chapell

Chapter Twenty-Two: SUICIDE OF A CHRISTIAN LEADER. . . 241
Wilson Benton

Chapter Twenty-Three: SUICIDE OF A FRIEND 253
Michael Horton

Chapter Twenty-Four: SUICIDE AFTER PASTORAL SCANDAL...261
   Jerram Barrs
Chapter Twenty-Five: SUICIDE OF A TEEN 269
   George Robertson

Appendixes
HELPS FOR HANDLING TRAGEDIES

Appendix One: Texts for Tragedies 277
Appendix Two: Helps for Conducting Funerals 281
Scripture Index. 293

EDITOR'S NOTE

NAMES OF INDIVIDUALS and occasional specifics of time or circumstance are changed in some personal accounts appearing in this book to respect the concerns and wishes of those involved. My debt is great to the pastors and people who shared the realities of Christ's love by the testimony of their lives in times of tragedy.

The Message of the Cross for the Mystery of Tragedy

WHILE STILL IN MY SEMINARY TRAINING, I had the privilege of being asked to pastor a small rural church. The opportunity to preach weekly, lead a congregation in worship, and "learn the ropes" of being a minister excited me. I thought I was getting a leg up on my seminary peers by being able so readily to apply our theology lessons to real-life situations. But I had no idea how *real* my real-life experiences would soon become.

The Challenges of Tragedy

Within weeks of taking the pastorate, the senior elder of the congregation was suddenly and unexpectedly hospitalized for an aggressive cancer. I had rarely been inside a hospital and had no idea what it meant to visit the sick, counsel the dying, and comfort the family. Yet I was immediately called on to do all of these. Then, within only a few days, I also had the responsibility of conducting this dear man's funeral.

Two days before the funeral, I phoned my homiletics professor, who also served as president of the seminary, and asked, "Dr. Rayburn, can you tell me what I need to know to do a funeral? We haven't covered funerals in class yet, and I have to do one the day after tomorrow." I will be forever thankful that the esteemed Dr. Robert G. Rayburn did not put me off. Instead, he invited me to his home for breakfast the next morning and, across the kitchen table, gave me a funeral-conducting lesson whose outline I still include in my lectures to students a generation later.

In no small measure, I and the other contributors to this book have included our sermons delivered during times of tragedy in order to aid pastors who have not had the privilege of such an across-the-kitchen-table lesson from Dr. Rayburn. Each of us has needed to prepare sermons in the face of tragedies, and we know the anxiety of trying to say appropriate things from God's Word that will comfort and strengthen God's people when emotions and faith are stretched thin. We pray that these messages will provide ideas and approaches to help other pastors on their path of preparation for some of the hardest sermons they will ever preach.

A Theology for Tragedy

In addition to offering suggestions for approaching different kinds of tragedy, these sermons provide insight into how to handle the theological challenges of human suffering. Each of the pastors in this volume has a Reformed theological perspective, believing in the sovereign control of God over all things. We can recite with enthusiasm and conviction the Reformation principle that God watches over me in such a way that not a hair can fall from my head apart from his will (Heidelberg Catechism Answer 1). We also believe in God's "most holy, wise, and powerful preserving and governing all his creatures and all their actions" (Westminster Shorter Catechism Answer 11). We believe these declarations of God's sovereign control of all things because Jesus declared the same: "Are not two sparrows sold for a penny? Yet not one of them will fall to the ground outside your Father's care. And even the very hairs of your head are all numbered" (Matthew 10:29–30).

Our Lord created all things (Ephesians 3:9); in him all things hold together (Colossians 1:16–17); and he sustains all things by the word of his power (Hebrews 1:3). Nothing exists or occurs apart from his will. All of these affirmations of our heavenly Father's control of all things comfort us until tragedy comes. Then the tragedy becomes the reason behind inescapable questions and—for some—faith-altering accusations: "If God is in control, then why did this happen? How could a loving God allow such things, much less include them in his will for us?" A young pastor who had just welcomed a second severely disabled child into this world wept in my arms while objecting, "I would not do such cruel things to my child; so why does my heavenly Father do them to me?"

Theologians will try to answer such questions with distinctions between God's decretive and permissive will. Still, the spiritual complexities and human consternation that accompany any explanation of God's sovereignty in *all* things ultimately outstrip our theology. Our logic reaches a dead end beyond which our hearts cannot go, if the pain and suffering of this world are God's doing. Yes, we can (and should) quickly retreat to the explanation that the tragedies we face are a product of the fallen world our human predecessors twisted into our present reality. But such an explanation does not easily withstand the blast of human objection from God's own declaration: "I bring prosperity and create disaster; I, the LORD, do all these things" (Isaiah 45:7).

Whether God actively creates disasters or allows the forces of evil that he *could* stop, we expect something different from One who calls himself our Father. If God creates disasters, then his love is at best a mystery and at worst a charade. If he allows the evil he could stop, then he remains accountable for the damage in its wake. We might, of course, suggest that the only disasters that God creates or allows are those that befall his enemies. If this were true, we could excuse earth's calamities as being a dimension of divine justice. Indeed, the Bible contends that God punishes his enemies with catastrophe (Isaiah 47:11). But the Bible also reminds us that bad things happen to good people (Ecclesiastes 9:1–3).

The Mystery of Tragedy

In order for the human heart to maintain love for a sovereign God, faith must affirm what it cannot prove: "In all things God works for the good of those who love him, who have been called according to his purpose" (Romans 8:28). We must believe that God has a good purpose for the awful things that occur to us. Just as a straight line can be drawn with a crooked stick, biblical faith requires the confidence that wicked and tragic circumstances can be turned to loving purposes by God for his people. Such conclusions are drawn in the earliest pages of Scripture. Joseph says to his brothers about their sale of him into slavery (when they could not know that his presence in Egypt would ultimately result in their family's rescue from famine), "You intended to harm me, but God intended it for good" (Genesis 50:20; see 45:5, 8).

But why should we believe in good "ultimate" purposes when the daily news about others and the regular experience of our own lives include so much inexplicable tragedy? How do we believe in the good purposes hidden behind bad experiences; and, how do we believe in a good God when bad things happen? Must our faith rest on an unproven heap of speculations, each ending with the surmise "there must be a reason"?

When my senior elder died within weeks of this inexperienced minister assuming the pastorate, there was no clear good purpose. I needed his wisdom; the church needed his stabilizing presence; his wife needed his help in her challenges of age. Perhaps the Lord, knowing that I would have greater leadership responsibilities in the future, cast me into the deep end of the ecclesiastical pool so that I would have to learn how to swim the trust stroke early. Perhaps the elder would have resented my encroachment on his leadership and would have taken action to discourage me from continuing in ministry. Perhaps the Lord needed me to sit across the kitchen table to hear the lesson from Dr. Rayburn that I would teach to a generation of students and the readers of this book. Perhaps, perhaps, perhaps ... Though all of these reasons are possible, none of them seems sufficient for taking a man's life, grieving his family, and crippling his church. If I were to base my trust in God on my speculations about what good may have resulted from this tragedy, then my faith would quickly crumble.

The Message of the Cross

So if faith in the ultimate goodness of God does not come from guessing what his good purposes may be, from where does it come? The answer from believers through the ages, and from the authors of the messages in this book, is the *cross*. We trust our sovereign God because he has shown us his heart at the cross. There, where any one of us would have stood and cried out, "This is wrong; God, you must stop this," our Savior made heaven's greatest good come out of earth's worst tragedy. At the cross we learn that God is good and can be trusted, even when everything seems wrong to human sight.

As I was pastoring the rural church attended by farmers and coal miners—people accustomed to hard lives—I heard a story that taught me more about the nature and foundation of true faith than I had gained in much of my seminary education. The story tells of a miner who, though a stalwart believer, was injured at a young age. He became an invalid. Over the years he watched through a window near his bed as life passed him by. He watched fellow workers marry, raise families, and have grandchildren. He watched the company he had served thrive without attempting to make adequate provision for his loss. He watched as his body withered, his house crumbled, and hope for better things in this life died.

Then, one day when the bedridden miner was quite old, a younger man came to visit him. "I hear that you believe in God and claim that he loves you," said the young man. "How can you believe such things after all that has happened to you?"

The old man hesitated and then smiled. He said, "Yes, there are days of doubt. Sometimes Satan comes calling on me in this fallen-down old house of mine. He sits right there by my bed, where you are sitting now. He points out my window to the men I once worked with whose bodies are still strong, and Satan asks, 'Does Jesus love you?' Then, Satan makes me look at my tattered room as he points to the fine homes of my friends and asks again, 'Does Jesus love you?' Finally, Satan points to the grandchild of a friend of mine—a man who has everything I do not—and Satan waits for the tear in my eye before he whispers in my ear, 'Does Jesus really love you?'"

Startled by the candor of the old man's responses, the younger man asked, "And what do you say when Satan speaks to you that way?"

Said the old miner, "I take Satan by the hand, and I lead him to a hill far away called Calvary. There I point to the nail-pierced hands, the thorn-torn brow, and the spear-pierced side. Then I say to Satan, 'Doesn't Jesus love me!'"

The cross of Christ is the warrant for confidence in God's promises of ultimate good, despite great heartache. Jesus' agony did not indicate that God failed, or that the faith of the one who died was weak. The suffering caused and inflicted by evil (Psalm 22:16) still was within God's will (Acts 2:23) and served a purpose so loving, so powerful, and so good that our eternity changed as a result (Isaiah 53:4, 10; Matthew 26:31; Revelation 13:8). Through Jesus' resurrection, we learn that our God has power over evil, but through the cross he gains power over our hearts. Though the human mind will reach its frayed end trying to reconcile earth's tragedies with God's goodness, the heart remains bound to God, knowing that the provider of the cross can mean no ill. Making much of the blood is neither maudlin nor manipulative; rather, the sacrifice of Christ is the heart's ultimate solace in times of greatest pain.

When we remember the cross, our faith in God's sovereign purposes strengthens and comforts our hearts, though tragedy comes and human answers fail. No less a faith stalwart than John Stott acknowledges the import: "I could never myself believe in God, if it were not for the cross."[1] The pastors who have written the messages in this book embrace these truths, acknowledging often the mysteries of the sovereignty of God in the face of tragedy, but affirming with greater frequency the necessity of confidence that his eye does not blink and his hand does not fail.

If our God has lost control or never possessed it, then we are at the mercy of the cosmic dice of fate. The Bible tells a different story, insisting that the Lord rides on the storms to deliver his people from this present evil world and

---

1. John R.W. Stott, *The Cross of Christ* (Downers Grove, Ill.: InterVarsity, 2006), 326.

to secure us for the next (Psalm 68:4, 33). We trust him, not because we can explain our circumstances, but because our God has revealed his character at the cross. The One who shed his blood for us can be trusted to love us; the One who gave his life for us can be trusted to provide what is best for us; and the One who purposed all this before the foundations of the earth were laid can be trusted to direct our paths to glory.

Sheep trust the shepherd whom they have learned is good, and we trust our Good Shepherd because he has laid down his life for us. The skillful shepherds of this volume further this trust by taking us often to the place where the Good Shepherd saved us, so that we will trust him to carry us when the darkness is too great to see our way or discern his.

Part One

PREACHING
in Response to
TRAGEDY

Chapter One

ABORTION

SITUATION

The following message was originally delivered to a coalition of religious, volunteer, and political organizations in a regional gathering on the thirty-fifth anniversary of the 1973 Roe v. Wade Supreme Court decision that allowed abortion on demand in the United States.

CONCERNS

My church is one of many evangelical bodies that have sought to inform its members and our community of the Bible's defense of the sanctity of human life at all its stages. The gathering for which this message was prepared included people of various religious backgrounds, political affiliations, and volunteer organizations who identified themselves with the pro-life movement. I wanted to say clearly what my biblical convictions were, but at the same time to differentiate those convictions from political agendas or secular priorities. For almost a generation the voice of the political right has often coalesced with evangelical priorities, making it difficult for many to separate religious conviction from political agendas—and difficult for some to stand for the sanctity of life without the sense of having to align with political entities. To encourage all to take a fresh stand for life on the basis of transcendent principles, I wanted to demonstrate that my convictions are biblical and more reflect obligations to God than to any political party or person.

Since the gathering included those who were very active in pro-life religious and political causes—persons weary from lack of success after more than three decades of endeavor—I felt the dual obligation of reinspiring them in the cause of defending the unborn and tempering the frustration that often led to demonizing opponents or others who are less zealous. In particular, I wanted to make sure that anti-abortion zeal did not obscure the grace of the gospel for those guilty of promoting or participating in abortion. This was not simply to honor the old maxim about hating a sin but loving the sinner, but also to maintain the credibility of the pro-life cause. When voices become so shrill in a righteous cause that they are indistinguishable from the sounds of hatred, then the righteousness advocated gets lost in the din of rhetoric. The gospel has the power to persuade when our message and manner proclaim its truth. My concerns were to make the Bible's objection to abortion clear and to make the gospel of Jesus Christ equally clear.

APPROACH

To emphasize that my intention was to be a representative of the gospel, I chose to base my words on a biblical text and to state that I was doing so because I was speaking primarily as a Christian and as a representative of the church. In this approach I was reflecting lessons learned by watching Billy Graham as he often addressed secular gatherings by introducing himself as a Christian who needed to speak to the Christians present while hoping that others would not mind listening in. By identifying both his position and his audience, Graham was able to speak with great freedom and without offense to very diverse audiences.

I chose to speak on a passage of Scripture that specifies the value of life in the womb. I sought to be honest about the frustrations and disagreements experienced by those in the pro-life movement and to use the authority of Scripture to say what the church must nonetheless teach about the value of all life. By underscoring the value of "all" life, I created a bridge to the responsibility that those in the pro-life movement have to value those who are guilty of abortion. Just as "not fully formed" life is valuable to God, so also are the hearts of those not fully righteous before him. My hope was to reinspire concern for the unborn with hearts that were committed to the full scope of gospel priorities.

GOD'S KNITTING

An Address to the Missouri Pro-Life Community in Behalf of the Pregnancy Resource Center

Bryan Chapell

¹¹If I say, "Surely the darkness will hide me
and the light become night around me,"
¹²even the darkness will not be dark to you;
the night will shine like the day,
for darkness is as light to you.

¹³For you created my inmost being;
you knit me together in my mother's womb.
¹⁴I praise you because I am fearfully and wonderfully made;
your works are wonderful,
I know that full well.
¹⁵My frame was not hidden from you
when I was made in the secret place,
when I was woven together in the depths of the earth.
¹⁶Your eyes saw my unformed body;
all the days ordained for me were written in your book
before one of them came to be.

—Psalm 139:11–16

Preliminary Remarks

I want to thank our local Pregnancy Resource Center for the opportunity to speak to you in behalf of the pro-life concerns that motivate so many of us to be here. When we unite around the cause of the unborn, we come from many different churches, organizations, and perspectives—and with varying contributions to make toward this vital cause. Tonight I want to come to you as what I am, a representative of the church, and to talk to you about the role of the church in this cause. In doing so, I do not want to minimize or diminish the importance of the roles that others have, but rather to acknowledge my inadequacy in telling you what should happen in your organizations or political structures or individual efforts to combat abortion. I am concerned to say what the church should say and do, because that is the arena in which I serve and for which I am responsible to determine if my actions are as diligent, responsible, and caring as my God requires. For those of you whose pro-life concerns even partially involve church ministry, and I would guess that is most of us, I would invite you to listen to see if what I believe God requires is being reflected in me, in your church, and in you.

In the church our pro-life concern must be based on a higher authority than personal preference or even principled concern for others. For this reason we look to Scripture such as Psalm 139:11–16, and ask God to give us understanding by praying together. Please pray with me now. *[After a brief prayer, the message began as indicated below.]*

Introduction

"Knit one, purl two. Knit one, purl two ..." This is the traditional chant of expectant motherhood. In our culture it is yet a caricature that when a mother is preparing for a new baby, she takes up knitting. There is a picture in this psalm that is wonderfully related. For while the mother may be knitting *for* the child in the womb, the Bible says that God is actually knitting *the child* in the womb. The image of such tender — dare I say, maternal — care being expressed by God for the child in the womb says much about our understanding of the innate value and personhood of the unborn child. But as beautiful as this image is, the subject that I must address today remains difficult.

There are a number of reasons for the difficulty. First is the apparent complexity of the issue of abortion as it has been argued for the last several decades. I have been preaching for more than thirty years, and as I reviewed the right-to-life sermons I have preached over this period, I was astounded at the range of issues we have had to consider in the abortion wars of this nation. Battles have raged over such things as:

- what Medicare will or will not provide; what the military will or will not provide; what foreign aid should or should not provide.
- what schools can or cannot say; what counseling clinics can or cannot say; what parents can or cannot know.

- at what term an abortion can be performed; what techniques can be used; what research can be allowed; what tissue can be used.
- what notification may be allowed; what information may be required; what delay may be required; what pictures can be shown.
- what degree of danger to a mother's health warrants abortion; what degree of damage to an infant's wholeness justifies abortion.
- what protest strategy to use; what picket distance to keep; what signs to hold; what language to use; what marches to join.
- whether to allow civil disobedience; whether to go to prison for our convictions; whether to kill others for our convictions.
- what legislation to support; what agencies to aid; what co-belligerents to join; what amendments to advocate; what candidates to elect; what commercials to air.
- which mothers to shelter; how, in an ethical way, to invite them to such shelter or to counsel.
- what infants to adopt; where to get them; how to "advertise" their availability.
- whether to lobby for what is winnable with a long-term plan for incremental progress; whether never to compromise and accept only a total ban on abortion.
- whether to secede from the political process or a particular party; how to vote or whether to revolt.

Some of these battles have been fought between Christians and the secular world; some have been fought between Christians and other Christians of varying perspectives. Yet, despite all the battles, abortion continues, and I fear our concern regarding it is flagging. I may be wrong, but my sense is that the pro-life forces in the church are nearly spent. Maybe you sense some of the reason for this exhaustion as you examine your own reaction to the list I just read. My guess is that while you were initially attentive, you eventually got bored with the list of all the issues—and it only took about two minutes to read, not thirty-five years to slog through.

Beyond the simple limit of our attention spans there is a certain lack of reward in being concerned about this issue. The lines of dispute are well entrenched. The society is deeply divided. The warriors of both sides are battle hardened. The average person is tired of it all, and there doesn't seem to be much probability of change on the horizon. To wade into the battle is only to open yourself up to pain. Pastors and other church leaders know that when it comes to addressing abortion, you will inevitably be attacked, either for saying too much or for not saying enough, for talking to certain people or not attending certain meetings deemed important for you. You will be called an "insensitive fascist" by pro-choice advocates in the church, who believe that any message against abortion shows insensitivity to women and disadvantaged children. At the same time, you will be labeled a "liberal coward" by right-to-life proponents in the church, who will say that your latest words and efforts were not strong enough, frequent enough, or public enough. The result is that pastors and sessions are simply tired of being pressured, yelled at, guilt-tripped, and outmaneuvered by parishioners with an abortion agenda, whatever it may be.

We just get tired of it all. The seminary I serve may be a case in point. For while remarkable efforts have been made by our professors—who have written books and articles, led marches, joined pickets, helped write legal briefs, and even crossed historic faith tradition boundaries to join with faculty and students of sister institutions to mark the travesty of Roe v. Wade—my sense is that we do not speak or pray or think or labor about the issue as much as we once did. Too many years of trying can wear down the best intentions, especially at an institution that tries to reflect the character of Christ and senses that to speak consistently against abortion is to cause us to be identified with other voices with which we are uncomfortable—voices often shrill, hateful, and contemptuous, even of fellow believers.

It is just not very pleasant to speak about abortion. So why bother? The most compelling reason struck me vividly as I prepared a sermon to address another anniversary of Roe v. Wade. In reviewing many years' worth of my own sermons on the abortion topic, what caught my eye and again captured my heart was not the debatable issues but the growing numbers that I have used in those sermons over the years: 6 million, 8 million, 9 million, 16 million, 22 million, 27 million, 32 million, 35 million, 37 million and counting—the number of unborn children whose lives have been ended by abortion.

My fifteen-year-old son, when I told him that figure, simply said, "Dad, that is fifteen cities the size of St. Louis!" Think of that as you look around you and as you drive home. The loss of life to abortion is the equivalent of everyone around you being exterminated, and fifteen times more. The magnitude of this tragedy, the immensity of this evil, the loss of 37 million children knit by God *and* shredded by men, demands that we speak, renew our zeal, refresh our compassion, and reignite our commitment to speak for "the least of these" that are so precious to God, regardless of the discomfort to us.

In the face of such great evil, we *must* continue to ask: What should the church say and do?

What Must the Church *Say* about Abortion?
The Unborn Child Is a Work of God

The child in the womb is made by God. The psalmist says that God "knit me together in my mother's womb" (Psalm 139:13). But there is more going on in this process than the merely anonymous workings of chemical and mechanical forces.

The child in the womb is seen by God. The psalmist says, "My frame was not hidden from you when I was made in the secret place, when I was woven together ... Your eyes saw my unformed body" (Psalm 139:15–16). Neither the darkness of the womb nor its inaccessibility to human sight hides the child from God. God sees in the darkness (the darkness is as light to him, the psalmist says in verses 11–12), and he sees the child, whose mature body is yet unformed (verse 13).

As I prepared this message, I was on an airplane. The man next to me was playing peekaboo with a child in the seat ahead of him. When the child hid his face with his own hands, the man would pretend not to see, but when the child put his hands down, the man said, "I see you." This simple game has special significance for our subject, as we recognize that this Scripture tells us that God says of a child still hidden in the womb, "I see you." The phrase says something about God's awareness of and care for the "person" who is in the womb — and this is the point that the psalmist will now drive home.

The unborn child is known by God. The psalmist says that God does not merely see the child's forming body, but foresees his life: "All the days ordained for me were written in your book before one of them came to be" (Psalm 139:16). The words deny the raw science that tells us that the forming child is simply "a conglomerate of protoplasm" or "the by-product of conception." God records the days of the child before one of them comes to be.

How many young mothers keep a book of the first year of life of their babies — books of hospital pictures, coming home pictures, birth weights, growth measurements, and locks of hair. Each entry is a statement of how precious that little person is to the mother. And God, with a degree of tenderness that is hard to take in, says, "Before you were born, I started keeping a book on you of all that I knew that you would be." What more powerful statement could there be of the personhood of the child in the womb than that God already counts him or her so precious as to put that child in his book.

The fact that God is not limited to our timing is a powerful argument for the personhood of the unborn. Human minds try to assess when life begins biologically, but the Bible tells us that God gives his children his care and purpose even before they are created. God says to Jeremiah, for example, "Before I formed you in the womb I knew you" (Jeremiah 1:5). Paul reminds us that we were actually loved before the creation of the world (Ephesians 1:4).

The unborn child is *a work of God*—made by God, seen by God, known by God. But all of these aspects of the child's relationship to God signal more than the workmanship of the baby in the womb. They also signal that the unborn child is *a wonder of God.*

The Unborn Child Is a Wonder of God

The best statement of this wonder is in the psalmist's reflection on the process by which the child is made. The psalmist says to God, "I praise you because I am fearfully and wonderfully made" (Psalm 139:14). The human body brought out of microscopic dimensions with all of its intricate processes, mechanics, abilities, and beauties simply causes the psalmist to pause and marvel in praise to God. But then the wonder takes on one more dimension. The psalmist recognizes that the human body in the womb is wonderful, not merely because of the marvelous process of its creation, but because of its connection to the Creator. He says, "Your works are wonderful, I know that full well." Ultimately the child is a wonder because of the Craftsman who fashioned that child.

What if you were to come across a painting in your grandmother's attic that was signed by Rembrandt or da Vinci or van Gogh? Even if you could not recognize all the artistry in the painting, the name of the one who created it would convince you of its value. You could say, "I know that a Rembrandt is worth something, even if I know nothing else." And the fact that the child in the womb is made by the hand of *God* says that this child is a wonder. This masterpiece is not a Rembrandt or a da Vinci or a van Gogh. No, this work is far, far better: it's a Yahweh, a God-work of art, and thus it is a precious wonder.

These two thoughts—that the unborn child is both a work of God and a wonder of God—should, at least, form a foundation for what the church *says* about abortion. And what the church *does* should be built on that foundation.

What Must the Church *Do* about Abortion?

To answer this question I am not going to focus on political strategies or picketing life-chains or the debates of the public square. I do not mean to minimize the importance of such measures or to say that the church has no role in them. Rather, my intention when answering what *the church* should do about abortion is to *call the church to what the church does best.* I want to challenge you to consider the unique contribution that the church can make, to recognize that some of our tensions and frustrations with each other may result from trying to force the church into patterns and practices that are outside her divine design. As a result, in our churchly attempts to influence secular culture, we may have been too quick to seek alternatives to the spiritual forces that are the true and greater powers influencing the direction of any society. And it is these spiritual forces that must be the chief preoccupation of the church.

If, as Scripture declares, it is true that we wrestle not against flesh and blood but against powers and principalities, the rulers of darkness and *spiritual* wickedness in high places (see Ephesians 6:12), then what should the church do? The answer is that the church must engage in spiritual warfare with the spiritual weapons of God's truth, grace, and love.

Teach the Truth (about Each Child)

The fact that the child in the womb is a work and a wonder of God gives the church the right and *responsibility* to insist that, though unseen by the world, the babe is a *child*, not a choice, a *person*, not a lump of protoplasm. This is the most critical truth that the church must say. We must not believe that such statements are useless or will always fall on deaf ears.

The reason that pro-abortion advocates are so zealous that expectant mothers not be shown pictures or models of pre-born children is that when mothers see what is being destroyed by abortion, their hearts resonate with the biblical perspective that the unborn child is precious. The prestigious *New England Journal of Medicine* reports that when mothers see an ultrasound image of the child, an emotional bonding takes place even before the child's movement is felt. When technology lets us see what the psalmist says that God already sees in the womb, then the divine imprint on the human heart whispers in the most powerful and deep chords, "This child is precious, and destroying this little one is wrong."

Actually, most people believe this already. Survey after survey will tell us that most people believe abortion is wrong. They *also* believe that it is wrong for the government to be involved in abortion decisions because they fear "Big Brother" involvement in forcing the birth of damaged children or the children of rape and incest victims (these subjects must be addressed at greater length another time, though I will speak of my own family's related experience in a few moments). Still, most believe that abortions of healthy children for the sake of convenience are immoral and wrong. We should not lose sight of the moral ground that has been won, lest we give up or retreat, thinking that our efforts have not had any results. The church must keep saying over and over again, "The child in the womb is precious." Such statements are making an impact.

But it is not enough to say that the child *in the womb* is precious. I took care to say earlier that the church must assert the value of *each* child of God. The psalmist's words do not refer merely to his own pre-born state when he marvels, "I *am* fearfully and wonderfully made," or speaks to God at the beginning of the psalm: "You know me. You know when I sit and when I rise; you perceive my thoughts ... you are familiar with all my ways ... you lay your hand upon me. Such knowledge is too wonderful for me, too lofty for me to attain" (Psalm 139:1–6). Key in the abortion battle is not simply to affirm how precious the baby is to God, but to declare how precious is the mother (another child of God) whom God made and knows and touches.

In an insightful article in *Christianity Today*, Frederica Matthewes-Green explains the importance of placing value on the mother:

> The "It's a baby!" message alone strikes the muddled middle [by this she means people who are not strongly allied with either pro- or anti-abortion advocates] as failing to take seriously the woman's plight. Our apparent willingness to dismiss those difficulties as "inconveniences" strikes many as either callous or wildly naive.
>
> Additionally, our opponents interpret this appeal as personal attacks on them. When we say, "Abortion is an immoral act because it kills a baby," they hear, "People who favor abortion are immoral people." I had long wondered why, at debates, I would attack abortion, and my opponent would not defend abortion but attack me.
>
> I came to realize that the "It's a baby!" message, important as it is, does not offer all the solutions we'd hoped it would, and in some instances creates more misunderstanding. It is a baby, and that ought to be the first point in presenting the pro-life position persuasively. But the conversation needs to move beyond that point.[1]

Matthewes-Green says the point to which the conversation must move is insistence that abortion damages the mother physically, emotionally, and

---

1. Frederica Mathewes-Green, "Wanted: A New Pro-Life Strategy," *Christianity Today* (January 12, 1998), www.christianitytoday.com/ct/1998/january12/8t1026.html.

spiritually. I am not going to document what you already know about the truths of these arguments as much as remind us of the importance of saying that *both* mother and child are precious to God. Yes, "It's a baby." Yes, "It's a child, not a choice." But because both mother and child are precious we also say, "Mothers hurt when their babies die." The Feminists for Life organization captures something of this truth with its motto: "Abortion hurts women, kills children, and destroys families."

Somehow we must keep in tandem our concern and God's concern for the mother as well as the child when we speak, because both are works and wonders of God. Keeping this in mind does two things: it modifies what we should be willing to say in the abortion debate, and it gives us a powerful spiritual weapon in persuading women not to have abortions.

If the mother is precious to God (and not only a mother *considering* an abortion but even those mothers *providing* abortions as nurses and doctors), then we must deal with each mother as a fellow image bearer of God. Hateful, disrespectful, and demeaning speech and actions must be challenged in the light of what God says about each of his children. Whatever we say, we must say it in the light of the truth that each child of God—unborn and born—is a work and wonder of God, precious to him. Although I want to be cautious in what I say here so as to avoid creating misunderstanding, when I have picketed, I have refused to carry signs that identify pro-abortionists as "murderers." I *do* believe that abortion kills. However, murder, by strict biblical definition, implies a destructive motive, and I recognize that some abortionists believe—truly believe—that they are doing something courageous and noble, and it is not always the best approach (as much as *I* believe that what they are doing is immoral) to accuse them of doing what *they* think is wrong and, therefore, murderous.

Our moral cause will not be advanced by speech that others view as unfair in its characterizations. We have to learn the lessons of our times. Why, after all, is it possible for a president's approval rating to stay high in the face of undeniable scandal or misconduct? I know the standard explanations are because no one really cares about anything but the economy, or because we have been calloused by the moral decline of our society. These reasons may explain why a president can survive scandals, but they do not explain the stunning rebuke of the Republican congress and the religious right in previous elections. The American people were not merely calloused to moral failing; they were incensed by what they perceived as hateful speech and tactics in dealing with moral failures. In the mind of many Americans, the moral critics lost the moral high ground.

There should be hope for us in these indications of regard for fair and just expression, for they indicate that there remains a moral dimension to public opinion. People do act on what they perceive as good, and they will act in behalf of mother and child if we do not surrender the moral high ground by rhetoric that is biblically prohibited by the mandates to love our enemies and to pray for those who persecute—even those who persecute their own babies.

Not only does saying that both mother and child are precious to God modify our speech; it can also be a powerful spiritual weapon in modifying a mother's behavior. These are remarkable words from Frederica Matthewes-Green:

> I spent a year [in researching a book] ... seeking to discover the reasons most women choose abortion. I expected to find practical problems heading the list: financial needs, child care woes, pressures to drop out of school. Yet after reviewing several studies and conducting my own, no clear pattern emerged.
>
> But when I spoke with groups of post-abortion women, a nearly unanimous consensus appeared. Women had abortions, in nearly every case, because of relationships. Most often it was to please the father of the child, who was pressuring for abortion. (In a couple of cases, the woman spoke of lying on the abortion table, praying that a husband would burst in and say, "Stop, I've changed my mind.") The second most common reason was pressure from a parent, most often the girl's mother.[2]

Convincing a woman of her inherent value to God, regardless of what other people may think or threaten, is a powerful tool in the battle against abortion. It is not a political tool, but it is powerful leverage on the soul to say that the reason that you need not act against the instincts and desires of your own heart in order to placate another or secure their acceptance is that your Father God calls you precious. He looks at you in your darkness, despair, and shame and says, "You are mine." We can tell these women, "You don't have to do this to be loved or valued because you are a work and a wonder of God. You *are* somebody apart from the approval and acceptance of the person who is pressuring you to abort your child, because *you are precious to God.*"

Teaching the value of each child of God is what the church should do. That message is made more credible and powerful when we also preach the gospel of grace.

---

2. Mathewes-Green, "Wanted: A New Pro-Life Strategy," *Christianity Today* (January 12, 1998).

Preach Grace

The same psalmist who says that he is fearfully and wonderfully made also asks God to "see if there is any offensive way in me" (Psalm 139:24). The writer does not fear that his flaws will remove him from God's esteem. In fact, in God's love for what is flawed there is cause for special praise. We can be flawed and still be precious to God. You and I know the spiritual comfort of this grace, but we need to translate it to all the areas of our thought. For mothers fearing the birth of a flawed child, we should never minimize the horrors of living in a fallen world and the heartache of bearing children who are not healthy in mind and body, but neither should we allow the notion that what is not perfect is not precious.

I have a younger brother who has had mental disabilities since birth. I have wished for many things for him, but I have never wished that he were dead. I have discovered that part of the divine imprint on my own heart is to love as a precious gift one who is imperfect. If we really lose this capacity to care for the flawed, if all that we finally value are those who are whole, lovely, and well formed, then we will ultimately find we are incapable of loving any. For we are all fallen creatures in a fallen world, and if we must discard or kill what does not please us, then we will find there is no value in the old, the infirm, the incapable, or in our own imperfect lives.

Grace teaches us something different: that the unlovely are loved by God. This message may not only preserve the life of the unborn child who is in some way flawed or suspected of being flawed; it can also dissuade the mother who is seeking abortion. The shame that may be driving her to seek an abortion does not mean that she is unloved; a past mistake does not mean that she is unforgivable; even a past abortion does not mean that she faces eternal rejection. And the man who may be urging an abortion because of his own fear of shame or disadvantage or retribution may also find new incentive to protect the unborn when he discovers the embrace of grace.

That embrace will mean nothing, of course, if it is not accompanied by meaningful love. Thus, the church that would preach grace, must also demonstrate love.

Demonstrate Love

The grace of God is the magnet that draws persons away from sin. But if those who say they represent grace are unloving, that grace has no apparent power.

What does love require? It requires that we honestly identify sin and warn of judgment. The psalmist does that here. He speaks of the Lord slaying the bloodthirsty and promises to consider as enemies those who work against the purposes of God (Psalm 139:19–22). Love does not mean silence in the face of evil. We must speak against what is abhorrent to God and warn of divine consequences. But we do so out of concern, dare I say "love," for those who oppose us. Yes, abortionists are our spiritual enemies, but God says we are to love our enemies, and in this psalm he seeks the good of one who confesses offense.

I believe, and I think you believe, that an understanding of who God is and what he has done is what is ultimately needed to turn people away from abortion. But if those who supposedly represent this God present themselves as angry, hateful, and mean-spirited, then it is foolish to believe that their God will be perceived as anything different. To warn of sin's consequences and still to love is our calling, and it is the power of the gospel against the greatest of evils.

Most of you know now of the story of Norma McCorvey, the plaintiff in the infamous Roe v. Wade case that legalized abortion in this country. In her book *Won by Love*, she writes of one of the Christians who combined love with warning until she, who is in many ways responsible for the deaths of 37 million, turned to God.

The key person in the battle for Norma McCorvey's soul was a seven-year-old girl named Emily Mackey. Emily's mother worked in the Operation Rescue offices next door to the abortion clinic in Dallas at which Norma McCorvey worked. Biographer Gary Thomas writes:

> Emily's blatant affection, frequent hugs, and direct pursuit disarmed Norma [who was skilled at cursing and spitting on abortion protesters]. The little girl's interest was all the more surprising considering Emily made it very clear that her acceptance of Norma wasn't an acceptance of Norma's lifestyle. Early on in their relationship, Norma explained to Emily, "I like kids and I wouldn't let anyone hurt little kids," to which Emily responded, "Then why do you let them kill babies at the clinic?" [Hear the clear identification of evil, even in the child's innocent candor.]
>
> This childlike innocence cut open Norma's heart. Norma wasn't won over by compelling intellectual arguments ... Over time, Emily began to personify the issue of abortion—especially when [Emily's mother] Ronda broke down and told Norma that Emily had almost been aborted ...

"Miss Norma," Emily cooed one afternoon, "it would be sooo cool if you would come to church with us." [After many refusals, Norma finally said yes because she was tired of telling Emily "no."][3]

Many of you know the story of Norma McCorvey's conversion that took place when she did go to church. She claimed the love of Christ because she had known the love of one of his children. With that claim came a new conviction born of love and grace. Emily's mother recalls Norma saying over and over at a church service, "I just want to undo all the evil I've done in this world. I'm so sorry, God. I'm so, so sorry. As far as abortion is concerned, I just want to undo it. I want it all to go away." The power of love had triumphed, as it must through us as well when we face the evil of abortion.

The stories could be repeated many times of abortionists or abortion-considering moms who have been won by love—Bernard Nathanson, Joy Davis, others you know. I do not mean to imply that the victories will come easily or swiftly, but we must not abandon what we know to be God's way of turning the human heart. Spiritual warfare requires spiritual weapons, and these include truth, grace, and love. Love must be demonstrated by words and deeds of mercy that cost time, money, and sacrifice because these are the church's weapons in any cultural battle. Yes, the church should be at the forefront of encouraging her people to care for desperate mothers and unwanted children whose lives need protection. Love must be evident in us and be expressed by us for God's power to be present.

Most of you know as well that when Norma's conversion became public knowledge, not everything was all right with Norma. She spoke openly to reporters about still supporting legalized abortion in the first trimester, and this was used by both secular and Christian commentators to discredit her conversion and her commitments.

What you may not know is that a few weeks after her conversion, Norma was sitting in Operation Rescue's office and began looking at a fetal development poster. Later she said,

The progression was so obvious, the eyes were so sweet ... It hurt my heart, just looking at them.

[After running outside the clinic, it dawned on her.] "Norma," I said to myself, "They're right." I had worked with pregnant women for years.

---

3. Gary Thomas, "Roe v. McCorvey," *Christianity Today* (January 12, 1998), www.christianitytoday.com/ct/1998/january12/8t1031.html.

I had been through three pregnancies myself. I should have known. Yet something in that poster made me lose my breath. I kept seeing the picture of that tiny, ten-week-old embryo, and I said to myself, "That's a baby!" It's as if the blinders fell off my eyes and I suddenly understood the truth—"that's a baby!"[4]

"It's as if the blinders fell off," she said. The words are a cliché in culture, but they have deep spiritual meaning for us. The ultimate battle against abortion is a spiritual battle, as the blind are made to see. This ultimately is a battle not of the ballot box and the judicial bench but of the heart and soul. For this reason, I again say to you and to me that we must make sure the church does not fail to do what it does best, and this means it must exercise spiritual power.

Exercise Spiritual Power

We cannot let apparent success or failure, or cultural boredom with the issue of abortion, keep us from our ordained tasks. We must preach against abortion because the unborn child is precious to God, as Psalm 139 makes clear. We must equip the saints with the truth of God's Word about the value of life and about the consequences of opposing God's purposes. Such teaching and preaching must be sufficient to equip believers to stand for life and justice in whatever area of life God may call them to, whether that means defending life in courts and legislatures or engaging in conversations at our own kitchen tables—for our own statistics tell us that the abortion rate is not discernibly different among evangelicals than in the rest of our culture.

Such figures make it clear that the battle against abortion will not be won by a law or a court decision. The factors that led to and continue to fuel abortion are as diverse as the affluence of our culture that promotes selfishness, the entertainments that stimulate promiscuity, the careerism of parents and busyness of children that are dismantling family structures, the success agendas of local churches, the professionalism of the clergy. These matters will not change because we get the right political candidates in office. They are deep, intertwined parasites of the soul that even we have grown to love, and they will not be overcome except by the Spirit of God engaged through the prayers of his people.

We *must* pray. This psalm is a prayer that includes not only an appeal for God's care but also an appeal for victory over his enemies. We must pray

---

4. Thomas, "Roe v. McCorvey," *Christianity Today* (January 12, 1998).

consistently and diligently that God will remove this blight from our land and the spiritual lethargy from our hearts that keeps us tolerant of its presence and even feeding its growth. If prayer does not seem enough, then we have not perceived the true depth of the problem and recognized our helplessness against it apart from the power of God. Prayer is the power God provides, and we must employ it against the evil that is greater than we.

Long ago, Oswald Chambers said, "Prayer does not equip us for greater works — prayer *is* the greater work."[5] If we will humble ourselves and pray, then the church is not doing the least that it can do; rather, it is doing the spiritual work that it is ordained to do, and it does so knowing that all other work is vain apart from it. When we pray, iron bars yield.

At St. Nicholas Church in Leipzig, East Germany, brochures still tell the account of the prayer movement that culminated in 1989. For most of a decade, the prayer group had met, praying for justice in Eastern Europe. Mass demonstrations, political rallies, and legislative agendas took place in other parts of the country, but all had little effect. The prayer group numbers ebbed and flowed, with sometimes a dozen or fewer praying in the massive church. But in 1989, the Spirit ignited the hearts of his people, and hundreds, then thousands, began to come. East German troops blocked the exits of the autobahn on the days of the prayer meeting to keep people from driving into the town. Systematic arrests of prayer leaders occurred on days prior to the prayer meetings. Communist sympathizers were dispatched by the hundreds to fill up the seats of the church so there would be no place for the pray-ers to sit. But the pray-ers still came and stood both inside and outside to pray while the Communists listened to their prayers, and many of *them* thus became part of the cause. When the numbers of pray-ers reached the thousands, troops were called in to handle the anticipated revolt, but all the people did was pray, holding candles in both hands to show that they had no weapons. The spirit of prayer and hope swept the nation, and though it only lasted a few weeks, the party and Communist ideology lost all public support. The system collapsed.

Later, Horst Sindermann, a member of the Central Committee of Communists ruling the country, wrote, "We had planned for everything. We were prepared for everything. But not for candles and prayers."[6]

---

5. Oswald Chambers, *My Utmost for His Highest: An Updated Edition in Today's Language* (Grand Rapids: Discovery House, 1992), October 17.

6. This story is told by a variety of news sources widely available on the Internet. These words are quoted from a brochure provided in the foyer of St. Nicholas church in Leipzig, Germany.

Yes, we must politic and picket and publish, but the arm of man will not save us or these children. We must seek our God, with the church doing what it does best: testify to the truth of the preciousness of life, preach grace, demonstrate love, and pray. He is not deaf to our call, for his own heart chants, "Knit one, purl two; knit one, purl two." God is knitting children. We have the eyes to see it. May we have the faith to act on what we see in order to call on him in devoted prayer and patient petition to come down with power to change us, so that with renewed words and works we shall be divine instruments used by God to save these little ones.

Chapter Two

CHILD ABUSE

SITUATION

Dr. Dan Doriani is pastor of the prestigious Central Presbyterian Church (EPC) in St. Louis, Missouri.[1] The death of his father brought not only grief but a flood of painful memories and conflicted feelings. So much of Doriani's life had been spent resolving not to repeat the abusive patterns of his father that he now realized he had not adequately considered the effects of the abuse on himself, his family, his ministry, and others similarly affected. After making tangential references to his experiences in a few sermons, Doriani ultimately felt he had to wrestle toward his own understanding, as well as others' need to apply the gospel to such pain. He did so by presenting an entire message on the subject of childhood abuse. Not sure of his own feelings or the reactions of all who would be gathered for a Sunday morning sermon, Doriani presented this message as part of a public lecture series sponsored by his church.

CONCERNS

Dr. Doriani indicates his major concern at the beginning of the message: helping others apply the gospel to their experience of abuse while not encouraging a crippling victim mentality in them or in himself. He adds that he aims "to equip pastors to minister to people who have suffered physical, emotional, or verbal violence." To do this he seeks to be empathetic with victims without becoming maudlin, and true to himself without being insensitive to those

---

1. Dr. Dan Doriani has pastored churches in Pennsylvania and Missouri, been a professor at Geneva College and Covenant Seminary, and authored ten books, including three commentaries (Matthew, James, and The Sermon on the Mount), two books on family and gender (*The Life of a God-Made Man* and *Women and Ministry*), and three on Bible interpretation (*Putting the Truth to Work*, *Getting the Message*, and *Beyond the Sacred Page*).

who experience and process abuse differently. He is careful to specify the nature of the abuse he experienced and to direct those who have experienced other forms of abuse to other sources of help. He wants to be honest about his pain while properly honoring his parents, showing deference for their own difficulties, and yet clearly identifying their sin and culpability. Finally, he wants to provide some biblical guidance for those journeying through recollected pain, present shame, and residual anger.

APPROACH

The first half of the message is biographical and intensely honest about the physical and verbal abuse Doriani and his brother endured. Those who know Doriani know that this sharing of personal pain is atypical, and in various ways he reveals his struggle to maintain his own sense of "manliness" while acknowledging a painful past and its effects on him. In the best sense, he offers redemptive vulnerability, being transparent about his suffering in order to minister the gospel rather than merely solicit sympathy.

The second half of the message points toward biblical paths of healing. Some of the gospel truths addressed are as surprising as they are insightful — and necessary. Doriani does not shy away from the need for victims to confess sinful responses and give thanks for life preserved, as well as the need to lament awful pasts and to forgive abusers. This pastor bravely acknowledges that no one can find spiritual wholeness without letting go of pain, shame, and anger — and he honestly confesses how difficult it is for even a pastor to do so. This message is not meant to be a final word, a comprehensive guide, or a counseling substitute; rather, it is a window into one person's experience that encourages others to enter similar doors to begin dealing biblically with their own hurt.

THE MESSAGE

VIOLENCE AND HOPE

Daniel Doriani

For where your treasure is, there your heart will be also.

— *Matthew 6:21*

A Personal Reflection on Violence[2]

Spankings stand at the center of my first two memories. In the first, I am very young. I defied my mother and kept playing with the knobs on our kitchen stove, so I deserved her discipline. In the second, I am four. I am hiding in my mother's closet for a long time, crying, trying to fathom what I did wrong, why my father hit me so hard, and why it hurt *so much*. It took me many years to realize that these "spankings" were actually beatings. But by the time I was seven, I knew that spankings were the least of my problems. There are things that hurt far more than a stick or a belt.

What Pastors Need to Know

I attended church every week for decades before I heard a pastor make anything but a passing reference to violence in the home. And when I finally did hear a message, it didn't come within a light-year of addressing my experience.

It is estimated that three million American men physically abuse their wives each year. Experts say that sexual abuse is more common than "ordinary" physical abuse. Counselors sometimes estimate that nearly half of the population has experienced some form of physical, verbal, emotional, or sexual abuse. Even if we suppose that counselors are unduly influenced by their profession, and we halve or even quarter the number, a serious pastoral problem remains. Clearly, pastors need to be able to address the problem of violence visited on children and women (possibly even men). We think first

---

2. I thank fellow pastors Clay Smith and Robbie Griggs and friends Susan Thomas and Lynn Morrissey for their careful review of this message. Their eyes strengthened it theologically and grammatically. I am grateful for their insights but responsible for my own errors.

of the pastor as counselor. Most who are currently suffering violence need encouragement to believe that their pastor will listen and take them seriously if they come to the office. And most have few ideas and little direction as they seek to understand their past and to find healing from it.

I believe pastors should also know how to address in sermons the issue of violence. My concern here is to equip pastors to minister to people who have suffered physical, emotional, or verbal violence. I describe four healing tasks in this message and urge pastors to mention them when they address the problem of violence. An additional purpose is to urge churches to be more honest about the darkest recesses of life. Many churches and many towns are full of confident, competent people who are more broken than we know or admit. We don't lie, but we aren't transparently honest or truthful either.

To compound the challenge, others who are not *currently* suffering carry deep wounds and yet, understandably, want to forget their past. This is true for several reasons. First, when the violence occurs, a great number of people endure the worst blows by disengaging or dissociating from their own experiences. They stand outside themselves; they may feel like spectators, as if the dreadful events are happening to someone else. In order to survive their ordeals, they learn to feel nothing. As a result, after the violence ends, when they escape, it's possible to pretend that nothing happened. If a memory surfaces, they think, "Why bring that up again? It's over. It's better to forget it and move on. It's too painful to remember."

Second, the wounded are often confused or ashamed by their suffering. They wonder, "How did I get into this position? Am I a fool? Did I do something to deserve this?" They also accuse themselves: "If I were a better wife [a better child], he wouldn't do this to me. If I avoided the things that set him off, if I were perfect, everything would be all right." Even if people overcome that thought, they may be ashamed of their past.

It can be humiliating to confess that one came from a violent and chaotic home. Sexual abuse can be especially complicated and difficult to overcome; rather than risk inaccurate generalizations, I refer readers to *The Wounded Heart* by Dan Allender.[3] The casualties of family battles can be frightened by their fear and helplessness or by their anger and dreams of revenge. The boiling pot of fear, anger, shame, and self-recrimination lead the wounded party to think it's easier to forget, easier to pretend that nothing happened.

---

3. Dan Allender, *The Wounded Heart: Hope for Adult Victims of Childhood Abuse* (Colorado Springs: NavPress, 1995).

Third, if a sufferer should decide to speak of the past, people from healthy homes can be skeptical. For more than one reason, I left home when I was sixteen. Over the next five years, I tried to tell four or five close friends or mentors just a little of my story. Their reactions, both verbal and physical, proved that they did not—could not—find a way to believe me. These were my best friends, including the woman who later became my loving wife. In retrospect, I understand why they doubted me. Until I began to share these things about myself, there was nothing in my persona that foreshadowed my story. Since my high school years, I have projected confidence—too much confidence, if anything. To protect myself, I had learned to project a certain toughness, maybe even nastiness (especially before my conversion), so people would think twice before messing with me. I didn't come across as a battered or shattered person. I wasn't on the floor weeping and cowering, so my story made no sense to normal people.

Even today, when we are far more aware of the problem of domestic violence, many people are slow to believe accusations, especially if the one reporting them seems to be fine. And many of us do seem healthy. We function well. We don't look depressed or vulnerable. When we tell the truth, we can get looks of blank disbelief. We can have accusations hurled at us: "Why would you make up such terrible stories about your parents?" Thankfully, some do listen. Some listen compassionately, and others hear and become advocates for awareness and change.

At this moment in our culture, a certain sort of person wants to bare the soul and all its wounds. A larger group likes to watch the train wreck, the horrible entertainment of lives colliding at high speeds. Another group watches in the hope of understanding their own miseries. Others are disgusted with the display. On the other hand, to be candid, at the most visceral level, I don't *resonate* with the wailing and lamentation. Emotionally or dispositionally, I share the mind-set of theologian David Wells, who is weary of emotionalism. Men used to be strong and stoical, he says, but now:

> They have been reduced to hugging and weeping. Their sense of self, as a result, is conflicted, confused, and evaporating ... America has become a very sensitive nation. There is always someone here who can be offended ... From all of this has arisen a busy and very profitable industry of healers, consultants, grief counselors, writers and various other purveyors of comfort to the fragile and afflicted ... In America, we have ... more counselors than librarians.[4]

---

4. David Wells, *The Courage to Be Protestant: Truth-Lovers, Marketers, and Emergents in the Postmodern World* (Grand Rapids: Eerdmans, 2008), 140.

I instinctively agree with Wells's derision of an unwarranted sense of woundedness and of exhibitionistic emotional displays. Everyone seems to have a tale of psychic blows. I know that my next remark will seem insensitive, naive, or worse, but I am compelled to say that some people exaggerate their suffering in order to gain sympathy and to villainize another person. This is especially likely to occur when a marriage is breaking up, but people seem to exaggerate childhood problems too. People have told me, with apparent sincerity, that they are scarred because their parents yelled at them five times during their childhood. It is not abuse if a mother once says, "You are *not* a princess," or a father once declares, "Do your homework, lazy bones." I believe it is sinful to yell at a child. Further, just as a single sentence of praise, spoken at the right time and in the right way, can bless someone for years, so too a sharp criticism, crafted to wound, can sting for years. Nonetheless, I hesitate to call a handful of unkind words "abuse." All abuse is sinful, but not all sin is abusive.

A Word about Words

So far, I have avoided the term *victim* and have spoken of *abuse* sparingly because the terms can be overused until they lose their meaning. Is everyone a victim? The problem with false charges of abuse is that they make true sufferers seem less credible and make them more reluctant to speak. Some people confuse paper cuts with shattered femurs. Self-indulgent or manipulative wailing makes it difficult to hear those who truly are broken.

For everyone who flaunts a wound, several pretend that nothing happened. Some bury their memories. For others, the blows remain too raw, too painful, even to contemplate. They say, "Dad was a mean drunk, and Mom couldn't control him. I left home and moved on with my life; I don't want to remember." Then something happens. The sutures break open, and it's impossible to ignore the broken flesh.

The church is a society of sinners, a society of the broken. But it's also a society that strives for holiness. *Too often our quest for growth, for wholeness and holiness, displaces the need to confess our sin and brokenness.* It is good to strive for Christ and to be Christlike. It is good to grow in grace. We rightly desire these things, but sometimes we feel pressure (or press ourselves) to *report* that we are doing well. Sadly, an excessive desire to make a good report leads us to say we're more healthy and holy than we really are. There is more brokenness in the church, more brokenness in church leaders, more brokenness in you and me, than we care to admit. We fear the consequences of true honesty.

The terms *abuse* and *victim* can cause additional problems. I have found that *abuse* makes some people think of sexual violence, when physical, verbal, and emotional cruelty have similar destructive power.

More important, I refused to think of myself as a victim. The word, the concept, felt so repugnant that it impeded my efforts to reflect on my past. I thought, "I am not a victim." Vanity was part of it; I am too proud to think of myself as defeated prey. Beyond that, victims are passive, and my brother and I were not passive.[5] We resisted; we fought back, however we could. We planned escape routes in case we had to flee, and we lifted weights in case we had to fight. We studied the enemy's moods; sometimes we provoked him, because we knew we could. Above all, we were neither cowed nor humiliated. A great many of the people you might call "victims" feel the same way. We are not victims; we are children of war who fought and survived.

A Sliver of My Story

My reflections won't make complete sense unless I tell a sliver of my story. I grew up in a home marked by physical, verbal, and emotional abuse. Over the years, my father hit us with his hands, with belts, with cords, with sticks — whatever was available to satisfy the urge. He destroyed our favorite possessions. At times, he refused to give us proper medical care, causing us serious danger at least twice. He threatened to kill us time without number. On two occasions, he actually did try either to injure or kill my older brother. These events led us to take his angriest death threats seriously. More than once we had to flee our house, sometimes into freezing winter rain wearing nothing but jeans and a T-shirt. Taking shelter under a nearby bridge, we weighed the dangers of hypothermia against the danger of his gun, for we dared not tell the truth to a friend or a neighbor or an authority.

When I was seven, he did something so pointless in its malice that I saw with perfect clarity: the man *wants* to inflict physical and emotional pain on me. I decided I wouldn't let him. I vowed to become hard, emotionally impervious to his cruelty: "I will be hard. I will never let him hurt me again." It was a preposterous vow for a seven-year-old, but I was earnest, and by the time I was ten, I had cauterized most of the nerves that feel emotional shock and pain. When he did something malevolent, I felt nothing.

---

5. In fact, I have two brothers, but one is much younger. His childhood was difficult, but our father did not subject him to physical or verbal violence.

This absence of feeling is common. Many make similar vows, especially victims of sexual violence. They survive intolerable abuse by feeling nothing.

I wish I had completely severed the capacity to feel pain, but the man realized that he still had me in one area—verbal abuse. He was a sophisticate in the world of insults. He told us we were worthless, helpless, hopeless, spineless, but above all, useless. He said it with contempt, voice trailing downward: "They're useless, absolutely useless." He said it with astonishment, as if it were a fresh but revolting discovery, as if he had just taken a gulp of rancid milk. As he would say, "Margie, this milk is *sour!*" so he said, "Margie, the boys are *useless!* Completely useless!" The voice grew louder with faux excitement. Oh yes, he had seen it before, but—eureka—there was fresh evidence! Sometimes he told us all about it in a calm voice, matter of factly: "You know you're useless, don't you? Both of you. Positively useless." He could rail and roar, but he also mastered the soft-spoken, soul-battering insult.

His theme was simple: you are worthless and always will be. But the variations were many: "You are helpless. Helpless as kittens. Like kittens, like *baby* kittens, like newborn *baby* kittens. Useless. Absolutely useless. And helpless. And you always will be. *Always.*" He paused portentously. "You know, you should do *something* useful. But no. You're worthless, completely worthless." He spoke this with a sigh, a shout, a moan. He hissed it, lamented it, roared it, caressed it. "Helpless, useless, worthless," spoken in every tone from tedium to disgust to rage. Three words, painted in a thousand shades of black.

We heard the "helpless, useless, worthless" mantra at least ten thousand times during our childhood. We had a short "you're worthless, useless, helpless" session every day for several years, but it could extend to forty or fifty minutes on some occasions. The shorter bursts we easily ignored. But sometimes he forced us to listen to protracted diatribes. The long harangues eventually stirred me to smoldering rage. I glared at him, silently disputing with him. "No. Not true. I'm *not* worthless. I have friends. I'm funny. I'm smart. My friends want me on their baseball and basketball teams. *You* are *wrong.*" So I attempted to resist. Still, the words had a cumulative effect that could overwhelm me as surely as if they were physical blows.

I must make one more observation, apologizing that I cannot say more, before we turn toward a positive plan for restoration: There are other traumatic events whose effects can be similar to violence. If a parent suddenly dies, if a marriage suddenly ends, the child can feel the same betrayal, the same deadness of soul, the same drive to live in pretense that we see in abused children. Therefore the four tasks outlined below may have value in other situations.[6]

Four Healing Tasks

I long ignored the effects of violence in my home. As an adult, I vowed and labored to make *my* family the antithesis of my childhood experience. God graciously gave me a loving and forgiving wife and three sweet and affectionate children. My career was humming along too. Life was good. But eventually I could ignore the past no more. I had to address my past, my wounds. Over several years of study and dozens of conversations with pastors, friends, and even a counselor, it became clear that the path toward healing had four parts: lamentation, confession, forgiveness, and thanksgiving.

Lamentation

Marriage and family therapist Ken Cope says, "We are taught that grieving is feeling sorry for yourself." If men are really strong, society says, we show no emotion. "Because we don't know how to be sad, we want to get to the end-stage of grief." We want "the benefits and results of healing," but not "the often long and painful process of grief." We are taught that tears are a sign of weakness and that we "must not wallow in [our] sorrow." As a result, we have unhealed wounds and ignore or discount our pains.[7] Women may hear all this and another line as well: "Your emotions are too much to handle and so must be kept under control or ignored."

Cope's comments label the hypermasculine desire to be tough, to be impervious to pain, to move forward. We don't want to *grieve*; we want to *have grieved*. Some will say, "If Jesus could be silent in his torment and persevere through agony, then we can—and *should*—too!" They think self-pity is an ugly state, but they confuse self-pity with legitimate grief.

Pastors should know better. After all, the Bible is laden with psalms and oracles of lament, with historical accounts of lamentation. In Israel, death, calamity, war, consciousness of sin, and illness all led to lamentation. The people mourned and wailed. They poured out their grief as they fasted, tore their clothes, beat their breasts, sat in ashes, and put dust on their heads.

---

6. Readers might start with C. S. Lewis, *A Grief Observed* (New York: HarperOne, 2001), and Nicholas Wolterstorff, *Lament for a Son* (Grand Rapids: Eerdmans, 1987).

7. Ken Cope, foreword to *A Sacred Sorrow: Reaching Out to God in the Lost Language of Lament*, by Michael Card (Colorado Springs: NavPress, 2005), 9.

Wailing and cries of woe occur more than 150 times in the Bible. There is weeping or crying or tears another 200 times. These are large, impressive numbers, but not everyone is at ease with the Bible's emotional displays.

Yet we should identify with the wails and laments. Emotional expression, positive and negative, pervades the Scriptures, and it is important to assess the biblical data. Baylor University ethics professor Robert Roberts shows that the Lord both commends and commands a panoply of positive emotions such as love, joy, peace, patience, compassion, and gratitude. He also forbids evil emotions such as unrighteous anger, envy, enmity (hatred), rage, and anxiety (see Galatians 5:16–23).[8]

How can God command emotions? Emotions can sweep over us, but emotions are not *simply* waves of passion that overwhelm us. As Roberts says: "All standard emotions are concern-based construals."[9] That is, our emotions flow from our strongest convictions and values. As we experience events that threaten something we hold dear, we may feel anxious or angry. If an event promotes something we value, we may feel joyful or calm.

This inner dynamic explains how God can command emotions. First, his word teaches us what we should and should not value and how we should construe events. For example, if someone dear to us dies, we may grieve; indeed we *should* grieve. Jesus wept over the death of his friend Lazarus, even though he knew the man would soon rise. Yes, Paul tells believers, "We do not want you to ... grieve like the rest of mankind, who have no hope" (1 Thessalonians 4:13). True faith should temper grief (Genesis 37:31–35), but some grief is good and proper.

This takes us to lamentation. Indifference is never the right response to evil. A stoical, impersonal approach, which essentially denies that real misfortune or evil exists, is not biblical. Jesus *mourned* over sin. Unbelief made him *angry*. He took evil seriously, and so should we.

If *we* have sinned, we should feel remorse and repent. If *others* sin against God, it is fitting to grieve and lament. We may lament when we see one person sinning against another. And we are free to lament when someone mistreats *us*.

The Bible commands that we lament when we see evil. Jeremiah told Israel to "put on sackcloth, lament and wail" at the judgment about to descend

---

8. Robert Roberts, *Spiritual Emotions: A Psychology of Christian Virtues* (Grand Rapids: Eerdmans, 2007), 9.

9. Ibid., 16; see pp. 11–24.

on Jerusalem for her sins (4:8). Later he urged, "Now, you women, ... Teach your daughters how to wail; teach one another a lament" (9:20; see 9:10, 18; Ezekiel 30:2).

Jesus stated, "Blessed are those who mourn, for they will be comforted" (Matthew 5:4). It is good to mourn over our sin and the sins of our brothers (2 Corinthians 7:9 – 10). It is good to mourn the sins that pervade society and to wail over the oppressors who "trample on the heads of the poor ... and deny justice to the oppressed" (Amos 2:7). Psalm 119 mourned the disobedience of Israel: "Streams of tears flow from my eyes, for your law is not obeyed" (verse 136). James summoned sinners to mourn: "Wash your hands, you sinners, and purify your hearts, you double-minded. Grieve, mourn and wail. Change your laughter to mourning and your joy to gloom. Humble yourselves before the Lord, and he will lift you up" (4:8 – 10; see 5:1). Such mourning *is* blessed, for it leads to repentance and restoration. Surely it is better to mourn over sin than to shrug the shoulders in indifference. God will comfort those who mourn truly.[10]

Lamentation takes different forms. Some lamentation aims strictly to express sorrow. One time, when David was hiding from King Saul, he and his men had to leave their families unprotected for several weeks. Suddenly, a large band of Amalekites raided and burned their town, then took the women, children, and livestock as booty. When David and his men found their town burned and their families missing, Samuel writes, "David and his men wept aloud until they had no strength left to weep" (1 Samuel 30:4). The weeping was an end in itself.

So David, manly man that he was, mourned and wept. These moments show that it is, first, *natural*, and second, *good* to feel grief and to let tears flow. Again, there are nearly two hundred instances of weeping in the Bible. Jacob wept over Joseph's reported death (Genesis 37). David and Jonathan wept when they parted (2 Samuel 20), as did the Ephesian elders when they bade Paul farewell (Acts 20). Godly Josiah wept when he read the law and saw the extent of Israel's sin (2 Kings 22).

Weeping and lamentation can feel unnatural, especially to men. We are trained to be tough, stoical. But many good practices feel strange at first. When I lament, I'm inclined toward the form of lamentation I read about in one theological study, the angry lament that leads to action. I'm at home with

---

10. See Daniel Doriani, *The Sermon on the Mount: The Character of a Disciple* (Phillipsburg, N.J.: P&R, 2007), 18 – 20.

the disappointment or grief or anger that turns into a desire to *do* something or to ask God to intervene.[11] We might call this "activist lamentation."

But Scripture contains many accounts of people who rightly weep, even when action is impossible. This is most obvious when someone dies. But we can lament other losses. Children who suffered violence can and should lament their lost childhood, lament the loss of innocence and trust, lament what fathers or mothers or grandparents could have been, should have been, and were not.

It seems strange to lament or to weep over something that happened decades ago. When I start to lament, I'm afraid that I will lapse into self-pity or some other crime of weakness. But the alternative is to pretend that nothing happened, and that is simply false. So yes, it is right, even good, to weep, wail, mourn, and lament. When Solomon said, "There is a time to weep and a time to laugh," he had the courage to put the weeping first (Ecclesiastes 3:4).

Confession of Sin

The second task follows on the first. If it is right to lament the sins of others and the losses one endures as a result, then it is also right to lament and repent of our own sins. And "victims" must admit: we may be survivors, but some of our survival strategies were or are flawed, foolish, destructive, even evil. Some survive by yielding to hate; they dream of revenge. Others survive by refusing to feel. That may "work" in the short run, but in the long run it cuts off the possibility of love. In short, no matter how much a victim is sinned against, he or she also sins, and some survival tactics can compound that sin.

Once the process of review begins, sins readily come to mind. Let me mention a few. The most obvious is petty deception. Without words, we can invite the impression that our life is and always has been in good order. We let people think we have it all together because we don't want to look like prey. It is also a defense mechanism and a way to ignore the past.

Many of us choose a life of emotional indifference. While I was shutting myself off from my past and its sorrows, I was often shutting off the sorrows of others. I could listen, but I tended to listen analytically, to solve problems, more than connecting empathetically with another person's heart. Not many people can be loving and detached at the same time.

---

11. See C. C. Broyles, "Psalms of Lament," in *Dictionary of the Old Testament: Wisdom, Poetry and Writings*, ed. Tremper Longman III and Peter Enns (Downers Grove, Ill.: InterVarsity, 2008), 384–99.

Adults who suffered violence as children are prone to sins such as cynicism, a critical spirit, and suspicions and doubts about others. We resist authority; we rebel. We act hard or indifferent or angry in order to prevent new blows. Children from violent homes *must* learn to resist their parents if they hope to become independent adults. Nonetheless, adults from violent homes must realize that the hardness, the rebellion, disrespect, and show of arrogance that permitted survival are in fact sinful.

Here it is vital to define repentance. We must never confuse a grim resolve to "stop doing bad things" with repentance. Nor dare we confuse repentance with remorse or self-condemnation. Repentance is more than sorrow that we got caught and look bad or hurt ourselves or someone else. Repentance includes a change in perception. The repentant *see* that their strategies for self-protection have led to neither authentic nor loving relationships. Further, "true repentance admits helplessness" so that it is very different from penance, which presumes that the sinner has the power to make amends.[12] The Westminster Larger Catechism, question 76, brilliantly defines "repentance unto life" this way:

> Repentance unto life is a saving grace, wrought in the heart of a sinner by the Spirit and Word of God, whereby, out of the sight and sense, not only of the danger, but also of the ... odiousness of his sins, and upon the apprehension of God's mercy in Christ to such as are penitent, he so grieves for and hates his sins, as that he turns from them all to God, purposing and endeavoring constantly to walk with him in all the ways of new obedience.

The pastor/scholars who penned this knew that the truly repentant man grieves that he has offended God and hates the sin he has committed. The sinner may feel dreadful or empty. "He may have caused much damage or little. But the penitent refuse to despair. They turn from heinous sin to a gracious God. They know God is merciful. They also know true repentance entails a constant endeavor to walk with God in obedience. The repentant turn from sin once for all, yet we also turn to Jesus daily for mercy and for healing."[13]

But we have not finished our self-examination when we recognize the more obvious sins of hard-heartedness, anger, or protectiveness. Some sins are subtle. For example, from an early age, I dreamed about the father I would be. I

---

12. Allender, *Wounded Heart*, 202, see 197–212.
13. Daniel Doriani, *Matthew* (Phillipsburg, N.J.: P&R, 2008), 1:51.

thought about what a child loves, needs, and admires in a father and resolved to do and to be all of it. I determined to become the father my father was not—the perfect father. By God's grace, I repeated very few of my father's sins. My relationship with each of my children is full of love, respect, joy, and a fair dose of fun. Yet, as I stand before God, I must confess that even as I played and read and taught and worked with my children, I often stood back and admired my good-fatherish behavior. I became proud and found too much of my identity and significance in my skill or virtue as a father rather than finding it in Christ.

Sadly, I could continue to confess my sins for some time, but you see the point. We need to survey ourselves and ask: Am I imitating the sins of the person who was violent toward me? Or have I so repudiated his ways that I have fallen into another mistake, perhaps the opposite of his, but still a mistake? How have my survival mechanisms become a pattern of life that I follow even when it's unnecessary, that is, when no one is harming me? Have I become cold, angry, withdrawn, suspicious, despairing, cynical? Do I pull away from love or trust because of my past? If we answer yes to any of these questions, we need to repent.

When we repent, the Lord forgives. This takes us to the third task: Just as the Lord forgives us when we repent, so we must forgive those who mistreated us.

Forgiveness

Jesus teaches us to pray: "Forgive us our debts, as we also have forgiven our debtors." He adds, "If you forgive other people when they sin against you, your heavenly Father will also forgive you. But if you do not forgive others their sins, your Father will not forgive your sins" (Matthew 6:12, 14–15).

This is hardly the place to attempt a full theology of forgiveness. Mature pastors have read the books, prepared the talks, and counseled privately on the theme. I simply make a few remarks. First and most obviously, if the violent person freely repents, the wronged party should freely forgive. If he refuses to repent (or cannot repent because contact is impossible), we still offer forgiveness as far as possible. That is, we refuse to hate him or hold a grudge. If he is alive, we pray for him and perhaps even strive to feel compassion for him. We don't curse him or wish that catastrophe befall him. We hope and pray that he sees his sin, repents, and finds restoration.

Many people hope to receive or to offer this forgiveness, but both parties may find that forgiveness is complicated. Let's briefly consider why this is so for the offender; then, we will consider the offended party.

Offenders can receive complete forgiveness or full restoration if and only if they repent before God and before the people they harmed. God always forgives the repentant, but humans are unpredictable. Some will be delighted to forgive; others will choose to remain distant or angry.

Further, some abusers "repent" poorly. They do so halfheartedly, while making excuses. Or they say they repent, while their sin continues unabated. The people around them inevitably wonder if the repentance is genuine. If the "repenter" declares remorse yet returns to the same sins again and again, we must wonder if he simply feels bad or hopes to purge guilt.

I say more about the offended party through my own story. When I saw things clearly, I knew that my talented and entertaining but troubled father deserved my pity and that I needed to forgive him. But such clarity of vision was rare. When I thought about my father from the safety of my home, hundreds of miles away, I could summon a sense of compassion. But my pity quickly evaporated when I visited my parents and he began to commit familiar sins.

It is easy to forgive in the abstract, when the sin and the sinner stand at some distance. One of Dostoevsky's characters stated the problem this way: "The more I love mankind in general, the less I love people in particular, individually ... I often think passionately of serving mankind" and even of dying for the sake of humanity, "yet I am incapable of living in the same room with anyone even for two days."[14]

As with love, so with forgiveness: it is easy to commit to the principle of forgiveness but hard to forgive *this man*, standing here, especially if he never fully owns his misdeeds. There is, furthermore, no reason to think that violent people will excel at reconciliation. Some deny that they ever did wrong. Others blame everyone but themselves: "I was so drunk [or so drugged] that I didn't know what I was doing." Some offer fragments of an apology that ultimately are no apology at all: "I don't remember doing what you say I did, but if I did do it, I suppose I'm sorry."[15]

Beyond all this, men and women who suffer violence struggle with ambivalence. We are surprised that feelings of pain, anger, resentment, or vengefulness remain long after we say, "I forgive you." We wonder why the hurt of anger remains many years after the offenses stop. The child of war may doubt

---

14. Fyodor Dostoevsky, *The Brothers Karamazov*, trans. Richard Pevear and Larissa Volokhonsky (London: Quartet, 1990), 57.

15. These quotations, like others, are accurate but composite. They capture what one or more people said on one or more occasions.

himself: Did I do it wrong? Should I offer forgiveness again? Above all, why is it so hard, as the dictum says, to forgive and forget? Let's consider four answers to this question.

First, the phrase "forgive and forget" is misleading. We cannot erase memories at will, as if our mind is a computer and we can delete documents by executing the right command. The goal is not a blank mind; it is the end of hatred and the beginning of restoration.

Second, forgiveness is more than a feeling. To forgive someone is essentially to hope, to pray, and, if appropriate, to work for the offender's good. The forgiving person relinquishes, in principle, his interest in revenge. He does not want to see the "sinner" suffer.

Third, if the offender is impenitent, or if the relationship otherwise remains troubled, emotional turmoil is bound to continue. To put it another way, when we offer forgiveness, we have appropriated the work of Christ in this age. *But the relationship remains in this age, not in the age to come.* To offer forgiveness is to gain the fruit of the cross, but not yet the fruit of the resurrection. When we forgive, we live in the legal sphere, which is the sphere of justification rather than the moral/relational sphere, which is the sphere of sanctification. Forgiveness, like justification, is immediate and absolute. Healing, like sanctification, is partial and progressive. If the offender does not (or cannot) pursue positive change, we cannot expect to *feel* much better.

Fourth, our emotions are often at odds with our will, mind, and heart. Our emotions are neither more nor less fallen than our other faculties. Therefore emotions can mislead as surely as the mind can mislead. Specifically, emotions (like reputations) are often a lagging indicator. Reality can change faster than our feelings about reality. Therefore, we may not *feel* that we have forgiven someone, even if we have forgiven them, as we defined forgiveness two paragraphs above.

In short, the process of forgiveness can go wrong in a number of ways. To return to my story, I had a sound *theology* of forgiveness before I was thirty, and I taught it, preached it, and counseled people about it. Yet I struggled to forgive my father. I tried to ignore my past. When I did remember it, I often felt an angry resolve: "I'll never be like that." When we talked about the past at family gatherings, I now see that we typically framed the issue of forgiveness incorrectly. My mother urged forgiveness through a reasonable but misguided question: What are the reasons or grounds to extend him mercy?

If we asked, "Are there *reasons* to offer mercy?" the answer had to be "yes"—and our mother often recounted them: His father was an opera singer who toured extensively. A European tour led to Russia, where the Communist authorities seized the family's passports and illegally detained them for twelve years. His mother ignored him during concert tours and suffocated him between them. He survived Stalin's purges and, like many who did, became paranoid. He was an alcoholic and often depressed. His first wife committed suicide. During America's "Red Scare," he lost the best job he ever had—teaching Russian at a major university. He detested Communism, but once someone called him a spy, no amount of evidence could exonerate him. Given these woes, my mother reasoned that we *ought to* excuse and forgive his behavior. There is no doubt that the man suffered much. She wanted us to ask, "What would I do if I suffered as he did?"

It seems necessary to conclude, "Therefore he deserves to be forgiven." But that statement conflates separate concepts. We may say there is a warrant for pity, understanding, or patience. But no one *deserves* forgiveness or mercy, for it is an act of grace to forgive. Sadly, I didn't see this at the time. Instead, I followed my mother's *conception* of the issue—that it is legitimate to view the question legally, in terms of merits—but disputed her *conclusion*.

I argued that no one *deserves* to be forgiven for misdeeds on the ground of past sufferings. We are responsible or culpable for our actions because we are moral and spiritual agents. We can perpetuate a cycle of violence or sever it. The idea that we should forgive someone "because he suffered" implicitly nullifies human responsibility. Further, it denies that God is judge of all flesh, even though this theme runs the length of Scripture. In Genesis, the blood of Abel "cries out" to God from the red-stained earth, and he hears (4:10). In Revelation, martyrs stand before God's throne and cry out, "How long, Sovereign Lord, holy and true, until you judge the inhabitants of the earth and avenge our blood?" (6:10). Can mortal man silence a voice that reaches God's ear? While child abuse is *forgivable*, it is not, in the strictest sense of the word, *excusable*. It grieves me that anyone would even debate this. The history of the man or woman who crushes a child is, in the final judicial accounting, immaterial. Those who suffer violence do not gain a *right* to do violence at a later date.

Thus the question "What does the offender deserve?" takes the wrong approach. No one has a right to be forgiven because of extenuating circumstances.[16] Forgiveness is an act of mercy. Unfortunately, I was so busy arguing

---

16. I do not deny that circumstances count. They do, and they certainly affect questions about subsequent restoration and healing, but they are not the ground of forgiveness.

with my mother that I failed to see that she asked the wrong question. Because I was wrongly content to give the right answer to the wrong question (Does he deserve to be forgiven?), I ignored the obvious fact that God commands forgiveness. I never *declared*, "I'm under no obligation to forgive him" (I was *thinking* about these issues as little as possible). Nonetheless, between the debates and my refusal to engage my past, I never relinquished my grudging anger or my judgmental spirit.

To summarize, past suffering is no license for future sin. God's law is the same, whether our life has been blissful or tormented. Still, it is a mistake to frame the question of whether *forgiveness* should be offered through a legal category of *justice*. No one deserves to be forgiven, but neither does anyone have a right to stay angry and resentful. We forgive because Jesus' mercy invites and compels it. "Be kind and compassionate to one another, forgiving each other, just as in Christ God forgave you" (Ephesians 4:32).

We forgive because God forgives. Grace is unexpected, undeserved, beyond human accounting. This grace is alien to us, fallen as we are. Why should the Almighty feel compassion for weak humans? *Our rebellion against him made us weak.*[17] But God's ways are higher than ours. "Because of his great love for us, God, who is rich in mercy, made us alive with Christ even when we were dead in transgressions—it is by grace you have been saved" (Ephesians 2:4–5). Again, God "saved us, not because of righteous things we had done, but because of his mercy" (Titus 3:5). There is no reason, by our rights, for God to forgive sinners, but we thank him that he does. Because he re-created us in his image, we offer grace to others.

Giving Thanks

I said there are four healing tasks. Naturally, one can think of others, but I close with a few thoughts on the sweetest of them: offering thanks for the gifts God has already given. The apostle says, "Give thanks in all circumstances, for this is God's will for you in Christ Jesus" (1 Thessalonians 5:18). This does not mean we give thanks for the violence itself, which is evil. But pastors must lead those who have suffered violence to see that there are reasons for gratitude. First, the Lord preserved life through the violence. He sent friends or allies who enabled "victims" to survive. He sent relatives, fellow believers, counselors, perhaps even public officials, to intervene, lend aid, and assist in the process of rebuilding a life.

---

17. Would we feel pity toward Cain if he lamented that he was an only child?

I have found great joy in thanksgiving for the way my brother and I stood together in the darkest hours. I treasure every friend who was glad to see me and so allowed me to deny the mantra that I was worthless, hopeless, useless. Pastors can lead their people to thank the Lord for every friend, teacher, and ally who loved them, encouraged them. If a man detached from life in order to endure, then thank the Lord for the capacity to separate from the worst times and so to emerge with fewer scars. We may even be able to see how our miseries made us better men and women. Above all, believers should thank the Lord for the grace that called us to himself, where we find hope and healing. The way people give thanks will inevitably vary, and one will join in more readily than another. Yet we must learn to trust God's providence. One day all of God's children must be able to say with Joseph, "You meant evil against me, but God meant it for good" (Genesis 50:20 ESV).

Chapter Three

COMMUNITY
TRAGEDY

SITUATION

As pastor of Redeemer Presbyterian Church in New York City, Dr. Tim Keller[1] bore heavy responsibilities after the terrorist attacks against the World Trade Center on September 11, 2001. The horror that the nation experienced through shocking video of gigantic buildings struck, set ablaze, and collapsing in clouds of smoke and dust was experienced firsthand by the people of Manhattan, where Keller ministers. Thousands were killed; families were devastated; friends were lost; businesses and livelihoods of generations were gone in the fraction of one day. President George W. Bush declared "a war on terror" to prevent future attacks. But as toxic building dust settled over the homes and businesses of Manhattan, terror, grief, and rage had already settled into the hearts of the people. Thus, on September 16, the Sunday following the attack, Keller preached a sermon titled "Truth, Tears, Anger, and Grace." Before September 11, 2001, Redeemer Church had an average attendance of 3,000. On the Sunday after the attacks, there were 5,100 people in attendance. In the months following, the attendance leveled off to approximately 4,000.

CONCERNS

The simple title of the sermon well expresses Dr. Keller's central concerns: to bring biblical truth to grief and rage, so that grace may be known amidst

---

1. Dr. Tim Keller has pastored churches in Virginia and New York and taught full-time at Westminster Theological Seminary. A highly influential preacher, he teaches many how to minister in contemporary culture and models such ministry in pastoring Redeemer Presbyterian Church (PCA) in New York City. His books include *The Reason for God*, *The Prodigal God*, *Counterfeit Gods*, and *Generous Justice*. His numerous online resources bless thousands and are available at www.redeemer.com/learn/resources.

terror. Not as obvious from the title of the sermon but evidenced in the ministry of the church was a dual responsibility. Redeemer Church was (and is) known as a church that is willing to ask and answer tough questions regarding the Christian faith. Everyone who attended on that poignant Sunday following 9/11 knew that the pastor not only needed to give comfort and perspective to his congregation but also had to provide a defense of God and the gospel to the many visitors who came seeking explanation and hope. On one level, the church and its message were being sought for comfort, but on another level the church was also on trial—Would it have anything meaningful to say in the face of horror?

APPROACH

In his sermon on September 16, 2001, Dr. Keller uses the account of the death and resurrection of Lazarus as an analogy for dealing with the devastation of the terrorist attack on the World Trade Center. He says that Jesus moves through the ruins of Lazarus's tragedy to teach us how to deal with truth, tears, anger, and grace. Dealing first with Mary's tears, Keller says that Jesus does not simply fix the tragedy but enters into her grief.

Next, Keller deals with Jesus' anger. In contrast to contemporary commentators on both the left and the right whose anger was poured into essays about the attacks being a judgment on America, or into hatred against people unlike ourselves, Jesus' anger went another direction. Jesus' anger was at death. In contrast to contemporary story lines about judgment and hatred, the gospel story line is about resurrection.

Keller then talks about the truth that Jesus discussed with Martha. The Savior offers not simple consolation but resurrection in response to belief. This leads to a brief presentation of the gospel, making resurrection available to those now hearing Christ's truth. Those who do not really believe are invited to keep coming to the church to explore the claims of Jesus.

Finally, Keller develops the point of grace. Christianity alone of all the religions tells us that God lost his Son in an unjust attack. Jesus knew that the only way to provide for Lazarus's resurrection and ours was for himself to be killed. In giving himself for us he proves the love of God despite the tragedies we face. Thus, while Jesus provides what is best for tears, truth, and anger, he also provides what we need most—the grace of his care. Keller concludes that the grace of Jesus "is what you need most, and that is what he came to give. That is what we are going to keep giving here."

THE SERMON

TRUTH, TEARS, ANGER, AND GRACE

Tim Keller

[1]Now a man named Lazarus was sick. He was from Bethany, the village of Mary and her sister Martha. [2](This Mary, whose brother Lazarus now lay sick, was the same one who poured perfume on the Lord and wiped his feet with her hair.) [3]So the sisters sent word to Jesus, "Lord, the one you love is sick."

[4]When he heard this, Jesus said, "This sickness will not end in death. No, it is for God's glory so that God's Son may be glorified through it." [5]Now Jesus loved Martha and her sister and Lazarus. So when he heard that Lazarus was sick, he stayed where he was two more days, [7]and then he said to his disciples, "Let us go back to Judea."

[8]"But Rabbi," they said, "a short while ago the Jews there tried to stone you, and yet you are going back?"

[9]Jesus answered, "Are there not twelve hours of daylight? Anyone who walks in the daytime will not stumble, for they see by this world's light. [10]It is when a person walks at night that they stumble, for they have no light."

[11]After he had said this, he went on to tell them, "Our friend Lazarus has fallen asleep; but I am going there to wake him up."

[12]His disciples replied, "Lord, if he sleeps, he will get better." [13]Jesus had been speaking of his death, but his disciples thought he meant natural sleep.

[14]So then he told them plainly, "Lazarus is dead, [15]and for your sake I am glad I was not there, so that you may believe. But let us go to him."

[16]Then Thomas (also known as Didymus) said to the rest of the disciples, "Let us also go, that we may die with him."

[17]On his arrival, Jesus found that Lazarus had already been in the tomb for four days. [18]Now Bethany was less than two miles from Jerusalem, [19]and many Jews had come to Martha and Mary to comfort them in the loss of their brother. [20]When Martha

heard that Jesus was coming, she went out to meet him, but Mary stayed at home.

²¹"Lord," Martha said to Jesus, "if you had been here, my brother would not have died. ²²But I know that even now God will give you whatever you ask."

²³Jesus said to her, "Your brother will rise again."

²⁴Martha answered, "I know he will rise again in the resurrection at the last day."

²⁵Jesus said to her, "I am the resurrection and the life. The one who believes in me will live, even though they die; ²⁶and whoever lives by believing in me will never die. Do you believe this?"

²⁷"Yes, Lord," she told him, "I believe that you are the Messiah, the Son of God, who is to come into the world."

²⁸After she had said this, she went back and called her sister Mary aside. "The Teacher is here," she said, "and is asking for you." ²⁹When Mary heard this, she got up quickly and went to him. ³⁰Now Jesus had not yet entered the village, but was still at the place where Martha had met him. ³¹When the Jews who had been with Mary in the house, comforting her, noticed how quickly she got up and went out, they followed her, supposing she was going to the tomb to mourn there.

³²When Mary reached the place where Jesus was and saw him, she fell at his feet and said, "Lord, if you had been here, my brother would not have died."

³³When Jesus saw her weeping, and the Jews who had come along with her also weeping, he was deeply moved in spirit and troubled. ³⁴"Where have you laid him?" he asked.

"Come and see, Lord," they replied.

³⁵Jesus wept.

³⁶Then the Jews said, "See how he loved him!"

³⁷But some of them said, "Could not he who opened the eyes of the blind man have kept this man from dying?"

³⁸Jesus, once more deeply moved, came to the tomb. It was a cave with a stone laid across the entrance. ³⁹"Take away the stone," he said.

"But, Lord," said Martha, the sister of the dead man, "by this time there is a bad odor, for he has been there four days."

⁴⁰Then Jesus said, "Did I not tell you that if you believe, you will see the glory of God?"

⁴¹So they took away the stone. Then Jesus looked up and said, "Father, I thank you that you have heard me. ⁴²I knew that you always hear me, but I said this for the benefit of the people standing here, that they may believe that you sent me."

⁴³When he had said this, Jesus called in a loud voice, "Lazarus, come out!" ⁴⁴The dead man came out, his hands and feet wrapped with strips of linen, and a cloth around his face.

Jesus said to them, "Take off the grave clothes and let him go."

—*John 11:1–44*

MARY AND MARTHA were facing the same problem we face today. They were looking at a tragedy and saying, "Where were you, Lord, in all of this? How do we make sense of this?" Jesus moves through the ruins with four things: truth, tears, anger, and, finally, grace. The truth he wields with Martha; the tears he sheds with Mary; the anger he directs at the tomb; and the grace he extends to everybody. Let's look at the way these four things fit together.

The Tears of Jesus

Let's begin with the tears of Jesus. What do we learn from them? When Jesus reaches Mary, she asks him a major theological question: "Lord, why weren't you here? You could have stopped this." She asked him a question, but he couldn't even speak. He just wept. All he could do is ask, "Where have you laid him?" He is troubled. He is deeply moved.

This reaction is startling because when Jesus enters this situation, he comes with two things that you and I don't have. First, he comes in knowing why it happened. He knows how he is going to turn it into a manifestation of the glory of God. He knows what he is going to do, and that in ten minutes they will all be rejoicing. When you and I enter into these tragic situations, we have no idea.

The second thing he has is power. He can do something about the problem. You and I can't do a thing to undo it. Yet still he weeps. Why? Why doesn't he just come in and say, "Wait until you see"? If you knew you were about to turn everything around, would you be drawn down into grief, entering into the trauma and pain of their hearts? Why would Jesus do that? Because he is perfect. He is perfect love. He will not close his heart, even for ten minutes. He will not refuse to enter in. He doesn't say, "There's not much point in entering into all this grief." He goes in.

We learn two things from this. The first is simple but needs to be said: There is nothing wrong with weeping at a time like this. Jesus Christ was the most mature person who ever lived, yet he is falling into grief. It is not a sign of immaturity or weakness. The people who are more like Jesus don't avoid grief. They find themselves pulled into the grief of those who are hurting. There is something very right about that.

Jesus' tears also suggest something about our need to "fix it." There are a lot of people who are coming to New York to fix things. We are glad for them. They will try to fix the buildings. We need that. And eventually they will leave. But when Jesus weeps, we see that he doesn't believe that the ministry of truth (telling people how they should believe and turn to God) or the ministry of fixing things is enough, does he? He also is a proponent of the ministry of tears. The ministry of truth and power without tears isn't Jesus. You have to have tears.

Do we do volunteer work? Yes. Do we help the people who have been displaced? Yes. Do we help the people who are bereaved? Yes. But consider this. Over the next months and years, New York may become a more difficult, dangerous place to live economically, politically, vocationally, or emotionally. It feels like it today, does it not? But if that happens, let's stay. Let's enter into the problems.

The city is going to need neighbors and friends and people who are willing to live here and be part of a great city. It may be more difficult and expensive just to be Redeemer for the next few months and years; I don't know. But if that is the case, the best thing we can do for the city is to stay here and be ourselves, even though it may cost more money or take more time. Maybe we are going to have to be a little less concerned about our own careers and more concerned about the community. So let's enter in. Let's not just "fix it." Let's weep with those who weep. This is the first lesson about suffering, learned from the tears of Jesus.

The Anger of Jesus

The second thing we learn about suffering we learn from the anger of Jesus. Did you notice anything in the text I read that indicated that Jesus was angry? In verse 33, when Jesus saw Mary and the others weeping, it says, "He was deeply moved in spirit and troubled." But the original Greek word means "to quake with rage." In verse 38, as Jesus came to the tomb, it says he was "deeply moved." The original Greek word there means "to roar or snort with anger like a lion or a bull." So the best translation would be, "Bellowing with anger, he came to the tomb." This must at least mean that his nostrils flared with fury. It may mean that he was actually yelling out in anger.

This is relevant to us because we are all going through this corporately. Our shock and grief are giving way to fear and anger. There is a lot of rage around. In this passage, Jesus is filled with rage. So are we. What does Jesus do with it?

There are two things he does *not* do. First, he does not become a "Job's friend." Do you know what a "Job's friend" is?

In the book of Job, a series of terrible things happened to Job. His children died; he lost all of his money; he became sick. Job's friends said, "Clearly you are not living right! God must be judging you for your sins or these bad things would not be happening."

Does Jesus speak that way to Mary and Martha? Is he angry at them or at the victims today? Does he say, "If this young man, Lazarus, is cut off in the prime of life, he must be receiving judgment for his sins"? No. He is not mad at them.

He is also not mad at himself. Isn't that interesting? Here is the one who claims to be God, who could have prevented this, now filled with rage—but not at himself. He says to Martha, "I am the resurrection and the life," one of the most stupendous claims that anyone has ever made. He doesn't just say, "I am a healer." He says, "I am the resurrection and the life. I am the offerer of life." He is claiming to be God! But when he gets to the tomb, he does not demonize anyone, including the victims, and including God.

I bring this up because everyone who is speaking publicly about this event we're going through must put it into a narrative structure to make sense of it. You cannot make sense of things unless you find a story line. There are two story lines that people are using today that Jesus is rejecting here.

The first story line is that this tragic thing is happening because America is being judged for its sins. Interestingly enough, the left and the right are both using it. People on the left are saying that America asked for it because of our social injustice. People on the right are saying, "Look at all our immorality! God is punishing us." In both cases, the story line is, "God is punishing us." Blame the victims.

Let's think biblically about this. How do you decide whether God is mad at you personally or at your nation? How do you know whether God is mad at you or pleased with you? Do you decide by looking at how life is going? No. Jesus Christ—who was a pretty good person, don't you think?—had a lousy life! Rejection! Loneliness! Everything went wrong!

In Luke 13, some people come up to Jesus and ask about two incidents. One was a political massacre in which a group of people was killed by Pilate. In the other incident, a tower fell on thirteen people. The question is: Were they being judged? Were they worse sinners than the others?

Do you know what Jesus says? *"No."* And then he asks, "Why don't *you* repent?"—almost as if he is irritated with the question. How do I decide whether God is mad at me or pleased with me? I read the Bible. The Bible says, "Love God; love your neighbor." If I am not doing that, he is mad at me. If I am doing that, he is pleased with me. I can't decide. "I just lost my job so he is mad at me." "I was just in a car accident. I am paralyzed. He must be mad at me." That's not how it works! Jesus did not suffer for us so that we would not suffer. He suffered so that *when* we suffer, it makes us like him. The story line that God is judging America for its sins is not a good story line. Jesus is not mad at the victims.

There is another story line that seems to have more justification, and for that reason it is somewhat dangerous.

This second story line is to demonize our enemy. *We* represent goodness; *they* are absolute evil. There is more warrant to this story line because what happened *was* evil. Justice has to be done. But this story line overreaches. Miroslav Volf is a Croatian Christian who has been through his share of suffering. It so happened that he was speaking at the United Nations prayer breakfast on September 11. Enormous problems happen, Volf says, when we exclude our enemy from the community of humans and when we exclude ourselves from the community of sinners, when we forget that our enemy is not a subhuman monster but a human being, when we forget that we are *not* the perfect good but also flawed persons. By remembering this, our hatred doesn't kill us or absorb us, and we can actually go out and work for justice.

Jesus does not conform to the second story line. He does not say, "I am mad at God. Demonize God. Demonize Middle Easterners. Demonize anybody who is Muslim. Shoot out the windows of their mosques." What does he do with his rage? He does not direct it against the people who have done this or against God. He focuses his rage on death itself. He is angry at the tomb. And this is the story line that the best leaders are using.

Jesus says, "I am going to turn this death into a resurrection. I am going to bring out of this something even greater than was there before."

That's the gospel story line, by the way. Out of the cross comes the resurrection. Out of the weakness comes real strength. Out of repentance and admitting you are weak comes real power. Out of giving away and serving others comes real strength. Out of generosity and giving your money away comes real wealth. That's the gospel story line.

Our most effective civic leaders are not saying we are being judged, and they are not saying we are completely good and our enemies completely evil. What they are saying is that we can bring something even better out of this horrible event. Out of this death we can bring a resurrection!

Think about it. New York is filled with people who don't give a rip about New York. All they wanted to do was to get ahead. There was so much fun, so much money around.

Now do you want to be a part of it? Here is what could happen. What if New York became a community? Through this death couldn't there be a resurrection? Instead of a bunch of self-aggrandizing individuals and individualists, what if we actually became a community? What if the United States was truly humbled in realizing we are part of the rest of the world? We are not invulnerable. At the same time, we would become prouder in the best sense, in terms of the democracy project that we are. Out of this loss of goodness can come something even better. Out of this death we can see a resurrection. We can be a better city, better people, a wiser and better country. That is the right story line, and it actually incorporates what little truth there is in the others — our need to humble ourselves, to recognize the need for change, and to do justice.

Here's the point. Unless you learn how to handle your anger, unless you know what story line to put it into, you can be railing and angry against America or railing and angry against God. Or railing against the demons out there who all look alike so we can beat them up when we see them on the street.

Or out of this death can come a resurrection. That is what you should do with your anger. Don't get rid of it — be angry at death! As Dylan Thomas said, "Rage, rage against the dying of the light." Say, "I'm going to put this light on. I am going to make it brighter."

Somebody says, "That's pretty hard to do. First you tell me to keep my heart open and weep with those who weep. Then you tell me not to use my rage in a way that short-circuits this whole process. I don't know if I can manage that!"

That is why Jesus gives us a third thing. It's the ministry of truth—not just his tears, not just his anger, but truth.

The Truth of Jesus

Jesus says to Martha, "I am the resurrection and the life. Do you believe this?"

The governor and mayor, whether they know it or not, are using the gospel story line. It's the best one there is. The moralistic story line is, "We are the good people; you are the bad people." That doesn't really help much in the long run. When your stance is, "We are the good people. We have been telling you that you have been sinning, and now you finally got what you deserved," it doesn't work terribly well.

The gospel story line is the one that works. To the extent that it is working in our culture right now, we can bring a better city out of the ashes. But Jesus says, "I can give you something so much more. If you want an even greater resource—the ultimate power to handle this apart from a kind of altruistic wishful thinking—you have to believe."

He looks at Martha and says, "I can give you this power, but do you believe that I am the Son of God who has come into the world, that I am the one from heaven who has come down to this planet to die and rise again? Do you believe this?" He has a reason to ask, "Do you believe?" Because unless you believe that he is the Son of God who has come into the world, you don't have access to this incredible thing I am about to tell you. Martha says, "Yes, I do."

Do *you*? I hope you do. What I am about to tell you is contingent on your having a personal encounter in faith with the Son of God. Here is what he offers—not a consolation but a *resurrection*. What do I mean by that?

Jesus does not say, "If you trust in me, someday I will take you away from all this." He does not say, "Someday, if you believe in me, I will take you to a wonderful paradise where your soul will be able to forget about all this." I don't want a place like that right now. I am upset and mad about what we have lost.

But Jesus Christ does not say he will give us consolation. He says he is giving us resurrection. What is resurrection? Resurrection means, "I have come not to take you out of the earth to heaven but to bring the power of heaven down to earth—to make a new heaven and new earth and make everything new. I am going to restore everything that was lost, and it will be a million times better than you can imagine. This is the power of *my* future, the power of the new heaven and new earth, the joy and the wholeness and the health and the newness that will come, the tears that will be gone, and the suffering and death and disease that will be wiped out—the power of all that will incorporate and envelop everything. Everything is going to be made better. Everything is going to be made *right*."

Every year or so, I have a recurring nightmare that my wife is very flattered by. The nightmare is that my wife dies. Something has happened to her, and I'm trying to make it without her. My wife is flattered because it is obviously my greatest fear.

But let me tell you something really weird. I almost like having the nightmare now. Do you know why? Because the first minute after I wake up is so unbelievably great! To wake up and say, "Oh my, it was only a bad dream. Everything bad I was living through has come untrue." It is not like being awakened to have someone give me something to make it better, in the sense of, "Here's another wife." No. What I like about waking up is that the dream becomes untrue. It is a wonderful feeling to say, "It is morning. It was only a bad dream!"

Do you know what Jesus Christ is saying when he says, "I am the resurrection"? He is not saying that he will give us a nicer place. *He is going to make everything that happened this week be a bad dream.* He is not just giving you a consolation. He is going to make it come untrue. He is going to incorporate even the worst things that have ever happened to you. They will be taken up into the glory that is to come in such a way that they make the glory better and greater for having once been broken.

No one puts this truth better than Dostoevsky. *The Brothers Karamazov* contains this fascinating passage:

> I believe like a child that suffering will be healed and made up for, that all the humiliating absurdity of human contradictions will vanish like a pitiful mirage . . . In the world's finale, at the moment of eternal harmony, something so precious will come to pass that it will suffice for all hearts, for the comforting of all resentments, for the atonement of all the crimes of humanity, of all the blood they've shed; that it will make it not only possible to forgive but to justify all that has happened with men.[2]

I feel like I am looking into a deep abyss when he says that. I know what he means. What he is trying to say is that we are not just going to get some kind of consolation that will make it possible to forget. Rather, everything bad is going to come untrue.

---

2. Fyodor Dostoevsky, *The Brothers Karamazov* (New York: Macmillan, 1922), 247–48.

At the end of *The Lord of the Rings*, the hobbit Sam, who thought every-thing was going wrong, wakes up and the sun is out. He sees Gandalf, the great wizard. To me, this is the quintessence of Jesus' promise. Sam says, "Gandalf! I thought you were dead! But then I thought I was dead myself. Is everything sad going to come untrue?" The answer of Jesus is, "Yes." Someday will be the great morning, *the* morning, not m-o-u-r-n-i-n-g, but m-o-r-n-i-n-g, the great morning that won't just console us. Jesus will take all of those horrible memories, everything bad that has ever happened, and they will actually be brought back in and become untrue. They will only enrich the new world in which everything is put right—*everything*.

Do you believe this? Jesus says, "Do you believe this?" You say, "I *want* to believe this." If Jesus is the Son of God who has come from heaven, if he is the incarnate Son of God who died on the cross so that we could be forgiven, so God could someday destroy evil and suffering without destroying us, he paid the penalty so that we could participate in this.

Do you believe the gospel? If you believe the gospel, then you have to believe that. There are a lot of people in this room who do believe the gospel, but they haven't really activated it this week. That is what I am here to help you do. You have not thought about that. Your heart hasn't leapt. You haven't wept when you thought about it. I hope today is a start!

If, on the other hand, you do not really believe that Jesus is the Son of God, I ask you to keep coming and explore it. Jesus says, "Unless you believe in me, all this is just a pipe dream." If there is a God up there who has never become human, and you are down here hoping that someday you will be good enough for him to take you to heaven, it won't work. But if you believe in a God who is willing to come to die, to resurrect the whole world, a God who would come into our lives, *that* is the gospel.

C. S. Lewis wrote, "If we let him ... he will make the feeblest and filthi-est of us into a ... dazzling, radiant, immortal creature, pulsating all through with such energy and joy and wisdom and love as we cannot now imagine, a bright stainless mirror which reflects back to God perfectly (though, of course, on a smaller scale) his own boundless power and delight and good-ness. The process will be long ... but that is what we are in for. Nothing less."[3]

Do you believe that? "Do you believe this, Martha?" Then you can face anything.

---

3. C. S. Lewis, *Mere Christianity* (New York: Macmillan, 1960), 174–75.

Everyone is wondering what kind of power New York is going to put back. I know that God is going to put something back. In the new heavens and new earth, everything we have here — even the best things we have here — will be just a dim echo of what we are going to have there.

Finally, somebody says, "How do I know this is going to happen? I would love to believe this, but how do I *know*?" There is one more thing in this story you have to recognize. Jesus offered tears, truth, and anger, but did you notice the last line of the story, the last line of the text I read? It said, "From that day on they plotted to take his life."

The Grace of Jesus

After Jesus raised Lazarus from the dead, his enemies said, "Now he's got to go. He is the most dangerous man there is. We've got to get rid of him now."

Don't you think Jesus knew that when he was raising Lazarus from the dead? Yes, he did. Jesus Christ knew and made a deliberate choice. He knew that the only way to interrupt Lazarus's funeral was to cause his own. The only way to bring Lazarus out of the grave was to bury himself. The only way he could get Lazarus out of death was for him to be killed. He knew that.

Isn't that a picture of the gospel? We have a God who is so committed to ending suffering and death that he was willing to come into the world and share in that suffering and death himself. There are an awful lot of people praying to a general God — "I am sure that God somehow is loving us." I *don't* know that. Or rather, I know that only because Christianity alone of all the religions tells us that God has specifically loved us: God lost his Son in an unjust attack. Only Christianity tells us that God has suffered.

When somebody says to me, "I don't know that God cares about our suffering," I say, "Yes, he does." They say, "How do you know?" If I were in any other religion, I wouldn't know what to say. But the proof is that he himself was willing to suffer.

I don't know why he hasn't ended suffering and evil by now, but the fact that he was willing to be involved and that he himself got involved is proof that he must have some good reason. He cares. He is not remote. He is not away from us.

Isn't it amazing that Jesus was so different with Martha and Mary? Martha and Mary, two sisters with the same situation, same circumstances, same brother. They even had the same question. Martha and Mary asked Jesus the same question word for word. But in Martha's case, Jesus' words were almost a rebuke as he laid truth on her. In Mary's case, Jesus just wept with her. Why? Because he is the perfect counselor. Not like me. I try, but I tend to be a "truther." I tend to say, "I have all this information. I don't want to waste your time, so let me try to fix things." I want to say, "You need to know this and this and this." Sometimes you just need somebody to weep with you, and I am not the guy. Then sometimes you go to a counselor, and all the counselor wants to do is weep, when you really need somebody to tell you the truth and bring you up short.

But Jesus is the perfect counselor. He will always give you what you need. If you need truth—or if you need tears—he will give it to you the day you need it. He will give it to you in the dosage in which you need it. He will give it to you in the order in which you need it. He is the only perfect counselor there is. You need to go to him. You need to get his tears; you need to get his truth; you need to get his anger. You need all these things, but most of all you need to get his grace. That is what you need most, and that is what he came to give. That is what we are going to keep giving here.

Let's pray. *Now, Father, we ask that you give us the possibility of growth and healing as a congregation, as a people, and as a city because we have seen that your Son is the resurrection, and he died to prove it. With that hope we can face the future. Now we ask simply that you apply this teaching to our hearts in the various ways we need it applied so that we are able to be the neighbors and friends the city needs us to be. We pray this in Jesus' name. Amen.*

Chapter Four

NATIONAL TRAGEDY

SITUATION

While Pastor Tim Keller was dealing with the community impact of the terrorist attacks against the World Trade Center on September 11, 2001, thousands of pastors at greater distance were also trying to help people apply their faith to a national tragedy. As all air traffic disappeared from the nation's skies, as trucks vacated highways, as news reports barraged hearts with stories of family pain, and as the president declared war against further impending terror, worship communities across the country gathered to pray, to consider Scripture, and to try to understand God's hand in all this. In the nation's heartland, the students and staff of Covenant Seminary also gathered for prayer, worship, and understanding in a chapel service immediately following the events of 9/11.

CONCERNS

The 9/11 tragedy raised the usual questions that must be addressed by any caring pastor faced with a nation's anguish: Does God understand, care, and rule? But special concerns also arose as a consequence of both religious and political speculation about why these events had occurred. Was this divine judgment for national sin? Was this God's hand setting the nation straight, or had God simply removed his hand from a nation gone wrong? Did this tragedy prove the absence of God, or the triumph of his enemies? Particularly in the academic setting of a theological seminary, there is a temptation to provide quick answers about God's purpose and providence. My goal was to insist that we avoid providing answers hidden from human understanding and affirm with passion the undeniable love and care of God as demonstrated in his Word. My priority for these future leaders of thousands of churches was on displaying God's heart rather than trying to rationalize his actions in the face of insanity. My hope was that when future situations called for such sermons, these students would be prepared to proclaim God's sure love rather than feel the necessity of providing strident or speculative theological clichés.

APPROACH

My approach was similar to that of Tim Keller and, unknowingly, I chose the same text he chose to preach from on the Sunday following 9/11. The account of the raising of Lazarus leaves many unanswered questions: Why didn't Jesus prevent his friend's death? Why did he allow the grief of Lazarus's relatives? Why did Jesus grieve, knowing that Lazarus would return from the grave? Why did Jesus allow opposition to his ministry to increase, knowing it would lead to his demise? Though describing the tragedy in detail, the Bible does not provide answers to these questions. However, the Bible clearly shows Jesus' care for those who are hurting and clearly demonstrates that he can turn human tragedy to divine purpose. Although I gathered information from the wider text, I took the questions (really objections) that rise up in our hearts when we face tragedy and sought to answer them with a focus on the shortest verse in the Bible: "Jesus wept." When we face events that hurt, does Jesus understand, care, and ultimately rule? I sought to show the answers to these confusing questions through the clear lens of Jesus' tears.

JESUS WEPT

Bryan Chapell

> Jesus wept.
> —*John 11:35*

ON SEPTEMBER 11, 2001, a businessman sat in his hotel room in the Midwest watching news reports of a jetliner crashing into the World Trade Center. He knew that his son was on an international flight scheduled to land in New York sometime that morning. Silently, the businessman bowed his head and prayed to the God of love that it was not this flight. Then the man raised his head and again focused on the TV screen as a second airliner plowed into the second tower of the World Trade Center.

The effect on my friend of watching the second crash occur was stronger that he could have anticipated and more convulsing than he even now can fully explain. Believing that he may have just watched his own son being murdered by terrorists, the businessman—a lifelong follower of Jesus Christ—flushed with rage. Some visceral instinct caused my Christian friend to imagine himself with his hands around the throat of whoever had planned this horror. He visualized the same hands that had once held his infant son with uncontained love now squeezing a terrorist's throat with unrelenting force. My friend later said that in those moments following the crash he wanted to watch the eyes of the strangling terrorist bulge with the same terror he had just caused.

You and I now know that my friend was spared the death of his son because the airplanes that struck the World Trade Center were not international flights. Still, my friend's inner anguish is not over. This businessman ordinarily is a kind and gentle man. He takes his faith seriously and desires to honor God in all that he does. Today my friend struggles with how to face the rage that he felt that day. The anger that welled up in him after watching the jetliner crash was alien to his normal emotions, and the memory haunts him. He fears that the murderous hatred that erupted from his heart is an indication of a defective faith. My friend questions whether the images and emotions that are so contrary to his personality and principles may be indicators of a darkness in his heart that he dreads to confront.

The more he has considered his emotions the more my friend has become convinced and troubled that his rage — while directed at an imaginary terrorist — was derived from a much more identifiable source. In the moment that the second plane hit the World Trade Center, my friend had to consider whether the God he worshiped had failed to protect the son he loved. The anger, the rage, and the imagined strangling were not simply a reflex response to an act of terror by men; the reactions were also the result of a deep sense of betrayal by God.

My friend's displaced rage erupted from a very disturbing but readily discernible logic. If God is truly God and truly good, then personal tragedy betrays rational confidence in God. Reason alone cannot justify him or our faith in the face of such events. I know the usual answers to the questions that try to make sense of life's horror:

- I know that this is a fallen world that groans as in the pains of childbirth until Christ returns to renew all things.
- I know that the final chapter of these events (and all other tragedies) is not yet written as God works all things together for good.
- I know that, in the final day, he who knows the end from the beginning will judge evil and vindicate his justice.
- I know that when the world shakes, a frivolous and unrepentant society may fall to its knees in search of firmer foundations than this world can offer.

I know, I know, I know ... Yet, despite all these formulaic answers — as true, accurate, and useful as they may be — the horror of these events defies our reason. We are still forced to claim that God is good, even though planes with real people aboard crashed into the World Trade Center, the Pentagon, and a field in Pennsylvania, killing thousands, grieving tens of thousands, and propelling us toward a war that has already sent many thousands more to the diseased squalor of refugee camps where they will experience miserable lives and lingering deaths.

In the face of such suffering and pain, we need more than the formulaic answers that human reason can offer. Our hearts cry out, "Does God really understand what is happening? Does he care? Does he rule?" Something in our souls cries for a truth that is deeper and more certain than logical possibilities. We must know, not apart from reason but beyond it, that the God we trust is still trustable. For this cry of the heart, John provides this report of Jesus raising Lazarus from the dead. The gospel account connects our God to our humanity, so that what our minds cannot fully explain our hearts can still receive. When we must ask the most basic and plaintive of questions—"How can we believe that God is love in the face of tragedy?"—John answers with the plainest and most poignant of answers: "Jesus wept."

Consider the compelling questions that these simple words, "Jesus wept," answer.

Does God Really Understand Our Tragedies?

In showing us the context of Jesus' tears, the Bible answers with certainty, "Yes, God understands." The full account of Jesus raising Lazarus from the dead assures us that our God really knows both what *will* happen and what *has* happened.

Our God Knows What Will Happen

Repeatedly this account reveals Jesus' knowledge of future events. When first he hears of Lazarus's sickness, Jesus says, "This sickness will not end in death. No, it is for God's glory so that God's Son may be glorified through it" (John 11:4). This hint of Jesus' prescience becomes explicit as the account proceeds. After delaying his journey to Lazarus's bedside, Jesus then determines to go to Bethany with these words: "Our friend Lazarus has fallen asleep; but I am going there to wake him up" (verse 11). And when the disciples, with amazing dim-wittedness, think that Jesus is only talking about natural sleep, Jesus speaks plainly to them, saying, "Lazarus is dead, and for your sake I am glad I was not there, so that you may believe. But let us go to him" (verses 14–15). Finally, Jesus comforts a questioning and grieving Martha, who meets him on his way to the now-departed Lazarus, with the assurance, "Your brother will rise again" (verse 23).

By displaying Jesus' foreknowledge, John lets us know that the outcome of events does not elude our Savior, even if it exasperates his people. Their exasperation is as plain as Jesus' predictions. After his inexplicable (to her) delay, Martha says to Jesus, "If you had been here, my brother would not have died" (John 11:21). Later, Mary goes to where Jesus continues to wait outside her town to avoid his antagonists, and she questions him with words identical to her sister's: "Lord, if you had been here, my brother would not have died" (verse 32).

In both Martha's and Mary's words there resides implicit faith and implicit blame. They acknowledge that Jesus is able to heal, but at the same time they question why he did not come to save their brother. In essence, they say, "Lord, we believe that you are able to help us, but where were you when we needed you?" In this question, which simultaneously links faith in the Savior's power with doubt of his wisdom, we do not perceive the best systematic theology, but we do understand—because the words have been on our lips too. In a fallen world where mishap and heartache are certain, who has not felt how close companions are faith and blame as we question, "Lord, I believe you are able, but where were you when the cancer spread, when the deal was lost, when the center line was crossed, when my marriage unraveled, or when the towers fell?"

There is no immediate answer to such questions in this account. Rather, there is only the repeated assurance that the events have not escaped our God's sight. He knows what will come. The future does not surprise him and, in fact, fits into a plan for the glory of God (John 11:4) and the good of his people (verse 14).

Such assurance of our God's knowledge of what will happen is helpful, but it does not answer all of our questions. It does not even answer the problems of this account. For instance, if Jesus really knows that what will come is good, then why does he weep? If everything will turn out for the glory of his eternal purposes, then why are there tears, even for a second? The answer is that through the Savior, our God demonstrates not only that he understands what will happen but also that he understands what *has* happened.

Our God Understands What *Has* Happened

Lazarus is dead! In that stark and terrible fact there is sufficient cause for the King of all creation to weep. As his tears fall, the Savior tells us that death— even a death of a few days—is a disruption and corruption of the universe he made. Our Savior knows how death ravages our hearts and rends the peace of our world. He shows that the death of just one person, for even a brief time, jars the created order and causes the heavens to shudder. In our mortality the dire consequences of our first parents' sin, the pain of separation from loved ones, and the momentary victory of the Prince of Darkness are personally, visibly, and sometimes violently displayed. Jesus knows that something truly tragic has happened, and he weeps.

Jesus' tears affirm the propriety and validity of shedding tears over tragedy, even when we have knowledge of our God's ultimate victory. Knowledge of eventual good and glorious outcomes does not prohibit him or us from shedding tears over an immediate tragedy that we know has happened.

I have watched Jimmy Stewart's *It's a Wonderful Life* dozens of times. I know how it will turn out. I know that George Bailey's friends will rally around him, that Zuzu will get well, and that Clarence will get his wings—ignore that theology, please. Still, my knowledge of what will happen does not keep the tears from my eyes when a grieving and drunken pharmacist damages the young George's ears, when Mr. Martini ends up in the gutter, and when Donna Reed tells Jimmy Stewart to go away. Despite the good to come, the tragedy is still tragic in the present, still painful to watch, and still wrenching to my emotions. My heart resonates with the present reality of such pain, even when my mind knows that there will be a happy ending. In the same way that our humanity sympathizes with pain we know will soon cease, the Savior's tears reveal his understanding of our tragedies without denying that he knows what will come.

The tears that Jesus sheds in the face of death give us permission both to dry our tears and to shed them. Our tears dry with the solace of knowing that our God knows what will happen. For this reason, Christians fear tragedy and death less keenly than others because our God already knows the future and has provided for our good and his glory in it. At the same time, Christians feel death more deeply because we know that it signifies a corruption of our world so deep that even the King of creation wept to witness its devastating effects, and this King would die to heal them.

In our experiences of tragedy, we need both of these truths to gain comfort:

1. We need to know that our Savior, in his divinity, knows what will happen. I can have no peace in a fallen world if my God is guessing what will happen to my family or my work or my nation or my soul.

2. We need to know that our Savior, in his humanity, knows what has happened. He must be able to understand what causes me joy and pain, or else his knowledge of the events about me will mean nothing to me because they will have meant nothing to him.

Does our God know what *will* happen? This account of his raising Lazarus clearly answers, "Yes." Does he know what *has* happened? The Scriptures say with equal clarity, "Yes," and as proof they point us to this truth: "Jesus wept."

Jesus' understanding provides us a measure of comfort. We are relieved to know that he is not blind to our experience. But full peace remains beyond our reach until we are certain that he who has such knowledge of our world can truly sympathize with our sorrows.

Does Our God Really Care about Our Tragedies?

In declaring, "Jesus wept," the Bible answers with certainty, "Yes, he cares." Jesus' tears for Lazarus convince even the Jewish observers, who say, "See how he loved him" (John 11:36). This revelation of the feelings of the Savior, as troubling as it may be to our theologies of God's impassivity, pour understanding into our hearts that rational thought alone cannot supply. Consider some of the rational explanations recently offered to justify God in the face of our nation's recent tragedy:

- Some died, but many more were spared (because 50,000 persons could have been in the World Trade Center) — an explanation that makes perfect sense — unless you lost a loved *one*.
- Many despair, but some will repent — a rationale that comes dangerously close to justifying the terror of man as an instrument of the mercy of God.
- The tragedy was horrific, but wrath was warranted because of the sin exhibited in a nation of sensualism, materialism, and abortion — a judgment that should never be uttered, unless in the same breath we confess that a holy God could rightfully rend the earth and bring this building down on *our* heads for our sins.

These rational, theological explanations for why we may still trust God in the face of tragedy have some measure of truth and some degree of usefulness. But they will never offer sufficient explanations for

- the wives who lost husbands
- the businessman who lost 800 employees
- the firefighters and police who lost hundreds of comrades
- the children who lost parents
- the parents who now must send their children into harm's way on a foreign battlefield

While the explanations of our reason are good and necessary, we need something more to assure our hearts that our God really cares. That assurance resides not merely in the tenets of our theology but also in the tears of our Savior.

Our Theology Helps — But It Alone Is Not the Solace We Need

As a pastor I was once involved in disciplining a pastor for his wrongdoing. Officers of our church rationally, fairly, and conscientiously followed the letter of our standards for correcting a minister. Also, at each step of the process, we officially assured the minister and ourselves that we were acting out of concern for his good, as well as out of concern to protect the testimony of the church and the glory of Christ. Some years later, that disciplined and restored minister spoke to me and some other friends about his experience. He said, "My church's officers said they were acting out of concern for me. I do not doubt it. All of their actions were correct, and all of their words were reasonable. But I did not begin to experience healing in the church until I visited another pastor after my discipline. He knew of my situation and of my sin, but when he first saw me, he did not say a word to me. Rather, he came to me, put his arms around me, and wept for me. Only then did I know that someone really cared about me."

When Jesus wept, he let us know that he cares — really cares — about our tragedies. Rational explanations of the actions and motives of God are necessary instruments in the medicine bags of effective physicians of souls. But dispensing pills of logical possibilities and reasonable theories are not sufficient to heal or comfort the human heart. I can constantly repeat and honestly believe the Westminster Shorter Catechism answer #11: "God's works of providence are his most holy, wise, and powerful preserving and governing all his creatures and all their actions," and still I may wonder in the face of this world's grief and groaning if God really cares. The complexities of our world and of our God cannot be fully contained in the formulas of the religious sciences of man. Answers plain enough and encompassing enough for the hurting heart come in the incarnate form of the God-man, Jesus. How do I really know that a sovereign God really cares? "Jesus wept."

In the vulnerability of the Savior is the undeniable message that our God cares. He makes this message clear, not only in the presence of his tears, but also in the message of his presence among us. He is the God who cares so much that he came not merely to shed tears but also — soon after this account — to shed blood in our behalf. As Dorothy Sayers wrote, "When [Jesus] was a man, he played the man."[1] His willingness to involve himself in my world, my misery, and my pain testifies of my God's care in terms that my theology cannot contain and my heart cannot deny. Jesus' pain is the ultimate solace for my own. Without the cross I do not have much to say to my world and to my neighbor about the providence of my God. Minus the cross I have

---

1. Dorothy Sayers, "The Greatest Drama Ever Staged" (London: Hodder & Stoughton, 1938), 2, www.gutenberg.ca/ebooks/sayers-greatest/sayers-greatest-00-h.html.

only the conclusion of Bernie Sayone, a Jewish survivor of Auschwitz: "Inside my heart I don't believe. God failed us. He was supposed to be our protector and guide. He took a vacation or something."[2] With the cross I can face the worst horrors of this world and, without pretending to possess full understanding or attempting to offer a fully acceptable explanation, still contend that my God cares. The evidence of his care is not in my circumstances but in his character. I trust him and turn to him, not because my circumstances are explainable, but because his care is unquestionable in the light of the cross and the tears that took him there.

Our Savior Himself Is the Solace We Need

Whenever there is a tragedy, people search not only for the truth of what happened but also of why and how. Few persons seem to understand that the ultimate truth of Scripture is a person. Jesus said, "I am the way and the truth and the life" (John 14:6). In the display of his character on the cross, we find truth so deep that we cannot plumb it and so dear that we do not doubt him. Engulfed, enveloped, and embraced in the knowledge of who he is, we find the truth we doubt the least and need the most: *He cares.*

For those of you who will be ministering to others as pastors or as parents or simply as friends, I pray that you will learn this lesson well. When bad things happen, we are often too quick to provide possible explanations for why the wrong is not really so tragic. We try to justify God by softening the circumstances. You will face circumstances that *cannot* be softened. This is a fallen world with hard and horrible circumstances. They may be so terrible that any attempt to say that this tragedy is really a "good thing" because it may have a good outcome will sound either hollow or callous. The answers we need will be found, not in explaining our circumstances, but in understanding God's character. In the testimony of our Savior who wept, we learn that we do not have to minimize the pain of a fallen world to assure others of a God who cares. As we gaze deeply into the eyes of the one who created us and gave himself for us, we may *know* that he cares. We *see* the care in the tears in his eyes.

But if he understands and cares about our lives, then why do the tragedies still come? Even if we trust God's wisdom and care, we may doubt his divine power because we do not see him controlling the tragedies that assault our world. So we have a final question to answer in order for our hearts to find comfort.

---

2. Quoted in an article in the *St. Louis Post-Dispatch*, October 11, 2001.

NATIONAL TRAGEDY · 81

Does Our God Really Rule over Our Tragedies?

If we claim that God is all-powerful, all-knowing, and caring, then we should expect his purposes to triumph. Questions about the rule of God are fair. The Bible itself introduces such questions when the Jews, observing Jesus' tears, ask, "Could not he who opened the eyes of the blind man have kept this man from dying?" (John 11:37). How can we talk about the triumph of our God's rule when tragedy so frequently seems to overshadow his hand? This account of Jesus' power over death clarifies our understanding of God's rule by allowing us to focus on one event to see the divine wisdom at work over all. What does the account of our Lord's raising of Lazarus teach us?

God's Triumph May Take Time

Various aspects of time converge in this passage, and each tick of the clock discloses another dimension of God's ultimate control of events. Delay may come, but his design remains sure.

Delay may come. Already I've noted the delay in Jesus' coming that seemed to exasperate his followers. John's account makes it clear that Jesus knew that Lazarus was sick for two days before the Savior started for Bethany, and that Lazarus was in the tomb for four days before Jesus approached his friend's tomb (John 11:3, 6, 17). Why the delay? We do not know entirely, except that Jesus seems to be ensuring that Lazarus is most assuredly dead and thus is the recipient of an undeniable miracle proving the lordship of Jesus. Jesus explains to his slow-to-understand disciples, "For your sake I am glad that I was not there [when Lazarus died], so that you may believe" (verse 15).

From the vantage point of our current perspective we understand that the passage of time (even though it contained significant hurt and grief for Lazarus's loved ones) was a means of confirming the ultimate glory of Jesus' work. Could he have worked faster? Yes. Jesus could have raised Lazarus from the dead in the blink of an eye from across the universe. Could he have kept Lazarus from dying? Yes. But then the events that confirmed Jesus' lordship would not have occurred. The triumph took time, but this did not mean that our God's purposes were not being fulfilled.

In the aftermath of the World Trade Center attack, an *ABC News* crew followed a mother and daughter as they went block to block, from police checkpoint to checkpoint, and from medical station to medical station in search of the head of their home. He had managed a restaurant in the second tower. The family had not heard from him since his cell phone went dead while he was describing the devastation of the first tower. As time passed, hope grew fainter and tears more frequent. Then, as they waited behind a police tape that blocked them from the devastation, the man they sought suddenly walked out of the ruins covered with dust. The screams of delight after such delay were irrepressible. It was as if the whole account was scripted for a too-good-to-be-true movie. But when the camera cut back to Peter Jennings, it was clear nothing had been scripted. He choked up and said simply, "Thank God. I didn't know how that was going to turn out."

Thank God that what takes time does not indicate that our God's purposes are uncertain. Through the death and devastation of this fallen world, our God, in the person of his Son, is still moving toward us and moving all events toward his certain purposes. The more clearly we see the person and purposes of Jesus emerging from the tragic circumstances surrounding Lazarus, the more certain we are of God's sure hand.

God's design is sure. The design of God over time becomes even more apparent when we examine these events from an even larger time perspective. Within days of the raising of Lazarus at Bethany, Jesus told a parable about a certain rich man who ignores the misery of a poor man at his gate (Luke 16:19–31). Both men die. Then, the rich man in Hades asks Father Abraham to allow the poor man in heaven to return from the dead and to warn the wealthy relatives of the torment awaiting the unrighteous. "They will believe and repent if someone goes to them from the dead," says the man in torment (paraphrased). Replies Father Abraham, "If they do not listen to Moses and the Prophets, they will not be convinced even if someone rises from the dead" (Luke 16:31).

The name of the poor man in Jesus' parable is not incidental. His name was Lazarus! Further underscoring the appropriateness of Jesus' parable, the apostle John tells us that when Jesus raised the real Lazarus from the dead, the Jewish officials did not believe and repent either. Instead, they plotted with greater zeal to destroy Jesus (John 11:45–53, esp. verse 53). Then, when the rulers later succeeded in their plot to kill Jesus, and he himself would rise from the dead, they *still* would not believe.

Each aspect of these gospel narratives, taken in isolation, has elements of inexplicable tragedy. But observed over time, they display a divine design of amazing intricacy and precision:

- the irony of the name chosen for the character in Jesus' parable
- the parallelism of the resurrection of the fictional Lazarus, the real Lazarus, and Jesus Christ

- the timing of these events to prepare the disciples (and us) to understand both the significance and, even, the resistance that would
accompany their Lord's death and resurrection

Every detail in these events is coordinated to reveal that what takes earthly
time is not beyond heaven's rule:

Jesus' parable is a lens to understand Bethany.
Bethany is a lens to understand Calvary.
Calvary is a lens to understand eternity.

In fine and grand detail God demonstrates that he is working an eternal
plan that will not be thwarted by events that in immediate time contain the
tragic consequences and evidences of a fallen world. Each dimension of God's
revelation and resurrection is meant to help us understand that in God's timing all things (even present events that are truly and deeply tragic) will not
thwart his ultimate triumph.

What happens here in Bethany is a lens for us to look over all time and
all events to understand, not only that God's triumph may take time, but also
that God's triumph will surely come.

God's Triumph Will Surely Come

Jesus will pass this way again. A few weeks after this account of Lazarus's
raising, Jesus will take the path from Bethany to Jerusalem as the crowds
strew their cloaks and palm branches before him (John 12:1, 12). With shouts
of "Hosanna!" they will declare that it is time for him to declare his rule. But
though his time has not yet come, it *will* surely come. A few days later, the
same crowds will cry, "Crucify him," because his rule has not yet come, but it
will surely come. They will hang him on a cross and declare that his rule has
failed because rescuing angels do not come, but the angels *will* surely come.
Three days later, the divine rule of Christ promised through the ages *does*
surely come. Jesus declares his triumph over sin and death with resurrection
power.

God's triumph may take some time, but it *will* surely come. We do not
always understand the cause of the delay. Like Mary and Martha, we can
find ourselves saying, "But Lord, if you had shown your power earlier, this
tragedy would not have occurred." It is true that God's power can and will
destroy all evil. But if the Lord were to establish his rule over a fallen world
and exercise his justice against all sinful creatures immediately, then all the

dimensions of his glory, all the fullness of his harvest, all the purposes that have to ripen before this world comes to a close, would not materialize. This is the message of the parable of the wheat and the weeds. There Jesus tells us that if God were to pull up all evil by its roots now, then the growth of lives and events leading to the harvest of righteous persons would cease because our destinies are so interwoven with others' until Jesus comes again. God alone has the power and the wisdom to establish his ultimate rule over this fallen world when the time is ripe. So tragedy will have its day because his ultimate triumph has not come, but it *will* surely come.

Can it be true? Can we really abide in this hope of divine triumph when a fallen world so consistently and powerfully displays its corruption and entangles us in its misery? How do we respond when Jesus declares, "I am the resurrection and the life. The one who believes in me will live, even though they die; and whoever lives by believing in me will never die"? How do we answer when Jesus asks, "Do you believe this" (John 11:25–26)?

The answer to Jesus' question and our own doubts resides in this account of Lazarus. In order to explain how his resurrection power would ultimately rescue us from the miseries of this world, Jesus could have drawn stick figures in the sand or told a parable with a nifty plot. Instead, each tear of Jesus acts as a lens, drawing us to look in microscopic detail at who he is and what he can do. Through the lens of his tears we see him work with real flesh and blood to triumph over tragedy with the power of heaven. In the microcosm of the events surrounding Lazarus's death and resurrection, we learn that the love of God does not wilt in the face of tragedy, nor does the power of God retreat in the face of death. Death is allowed its moment so that we can clearly see proof of the Savior, who conquers death to save his people eternally.

Through the tears God brings us close to himself to enable us to see him who is the Lord over life and the Victor over death. When through his tears we see that Jesus knows our world, cares about us, and rules over the forces of the natural and the spiritual world, we learn that we can trust him in tragedy. Through Jesus' care for Lazarus we learn the reality of his power to turn back the consequences of the fall. Such expression of power in the face of tragedy will reach grand scale and have the greatest eternal consequence when our Lord will himself die to destroy Satan's rule forever.

Had we stood beneath the cross of Jesus Christ, our tears would have flowed down with his blood. We would have shaken our heads at the tragedy and been tempted to scold our God, "This can't be right!" But it *was* right. Though the triumph would take some time, it would surely come. Three days later, he would rise, right on time. The purposes of the risen Lord still will triumph in the time of his design. He yet fulfills the words of the prophet of old:

> The revelation of God's purposes awaits an appointed time;
>> it pants toward the goal,
>> and it will not fail.
> Though it tarries, wait for it,
>> because it will surely come and will not be late.
>
> —*Habakkuk 2:3, personal translation*

What proof do we have of such amazing statements? What basis do we have for such faith? Lazarus's rescue from the grave and Jesus' resurrection from the dead are the proofs in microcosm and grand scale that give us assurance in tragedy—near and far, small and great, personal and national—that our God understands, cares, and rules. How do we know? *Jesus wept.* Each tear in this tragedy is a lens to understand the power of God directed by love so strong that death cannot restrain its rule, time cannot blur its design, and tragedy cannot derail its triumph. This is how we know that God is love in the midst of tragedy: *Jesus wept.*

Part Two

PREACHING
AFTER THE LOSS OF A
CHILD

Chapter Five

SPECIAL NEEDS CHILD

SITUATION

Mary Rose was the first child of Ron and Tara Holms. Mary Rose entered the world with multiple birth abnormalities that immediately threatened her life and continually limited her mental capacity. She was expected to live for weeks but survived for five years—long enough for her parents to have another child, who experienced none of Mary Rose's difficulties. Though Mary Rose never spoke or walked, she developed rudimentary responses to her parents as they gave her round-the-clock care. She died near Christmas. Her passing into glory was unexpected and occurred shortly after her parents had sent friends a letter stating that her health was stable.

CONCERNS

I wanted to value Mary Rose. My primary concern and that of her parents was not to let her physical and mental impairments eclipse the beauty of her life. She was a child of God, a creation of his hand, and a treasure of life whom her parents had no trouble cherishing from the first moment of her birth. After her death, her parents were well aware that some would consider them blessed to now be without the burden of a child who required so much care. In response, they wanted everyone to know of the depth of their love for Mary Rose, the joy she had brought into their lives, the reality of their grief, and the strength that their faith had provided them through the trials of Mary Rose's life.

As their pastor, I wanted to honor the wishes of Ron and Tara to speak about how precious Mary Rose had been to them, but I didn't want them or others to fail to face the pain of her passing with gospel hope. I wanted to be honest about the trials they had faced, their present loss, and the blessing of the resurrection promises that God's Word makes to Christians. Mary Rose was already basking in the loving presence of her Lord, and she will ultimately be made whole in body and mind according to his heavenly promises. The message I preached needed to affirm Mary Rose's earthly value and offer her family the comfort of those promises.

APPROACH

I chose a psalm that exalts the goodness of God based on his eternal as well as earthly promises. My goal was not to expound the psalm verse by verse but to use its affirmations to identify both the consternation and comfort parents must feel when facing the presence and loss of a child with multiple challenges. I chose to identify with the parents in their pain and joy by speaking of my family experience with a brother who has mental disabilities. My intentions were to affirm the value of every child of God, to explain to all attending the funeral how deeply families can love special needs children, and to rejoice in the ultimate wholeness the Scriptures promise to such children through heaven's blessings.

THE SERMON

PRAISING GOD FOR THE BLESSING OF ONE SPECIAL LIFE

Bryan Chapell

¹I will exalt you, my God the King;
  I will praise your name for ever and ever.
²Every day I will praise you
  and extol your name for ever and ever.

³Great is the LORD and most worthy of praise;
  his greatness no one can fathom.
⁴One generation will commend your works to another;
  they tell of your mighty acts.
⁵They speak of the glorious splendor of your majesty—
  and I will meditate on your wonderful works.
⁶They tell of the power of your awesome works—
  and I will proclaim your great deeds.
⁷They celebrate your abundant goodness
  and joyfully sing of your righteousness.

⁸The LORD is gracious and compassionate,
  slow to anger and rich in love.
⁹The LORD is good to all;
  he has compassion on all he has made.
¹⁰All your works praise you, LORD;
  your faithful people extol you.
¹¹They tell of the glory of your kingdom
  and speak of your might,
¹²so that all people may know of your mighty acts
  and the glorious splendor of your kingdom.
¹³Your kingdom is an everlasting kingdom,
  and your dominion endures through all generations.

The LORD is trustworthy in all he promises
  and faithful in all he does.

—Psalm 145:1–13

I received the news of Mary Rose's departure the same day that the Christmas letter from her parents, Ron and Tara, arrived, sharing how well she was doing.[1] Mary Rose has been full of surprises all of her life. She surprised her parents when they learned that she would come into this world with burdens many children do not bear. She surprised the doctors in living much longer than they had predicted. She surprised us all by learning to smile so radiantly and regularly. She surprised us by teaching us how much joy can come in a package whose wrapper once seemed so damaged. She surprised us by teaching us how much strength God provides for the care of one so weak. She surprised us by not going home to him all the times when we thought she was ready, and then going home to him when we were not ready.

How should I talk to you about a child so full of surprises? When Ron called to ask that I speak to you, he simply said, "Exalt the Lord."

Why should we exalt the Lord in the face of this sadness? The psalmist answers, declaring that we should exalt him because "the Lord is good." And Mary Rose was not excluded from his goodness. Scripture says, "The Lord is good to all; he has compassion on all he has made" (Psalm 145:9).

We Exalt the Lord Because of His Goodness to Mary Rose

I know it is easy to question God's goodness with regard to one so damaged in mind and body, until we add to our understanding the words "but no more." Mary Rose was damaged in mind and understanding — *but no more*.

The psalmist tells us that the kingdom our Lord establishes for all he loves is an everlasting kingdom (Psalm 145:13). For this kingdom to be everlasting, the effects of the fall have to be reversed. The broken world has to be made whole, and those who live in that new world have to be made whole as well. This is precisely what the Bible promises: a new creation will come in which there will be no more tears or pain or infirmity (Revelation 21:4). Already Mary Rose exists in the glory of the Lord, seeing him face-to-face without limitation of body or mind (1 Corinthians 13:12).

She Will Be Like Jesus — Her Imperfections Will Be No More

When we see Mary Rose again, she will be like Jesus — made perfect in the radiance of his likeness. Her imperfections will be no more.

---

1. Individual names and some personal details have been changed as an expression of care for the family.

What will her body and mind be like, exactly? We don't know. Will she be a child, running and laughing with other children who have passed into glory, or will she be an adult of perfect stature, confident stride, and inexpressible beauty? We don't know. The Bible states that "what we will be has not yet been made known. But we know that when [Christ] appears, we shall be like him" (1 John 3:2).

She Is with Jesus — Her Longings Are No More

The Bible teaches us that to be absent from the body is to be present with the Lord (2 Corinthians 5:8). This is almost more goodness than we can take in. Mary Rose even now is in the arms of Jesus. We know that dear New Testament image of Jesus taking little children into his arms. That is the reality Mary Rose fully knows.

Her mother and father now ache for her absence, but if we could imagine the best way to ease their pain it would be to tell them that Jesus has their child. Perhaps we could compare this to how we would feel if we had been frantically searching for a lost child at the grocery store and then gotten word that she had walked to Grandma's house and was asleep in her arms. We would know such relief and thanksgiving and joy. Greater joy, even in the midst of our pain, is present now because Mary Rose is not with Grandma; she's in the arms of Jesus. He holds her. She knows his comfort. He has dried her tears. She is not afraid. She is not lonely.

Can we really say that she is not lonely? She is without her mommy and daddy and will be without them until they go to Jesus or he comes for them. Yes, we ache to think of their time apart. But there are two words of comfort from the Scriptures regarding this period of separation. First, in the same verse (1 Corinthians 13:12) that I quoted before — the one telling us that apart from this life, we shall see our Lord face-to-face — Paul adds these words: "then I shall know fully, even as I am fully known." The full import of these words is a mystery, but it is clear that God shares with us the depth of his heavenly understanding. To the extent that Mary Rose knows her parents' eternal security in Jesus and the certainty of her reunion with them, she is not lonely.

But what if it's a long time until she sees them again? Then we need the second word of comfort from Scripture: a thousand years in heaven's time are but as a yesterday already gone by (Psalm 90:4). In the measurement of eternity, all of our days here are but a passing breeze. The full span of our lives will go by for her as a blink of an eye. If time has so little meaning, and she already knows that she will be together again with her mommy and daddy, she is fine. She is fine!

Perhaps some may question if we can exalt the Lord for such blessings to Mary Rose, wondering if the heavenly promises apply to her. After all, she made no profession of faith; she could not acknowledge trust in so loving a Lord. For such questions, I take great delight and comfort in the apostle Paul's declaration that God counts the children of believing parents as "holy" to himself (1 Corinthians 7:14). Before they are able to claim him, God claims the children of believers as part of his holy family. We exalt the Lord because of his goodness to Mary Rose. She is with him; her imperfections will be no more, and her longings are no more.

We Exalt the Lord Because of His Goodness to Mary Rose's Parents

Perhaps it is beyond human understanding not to question how Ron and Tara could honestly repeat verses 9 to 13 of Psalm 145. Have they really experienced God's "mighty acts" and "glorious splendor"? Can they really testify, "The LORD is trustworthy in all he promises and faithful in all he does"?

How does the life of a child with so many problems and impairments give any indication of a mighty, glorious, and faithful God?

Did you read the Holmses' Christmas letter? Since I know the trials they have faced, I was struck with the joy and love that seemed to leap off the pages. They rejoiced in Mary Rose's progress. They delighted in her smile. They rejoiced in how their family had been knitted together by her care. They had learned to appreciate the greatness of other blessings, as measured against every small blessing of her life. They, like so many other Christian families who have experienced trial, instead of feeling abandoned by God, had a peculiar sense of his preserving. They sensed that apart from his care, this trial would have torn them apart, but because he was there helping them to endure and to love her and to love each other, they had a special sense of a divine hand upon their home.

If you have not been through such a trial with God's help, it's hard to explain how this can be. How can it be that trial does not turn to bitterness, and challenge actually gives you a greater sense of God's care rather than of his abandonment? I don't think I can explain this very well, but my experience with my mentally disabled brother Jeff has helped my understanding. Jeff made me sensitive to what other people experience as they care for children the world identifies as disadvantaged or disabled.

When I was a teen, I was greatly helped by an account from a TV movie. It probably wasn't a great movie, but it was God's gift to let a line of dialogue lodge in my mind. I have revisited that line many times. The actress playing the mother of a mentally disabled child said in the movie that when parents are expecting a child, we are like tourists anticipating a journey to a wonderful city we have not visited. We wait for that child as though we anticipate a trip to London for the first time. We read about what we will experience and try to anticipate everything we will enjoy. But when a special needs child comes into our lives, we discover that the plane that was supposed to take us to London has landed in a different place. For some inexplicable reason, we are not in London but in Paris. There is some initial disappointment and fear and anger that we are not where we wanted to be. But after we have been in Paris for a while, we discover that, although our journey has taken us to a very different place than we expected, Paris is wonderful too.

In this Paris of "Mary Rose," joy blossomed, and love grew as these two parents gave of themselves for the care of one who needed them very much. As they lived beyond their strength, and for another rather than for themselves, they discovered more of the nature of Jesus' love for them, and it made them even more able to express that love to Mary Rose and to each other. Of course they grieved then and now that Mary Rose could not know that love as fully as they gave it to her. But she does now, and she will again. For the joy of this knowledge, Ron and Tara exalt their Lord.

We Exalt the Lord Because of His Goodness to Us

What do you feel when you think of Mary Rose? You feel sorrow, as well as love for a child with so many shortcomings. How can you feel such things? You feel them because you are made in the image of God, and it is his delight to love the frail, faulty, and needy. Your compassion is a reflection of God's nature and of his redemption.

In Mary Rose we see the message of Christmas that should capture our hearts: God claims the lowly and needy as his own forever. In our Lord's blessing of Mary Rose we understand how we can come to him in our humility and woundedness and believe that he will still embrace us and love us. He is waiting not for the refinement of our perfections but for the acknowledgment of our need.

We all know that Mary Rose had a smiling ministry; we may not have yet grasped that it was God's smile. We have seen it before, when he smiled on a child in a manger, a king in swaddling clothes, and his Son on a cross. Yes, pain was there, but also the message that God loves the forlorn and will welcome those whose need of him is the greatest. In our love for Mary Rose we learn something of the nature of God that he planted in us. We need to learn to recognize the source of that love growing in our hearts so that when we are in need, we will turn to him and trust in him, despite our impairments.

He displays his glory by loving the meek and helpless, by using the weak things of the world to shame the strong, and by choosing the things that are not to nullify the things that are (1 Corinthians 1:28). For his glory he cares for the lowly more than those who lift themselves up, and for the fallen rather than for the faultless. For such great grace, we exalt him. Great is the Lord and most worthy of praise. Let us exalt him together for ever and ever.

Chapter Six

MISCARRIAGE OF
AN EARLY-TERM
INFANT

SITUATION

While many pastors glean from the wisps of biblical material to address the difficult but common experience of miscarriage, Pastor Dan Doriani[1] speaks from personal experience. Though the miscarriage he speaks of here took place more than twenty years in the past, the precise memories and the poignancy of their expression well demonstrate the past and present pain of such an experience. For this message, this pastor with a PhD puts aside his scholar's robe and speaks with the understanding of a skilled shepherd and the compassion of a still-pained father.

CONCERNS

Pastor Doriani addresses the expected subject of the spiritual state of infants who have died, but this is not his primary focus. He has three major considerations: First, he wants to help those who have not experienced miscarriage to understand the thoughts and needs of those who have. Second, he wants to help those who have experienced miscarriage to know that their turmoil, pain, and differing ways of handling it are normal, shared by others with similar experiences, and can be helped with the gospel. He especially wants

---

1. Dr. Dan Doriani has pastored churches in Pennsylvania and Missouri, been a professor at Geneva College and Covenant Seminary and authored ten books, including three commentaries (Matthew, James, and The Sermon on the Mount), two books on family and gender (*The Life of A God-Made Man* and *Women and Ministry*), and, three on Bible interpretation (*Putting the Truth to Work*, *Getting the Message*, and *Beyond the Sacred Page*).

to offer a word of gospel hope to parents who feel the strange guilt that often accompanies miscarriage. Finally, he wants to warn those who are grieving, and those who seek to offer comfort, about the blunders in speech and behavior that are likely to occur because our society's silence on this subject leaves many people ill prepared to handle it.

Approach

While Pastor Doriani brings appropriate biblical texts to bear upon the grief and questions that accompany miscarriage, his main tool of sympathy and understanding is redemptive vulnerability. He shares not only the facts of his own experience but also his disappointments, questions, doubts, pain, innermost thoughts, and even differences with his wife's processing of the same event. The rigors of self-examination are not meant to be self-indulgent or cathartic, but rather serve as disclosures that enable those who are suffering to know they are not alone in their experiences. At the same time, this caring pastor tries not to universalize his sorrow, allowing others to experience grief on their own terms. He validates the feelings of those who have connected deeply with an unborn child and allows for the emptiness of those who have not, with the knowledge that the gospel is wide enough to embrace both in whatever they are feeling and asking.

MISCARRIAGE: A DEATH IN THE FAMILY

Dan Doriani

When Rachel saw that she was not bearing Jacob any
children, ... she said to Jacob, "Give me children, or I'll die!"

— Genesis 30:1

"A voice is heard in Ramah,
    mourning and great weeping,
Rachel weeping for her children
    and refusing to be comforted,
    because they are no more."

—Jeremiah 31:15

The Loss, the Questions, the Pain

The weeping of Rachel confirms what we already know: there are few sorrows
that can compare to the loss of a child. And even the loss of an unborn child
can stir uncommon anguish. Many women understand exactly what Rachel
meant when, in a different context, she said, "Give me children, or I'll die!"

The loss of children is a heartbreaking theme, even in its lesser form — the
loss of an unborn child. Our third pregnancy ended in a miscarriage, so I
address the subject in the light of our experience, which began with a positive
pregnancy test. Our two daughters, four and two, were playing in the next
room when I heard the happy news. Soon afterward, I fell into a reverie that
revealed that I now wanted a son. I could not know that my girls would one
day become gritty competitors in an array of sports and become my partners
in running, hiking, and tennis. At that time, I occasionally fretted about their
love of fancy shoes and dresses. Even though I shared their affinity for tea

parties, I worried about the forms of femininity that led some girls to become cheerleaders rather than players. I wanted a son who would become a man's man, the kind who would rather score points than applaud them. In this way, I began to dream happy dreams of our child, whom I imagined as a boy. This was the way I felt the joy that we were going to have another baby.

My wife, Debbie, never shared my zeal. I ascribed her subdued response to the rigors of pregnancy and the first year of motherhood; no one could say we had easy babies. But she resisted that line of thought. She would say, "Something is wrong," and then let her words drift off.

"But how can you know that?" I countered. "You've only been pregnant twice before. That's hardly a sufficient sample size for reliable generalization." We had a friendly dispute about this for a month. Our refrains were, "Something is not right," and, "How can you know?" Meanwhile, I had told our girls that they would have a little brother or sister. Debbie's intuition restrained her, so I took up the vacated role of chief celebrant. As I tried to pump Debbie up and led the girls into what I considered a healthy level of enthusiasm, I became ever more convinced that Debbie's fears were unfounded.

But she was right. About three months into the pregnancy, on July 3, Debbie began to bleed. We spoke to our doctor on the phone. He delivered a stirring lecture on the theme of complete bed rest. "You need absolute rest. If you can't do it at home, I'll put you in the hospital!" His lecture, his zeal, galvanized me. I was certain we could do it. And then all would be well.

Thirty-four hours later, at bedtime at the end of an uneventful Fourth of July, contractions started. By this time our physician had left town for a short vacation. An alien voice offered thin, vague advice: "Rest is essential; you don't need to rush to the hospital." Unsure what this meant, we stayed in our beds as sleepless hours spun by in bright pain and dark anxiety. The clock read 12:47, then 1:39. "This is worse than childbirth," Debbie lamented. In the past, contractions meant progress, but not today. The contractions had to stop; otherwise this was the worst sort of labor in vain.

I thought of our child over and over. *What is happening to him? Is there any hope? Is he dying right now? Should we go to the hospital? What would be the point?* We wondered who would watch our girls if we had to go in, as the perpetual need to arrange babysitting juxtaposed itself against eternal matters. Meanwhile the clock continued to hurl cold, red numbers into the darkness: 2:17, 2:49, 3:14, 4:22.

Near sunrise, we took the girls to the home of our best friends, Steve and Sue, and drove to the hospital. There we waited for the substitute physician to take flesh. He had not wanted to talk to us, and now it seemed that he didn't want to see us either. He took his time coming in.

By the time he did arrive, Debbie had withdrawn to an inner space where she battled to control her pain. I want to say, "She battled pain and despair," but that would not be right. She had never gotten very enthusiastic about this child, and now she knew it was time to abandon all hope. She had other work to do. So I battled my despair alone.

There were five people in the room now—the weary, impersonal physician; the weary, impersonal nurse; Debbie; the baby; and me. No one seemed to care about the questions I yearned to ask, for myself and my family: *What is happening? Is the baby dead?*

I thought I knew, but I longed to be sure, and the silence of the professionals silenced me. I told myself to wait, thinking, *Surely the doctor will explain things shortly.* But the doctor voiced nothing but grunts and terse commands.

Finally, my lips broke loose and I said something, but in my anxiety and exhaustion, I didn't ask the right question. The doctor muttered something inaudible. I tried again, and he offered technospeak: "We have an incomplete spontaneous abortion ... I need to remove ... [pause] ... the product of conception. There is some tissue here ... [pause] ... that I need to remove." With that, he hurled a bloody mass that landed on the floor with a flop and a spatter.

I screamed silently. "Tissue? That's not tissue, that's my baby! Why can't he say, 'I'm sorry, Mr. and Mrs. Doriani. Your baby has died?' He won't even call it a fetus! Doesn't he know what's happening? Why can't he say it: our child has died"?

So I began to realize: if life begins at conception, then miscarriage (what he called a "spontaneous abortion") is a death most untimely. A death in the family.

The behavior of two people still stands out, twenty years after that night and morning. On one hand, we have the physician, so cold, so impersonal and uncaring, so intent on unwanted "tissue" and the "product of conception." He even labeled the event an abortion—an incomplete spontaneous abortion. He seemed wholly unaware of the death of a child and the grief of two parents. His cold manner and clinical language led me to suspect that he did perform abortions and to wonder why our beloved obstetrician would have such a partner. Weeks later, I learned that the man was, in fact, staunchly pro-life. Sadly, his pro-life principles didn't lead to a pro-life speech or manner that day.

The second person was an old friend named Willard. At nearly 7:00 a.m., I stepped outside the hospital room to find some water and to clear my head. As I walked down the corridor, I was astonished to see Willard sitting in a stray chair not far from our room. "Willard," I practically shouted, "what are you doing here?" Quickly drawing an erroneous conclusion, I asked, "Are you OK? Is everyone all right?"

"I'm fine," he replied calmly. "When you dropped off the girls, Sue and Steve called me and asked me to pray. But I decided to come to the hospital." So Willard had prayed and waited outside our room for nearly two hours on the off chance that he *might* see one of us for a moment, say a good word, and encourage us by his presence. And that, beloved, is *friendship*. *That* is Christlike love.

The First Days: Groping Painfully for Peace and Understanding

We went home a few hours later and made the mistake of answering the phone whenever it rang—and it rang and rang until it sounded like a jangling, howling snake. We felt we had to talk to family and friends who knew what had happened and wanted to stay in touch. But I foolishly kept answering until we realized we were forfeiting what we needed most—silence and solitude. That night, after tending to my confused daughters and weary wife, I crept into bed, knowing we had barely paused a minute to consider what had happened.

I was teaching at a Christian college and had to work the next day—or at least I *thought* I had to work. Word of our loss reached the office before I arrived, and soon the simplest question—"How are you doing?"—became a trial. How shall I answer *that* question for *this* person? I tried to mix honesty and evasion, while saying as little as possible: "Debbie is alright physically. Otherwise, I don't know how we are doing." But that seemed to satisfy no one. Everyone seemed to hold my gaze, to wait for me to say *more*, especially about my wife. They wanted to know how *she* was doing, not how *we* were doing.

I didn't want to talk about it, but it seemed to me that everyone was begging for more information. Their body language asked, "Can't you tell us more?" By my silence I replied, "Can't you see that I'm not ready to talk?" Even if I was gone by noon, I stayed in the building far too long. Somehow I couldn't see that I needed to grieve my loss. I had inhaled the "real men don't cry" model of manhood and hardly knew how I should feel or what I should do.

After a day or two, I was reticent to talk for another reason: I was flooded with unexpected and unanswerable questions. They troubled me because they bumped against some of my convictions about unborn children.

I wondered if our son (as I imagined) was in heaven. I hoped so; I believed so. But how could I be sure? If he is, would I meet him one day? Would he know me, in any sense, as his father? Would he be thankful for the providence that spared him from the sorrows of our lives?

But then, if he is in heaven, I reasoned, heaven must be largely populated with the unborn. Perhaps one-fifth of all pregnancies end in miscarriage. There are so many! Are all the unborn redeemed? It's reported that in some nations most pregnancies end in abortion. If so, are the people who do this unwittingly filling heaven with their monstrous practice? How does this affect the way we view their actions? Or perhaps none but the progeny of believers are in heaven. And are they among the redeemed, or among the angels, who never rebelled? It is hard to imagine the life of a never-born child in heaven.

I also had a darker fear. The Bible says so little about these matters. Could the orthodox doctrine be wrong? Maybe my child wasn't yet a person, not yet "my child." I wondered how my son, so small, so undeveloped, died. Like a higher animal, feeling but without self-consciousness? Like a worm, all but insensitive? Like a man, carried off by angels, rejoicing?

I suspect that I thought about these questions too much. I also suspect that I ran to these intellectual questions because I wanted to avoid my sense of pain, loss, and loneliness.

Then I began to understand my grief. If abortion is murder, then miscarriage is a death in the family. But a miscarriage is a strange kind of death. Where is the funeral, the gathering of family to mourn? There can be no eulogy. It is the death of someone whom no one knew, except (in a limited way) the mother.

If some of my questions were too intellectual, others were very real. First, everyone seemed to "know"—or assume—that women suffer more than men in these cases. Why, then, did I feel more grief, far more grief, than my wife? The answer was easy: Debbie always knew something was wrong, that something like this would happen. She had never attached herself to this child, and her detachment had spared her. I also watched our children. Why was one daughter stricken with the loss, while the other acted as if nothing had happened? Why do people experience loss so differently?

My second question was even more baffling: Why was I feeling polluted and defiled, as if I were guilty of something? A couple days after our loss,

I went running at night. Alone with God in the warm July darkness, the explanation slugged me like a barrage of hammers: I had observed an event that sounded and felt like an abortion—the abortion of my own child—and I had said nothing. The doctor's cool, detached talk of "tissue" and "product of conception," his manner as he threw that "tissue" on the floor—that must be what an abortion is like. At an abortion, I guessed, it would be psychologically impossible to say words such as *baby* or *dead*. It might not even be possible to say *fetus*. Yes, life had left my child hours earlier; it wasn't an abortion. But I had failed to defend the dignity of my child's life. By my silence I had sinned, against my conscience at least, and I needed to repent.

Leading Lessons

It was easy to see that our miscarriage didn't fit the typical pattern, but I don't think our case is exceptional in any ultimate sense. It is wiser to conclude that no two experiences of loss are identical. A miscarriage after ten weeks will differ from a miscarriage after twenty weeks. The loss of a first pregnancy will be different from the loss of a second pregnancy. A third or fourth miscarriage will be different from a first. In short, no two sorrows are identical, and even if the facts are the same, the people who experience them are not. Perhaps we should summarize the main lessons for the parents.

First, parents should expect to experience the loss of an unborn child in very different ways. Husbands and wives should give each other (and themselves) permission to respond honestly and without preconceptions about what is fitting. One parent may be devastated, the other only lightly troubled. As a result, would-be comforters should listen to their friends instead of prejudging the situation. Soon after our miscarriage, a certain woman strode up and declared, "I know this must be so hard for Debbie. It's always harder for the woman. The men don't care." She gave me an "all men are cold brutes" look and said, "So you take care of Debbie!" I'm sure she thought she was being helpful.

Second, a miscarriage is a different sort of death, but it is a death. The long cultural debate about abortion has sharpened our view of unborn children. When we affirm the humanity of a child, even in the womb, it can intensify our sense of grief and loss when the fetus dies.

I first wrote about my first reflections on our miscarriage three years after the event. By that time, the laughter and chatter of an eighteen-month-old girl filled up an already active house. The anguish had receded; each day has enough trouble of its own. But three years after our event, our second daughter, stricken as deeply by the miscarriage as a two-year-old could be, still spoke freely of dying babies. Few adults are so open. Common as it is, we rarely discuss miscarriage and hardly know what to do or say. More than two decades later, I admit that I still think about our lost child. My children are twenty-six, twenty-four, and twenty. My eye still sees the symmetry that should have been: twenty-six, twenty-four, *twenty-two*, twenty. I still wonder about that lost son at times. Would we have played basketball, baseball, football, tennis? Would we have discussed politics and philosophy and movies? Some holes are never filled.

Third, since we do continue to think through our view of unborn children, we should expect uncertainty. There is no protocol, no normal response. We are walking in the dark, so we will stumble.

Fourth, while I cannot know how the unborn die or how they experience eternal life, I am confident that believing parents can trust that their unborn children are with the Lord. Above all, they are members of the covenant family. As Peter stated, "The promise is for you and your children" (Acts 2:39). They never sinned or rebelled, and even if the taint of Adam's sin touched them in the womb, the work of Christ is sufficient to cure it. But we need not say more than that. It is enough to know that "the secret things belong to the LORD" (Deuteronomy 29:29) and that "the Judge of all the earth" will do right (Genesis 18:25).

Counsel for Counselors

Since I first wrote about miscarriage, I have had many conversations with women and men who lost a child. So then, what do you say to a woman who loses her daughter before she ever holds her? How do you comfort a man who cradles a son whose life is measured in minutes? Fortunately, there is a substantial consensus among people who have experienced miscarriages.

First, while a few escape an early-stage miscarriage without much sense of loss, most do not. The grief is compounded (generally speaking) if the pregnancy reached a later stage, or if the couple suffered repeated miscarriages, or if they are older or had difficulty becoming pregnant.

Second, while the Christian community could do better, everyone seemed to find friends or family members who shared their burdens well. They listened; they quietly helped with material needs. But we also endured miserable comforters who unwittingly intensified our pain.

So then, what is helpful and what is not? It helps, we agreed, when friends bring meals, send cards, take care of older children, and provide a warm embrace or a calming, silent presence. Willard came to the hospital and waited for nearly two hours to see me for barely two minutes. No one forgets that kind of sacrifice; it fairly shouts, "I love you."

Initially, most of us found that the simplest expressions of love were most helpful. We still remember friends who gently reminded us, "We love you. Even now, God loves you too."

It is important to give a grieving family time to be alone and to find psychological breathing room. Cards express compassion without invading privacy. When a friend takes the other children for a few hours, she gives the gift of solitude. Alone with each other, the couple talks (or not) and grows closer. Alone with the Lord they can learn anew why Jesus called the Holy Spirit the Comforter. When friends bring a meal, they need to look for clues that it's time to go. As in the hospital, it's best to err on the side of brevity. There is "a time to be silent and a time to speak" (Ecclesiastes 3:7). No one should push to know how the prospective parents feel. Persistent questioning forces the couple to either express or deny their feelings: Should we speak before we are ready? Or should we smile and choke back the tears?

No one likes the overconfident visitor. "I know how you feel" can bring anything but comfort. The knife of miscarriage never cuts the same way twice. Did my friends know how we felt when our pro-life doctor was substituted for by someone who *acted as if* he were comfortable with the demise of an unborn child?

Let me share some of the stories I heard. Two women told me the hospital kept them overnight—in the maternity ward! Who can know how that felt? One had a nurse bounce up asking, "Do you want your baby now?" Another who bore twins entered labor in the twenty-first week of pregnancy. As soon as the process of delivering a perfect boy and girl was finished, the process of dying began. Named and loved, the children lay in their parents' arms until no breath remained. Another couple wondered why they were stoical, almost unfeeling about their loss. Was something wrong with them?

So then, when someone says, "We know how you feel," skeptical parents think, *Do you? Do you know what the doctor said? Do you know that this was our last chance to have a girl? Do you know that our in-laws told us they are glad the baby died?*

Speaking of another baby is an especially bad idea. Perhaps the doctor has forbidden it; perhaps there has been infertility. Or it can seem to imply that the lost child is easily replaced, that the parents shouldn't be too upset.

Unsolicited advice often misses the mark. In Solomon's words, "Fools find no pleasure in understanding but delight in airing their own opinions" (Proverbs 18:2). One woman had three preschool children when she lost her fourth. "You should be glad," several people dared to say. "Why would you want a fourth?" Proverbs 15:2 rightly declares, "The mouth of the fool gushes folly."

One visitor told a mourning parent, "Maybe you weren't ready for another child." Maybe, but why did God, who opens and closes the womb, therefore allow the pregnancy to begin? This line of thinking invites people to question God's wisdom, love, and power at the worst time.

After our loss, someone told me, "Maybe God allowed your miscarriage so you can minister to others with similar losses." Maybe. But could not God, who is all-powerful, have taught me in another way? Would God, my loving Father, take away my child (just) to make me a marginally better comforter?

True friends know the value of silence (see Job 2:13). James rightly states, "Everyone should be quick to listen [and] slow to speak" (1:19). In times of distress, sufferers may need to be reminded that our Lord indeed reigns, but unwanted counsel has this flaw: It tries to interpret someone's experience before they even know what that experience is. Like steak in the mouth of an infant, it chokes. The wise comforter lets the grieving parents set the agenda. Simple words are amazingly helpful: "Can I do anything?" or "I'm available if you want to talk." One woman told me she wanted to talk and talk and talk after her miscarriage. She processed her experiences by talking about them. Some people speak so they know what they think, but most people think so they know what to say. Some people need to think for weeks before they are truly ready to speak. Wise friends wait patiently for that time and listen well when it comes. Another woman captured the thoughts of many when she said, "My friend helped me the most when she just listened, when she let me talk and cry."

A miscarriage *is* a death in the family, so this grieving is *right*. Yet, in time, the tears slow and then dry. The comforting friend helps by affirming two things. First, in the present, there is real loss — the death of *this* child. As David declared after the death of his newborn son, "I will go to him, but he will not return to me" (2 Samuel 12:23). Second, the comforter gives a friend space and time to be alone with our Lord, our Counselor. Ultimately, he alone must answer our questions, wipe away our tears, and comfort us with his love, now and forever.

Chapter Seven

MISCARRIAGE OF A LATE-TERM INFANT

SITUATION

Joshua was the third child but first son of this couple who had newly come under Pastor George Robertson's pastoral care.[1] Given the age of Joshua's older siblings, he may have been a "surprise" baby. Regardless, his family was elated at the prospect of his arrival. However, the joy turned to dread when they learned, near the delivery date, that Joshua had died. After a long, agonizing labor, their baby boy was stillborn. His parents, having been well-grounded in the Scriptures, though heartbroken, were steadfast in their confidence that they only held the "tent" of his soul in their arms and that his soul had gone to be with the Lord.

CONCERNS

Joshua's parents wanted a memorial service, but not just for their immediate family's sake. They were devoted believers, so they wanted those of their friends and family who did not know Christ to hear that God's covenantal grace gave them confidence — not their works, not external sacraments, not the inherent goodness of children. Robertson's church was centrally located in a theologically astute community. Not only was the denomination's seminary

---

1. Dr. George Robertson has pastored churches in Missouri and Georgia. He now pastors First Presbyterian Church (PCA) in Augusta, Georgia. A frequent teacher of preachers in seminaries, he is the author of *Deuteronomy: More Grace, More Love.*

nearby, but there were also three other seminaries of divergent theological perspectives in the same city. Friends and family members whose views of the death of children were influenced by all of these varying perspectives would be present at the service. Robertson's foremost concern was to shepherd these parents to the comfort that only the gospel could bring in their dark night of the soul. But he also had to be sensitive to their concern for the others present. He had to preach, as clearly as possible, a biblically and theologically informed message on the death of a covenant child without the sermon sounding like a seminary lecture. Thus, using hymn writer Katherine Hankey's words, he sought first to "tell the story" of God's Fatherly grace "for those who know it best," while allowing "the rest" to overhear the biblical assurances of Jesus' sovereign love for our covenant children.

APPROACH

Pastor Robertson determined that what everyone present needed most was a story about Jesus. Mark's account of the little children and Jesus (10:13 – 16) is the most straightforward telling of this event in the Synoptic Gospels (see also Matthew 19:13 – 15; Luke 18:15 – 17). And given that Mark's gospel was used in the early church to instruct new believers, he thought it would be wise to use this brief but brilliant account of that touching scene. The desire was to allow Jesus' persona to comfort those in attendance emotionally, while unpacking the biblical writers' carefully chosen vocabulary in all three synoptic accounts to build the infrastructure necessary to bear up under heavy theological questioning.

The Lord wonderfully comforted the grieving family with his Word the day this sermon was preached. But he also used this sermon as a helpful reference point for other parents and grandparents, some of whom, in future years, also would suffer the loss of a child. God's promises to our covenant children, implicit in this text, also became a guide for other church members regarding their approach to individual parenting and corporate children's ministry.

THE SERMON

JESUS' CHILDREN

George Robertson

> [13]People were bringing little children to Jesus for him to place his hands on them, but the disciples rebuked them. [14]When Jesus saw this, he was indignant. He said to them, "Let the little children come to me, and do not hinder them, for the kingdom of God belongs to such as these. [15]Truly I tell you, anyone who will not receive the kingdom of God like a little child will never enter it." [16]And he took the children in his arms, placed his hands on them and blessed them.
>
> —*Mark 10:13–16*

DEAR PARENTS, thank you for your courage and generosity in requesting this memorial service, which not only gives you the opportunity to grieve Joshua's death but also provides an occasion for us as your covenant family to express our love for you. Today, together, we climb into our Savior's arms to find the comfort of his promises, which are abundant to his children, their children, and their children's children. While by inference we may conclude that our merciful Creator is gracious toward all children dying in infancy, there is no need for the Christian to doubt his sovereign Redeemer's protection of covenant infants.[2] So as those to whom God has made the same promise that he made to Abraham—to be your God and the God of your children—let me urge you for now to lay aside your questions about what you do not understand and repose on what you may know for sure from scriptural promises, which are all "'yes' and 'amen'" in Jesus.

---

2. Among the Reformed this has been the consensus. The most thorough theological treatment of this subject was by Robert Alexander Webb, *Theology of Infant Salvation* (Harrisonburg, Va.: Sprinkle, 1907). The thesis of Webb's book can be summarized by the Canons of Dort (1619): "Since we are to judge of the will of God from his Word, which testifies that the children of believers are holy, not by nature, but in virtue of the covenant of grace, in which they together with their parents are comprehended, godly parents ought not to doubt the election and salvation of their children whom it pleases God to call out of this life in their infancy" (1.17).

Come with me now and observe the comfort these parents experienced in the love of Christ for their children. [Pastor Robertson then read the biblical text as presented above.]

Jesus' Powerful Love for His Little Ones

While I was actively teaching seminary classes, the infant child of one of my students died of SIDS while in his crib in the family's on-campus apartment. In the funeral service for that covenant son, their pastor related the story of a new pastor who visited the home of one of his parishioners and noticed a large round stone on the floor engraved with the words "the moon is round." The pastor, of course, was perplexed, so he asked the woman for an explanation. She informed her visitor that a young friend of hers had died of cancer at fourteen years of age. During the two years of the young girl's struggle, she had kept a notebook of Bible verses that had comforted her in her suffering. After the girl died, friends and family began to read her journal. In the middle of the book was an index card with no verse written on it, just this statement: "The moon is round." Of course they did not understand the cryptic statement at first, but eventually the meaning became clear: When it is dark and only a sliver of the moon is showing, what do you know? You know that, though you cannot see it, the moon is round. The teenaged saint believed that though she could not see enough into God's providence to understand everything that was happening to her, she still knew that God is gracious.

Mary and Daniel,[3] you practiced this kind of faith throughout the process of Joshua's birth. Rather than questioning what you did not understand about God's ways (a questioning that the psalmists certainly show us that God allows us to do), you spiritually camped on what you knew about God's character as revealed in Christ. Very specifically, you focused on what you knew about Jesus' care for the children of believers. In so doing, you learned such truths from texts such as the one we've just read. Here, by Jesus' proactive generosity, we may discern what he thinks about our children and find immeasurable comfort.

To appreciate the promises embedded in Jesus' actions requires proper *identification* of these children handed to the Savior for his blessing. While Matthew and Mark use the generic word for *child*, Luke is very specific. These were babies (*brephē* in Greek), still nursing perhaps. These babies had

---

3. Individual names and some personal details have been changed as an expression of care for the family.

to be *carried* to Jesus; they did not break free from their parents and run into his arms like a kindergartner to Santa Claus. They could not come on their own accord. Before they could even recognize Jesus, much less pronounce his name or repeat a catechism answer, they were *brought* to Jesus. Likewise, Joshua did not have to have the ability to lift himself to Jesus; the Shepherd took this little lamb into his arms.

Next, notice Jesus' *ire* over his disciples' attempt to rebuff these parents, perhaps supposing that Jesus was too busy to fool with babies. Jesus was angry; in fact, he was indignant, and it was the anger of love. Throughout his earthly ministry, Jesus demonstrated his love for children. Obviously, he had attentively observed children at play, because he described their activities so as to teach spiritual lessons to adults (Matthew 11:17). Loving the voices of the ones he created, he refused to hush them when they yelled, "Hosanna!" during his triumphal entry (Matthew 21:15–16). Because Jesus had made it a practice to listen to them, the Word of the One who was infinitely strong, says that strength comes from the mouths of babes (Psalm 8:2). Only one who had studied the child's heart would turn to a child for an example of humility when his disciples were arguing over greatness.[4] And because he loved children with the protective passion of his Father, he warned that it would be better for someone to try to swim with a millstone around his neck than for that person to cause a child to stumble (Luke 17:2). So it is no surprise that when someone tried to keep a baby from his blessing, Jesus became furious. Such fury reveals great love. Listen to this poetic description of God's anger against any who hinder or harm a child:

> And these, all these are mine
> I know each sinew of their small frames
> I hear their fear of night
> I watch their fun
> And when they laugh, so do I
> In joy I see them invent themselves
> Even their shyness is a delight to me
> I cherish their innocence
> And these, all these are mine
> And if, when I return,
> I find just one who has been defiled

---

4. J. Norval Geldenhuys, *The Gospel of Luke* (Grand Rapids: Eerdmans, 1951), 455n.

One desecrated by your corruption
One invaded by your lust
One chained to your perversion
One burgled of purity
One dominated by your tyranny
One diseased through your indulgence
One famished by your inequity
One reliant on your base favours
One separated from Me through your wicked fancy,
One, who once was Mine
Then I promise
You will never see the sun again
All you will receive is darkness
It will have no end
And you will not know peace
It will be terrible and just on that day
Because these, all these are mine.[5]

Jesus' Heavenly Desire for His Little Ones

Jesus' earthly love for these children of believers was merely reflective of his eternal *intention* for them. Mark tells us that he gave the kingdom to them. Some gloss over Jesus' startling announcement in verse 14 by claiming that the Savior was merely using these children to form a comparison. They read the verse like this: "The kingdom belongs to those who are *like* these." This rendering points merely to a comparison, but the Greek pronoun translated "such as these" (*toioutōn*) is not used in comparison but rather for identification.[6] For instance, the same word is used in Hebrews 7:26: "Such a high priest meets our need—one who is holy, blameless, pure, set apart from sinners, exalted above the heavens." The author of Hebrews was not saying that any priest who fit that bill would do. Jesus is the only possible reference. Likewise, Jesus is not saying in our text that the kingdom of God belongs merely to those who become like children—he will say that in the next verse; rather, he is saying it belongs to *these* children. While no one has the authority to make that declaration over every single child, *these babies* brought to Jesus by

5. Stewart Henderson, "Broken Image," quoted in Raymond Brown, *The Message of Deuteronomy* (Downers Grove, Ill., InterVarsity, 1993), 236.

6. John Murray, *Christian Baptism* (Phillipsburg, N.J.: P&R, 1980), 61.

their believing parents—before the babies themselves were able to speak or read or walk down an aisle—were identified as members of the kingdom of God whom he had sovereignly claimed without their cooperation. Of course they were born sinners, but because God is sovereignly gracious, he is able to apply the redemption purchased by Jesus Christ to any he chooses, even if they are not yet capable of laying intellectual claim to such truths.[7]

By now it should be clear that Jesus has also designed that our children *imitate* true gospel living for the world. After his bold declaration of these children's citizenship in heaven, Jesus appeals to a child's simplicity as a model for kingdom living. Their readiness to be held by him is the proper response for any sinner to the Shepherd-King. The Shepherd who holds your child this morning is the same Shepherd whose arms are outstretched to embrace you, the parents.

Children receive gifts readily, but adults are sometimes more reticent to accept something they did not earn. Sometimes that reticence can even prevent them from receiving the grace of salvation. To you this morning, Mary and Daniel, Jesus is extending the gift of gospel comfort. Do not be shy to open that gift with the same kind of vigor and determination with which a child opens a wrapped present. You need this gift, and it will comfort your soul.

Children also simply receive whatever we teach them about the Lord and his works. If we tell them that God made the world, they accept it. If we tell them that Jesus loves them, they accept it. If we tell them that Jesus does not want them to do something, they may do it anyway, but they accept without question that Jesus does not like it. However, adults will argue with Jesus every step of the way. When your Savior tells you today that the kingdom of God belongs to your child, do not argue; just accept it as a child.

Jesus' Intimate Knowledge of His Little Ones

Finally, you must find comfort in Jesus' *intimate* actions. They absolutely convince us that he loves our children. Notice how the Lord took these children

---

7. Westminster Confession of Faith 10.3. In 1903, the PCUSA adopted this interpretation of the Confession's statement regarding the death of elect infants: "With reference to Chapter X, Section III, of the Confession of faith, that it is not regarded as teaching that any who die in infancy are lost. We believe that all dying in infancy are included in the election of grace, and are regenerated and saved by Christ through the Spirit, who works when and where and how he pleases." Reformed theologians who taught this include Charles Hodge, B. B. Warfield, Herman Bavinck, Louis Berkhof, and Loraine Boettner. See William Hendriksen, *The Bible on the Life Hereafter* (Grand Rapids: Baker, 1975), 100–104.

in his arms and embraced them. Sometimes our body language speaks much more than our words. Jesus did not wave at them or pat them on their heads or merely shake their hands. Rather, he *embraced* them—because he loved them. Our children belong to him first and are merely loaned to us as parents. Jesus' hug demonstrates a divine love that came before ours and extends into eternity.

But not only did Jesus hug these kids; he put his hands on them and blessed them as well. In the Old Testament, when a faithful Jew put his hand on someone and blessed him by God's command, it was regarded as an incontrovertible imparting of grace.[8] Now sometimes finite sinners did not hear God properly, or they placed their hands on the wrong person. But there is no margin for error here: God himself placed his hands on these children and imparted grace to them. God still places his hands on our children's heads and says, "Your children are born to me" (see Ezekiel 16:20). I do not know the destiny of an unbeliever's child, because the Bible does not make promises to unbelievers' children. Given all that we know about God, we are inclined to believe that all go to heaven who die in infancy. Still, we must confess that the Bible, which is addressed to God's people, does not specifically address this subject. However, the Bible is not silent about God's specific regard for the children of believers and his ownership of them.[9]

Jesus' actions of embracing and blessing these children explain how we can know that Joshua is in heaven. Little Joshua had a sinful nature even in his mother's womb (Psalm 51:5; Romans 5:12, 18–19; Ephesians 2:3). No one would have to teach him how to whine or disobey; he would grow up knowing how. So how could he get to heaven without professing faith in Jesus Christ? The same one who took these children in his arms while they were babies and gave them grace is the same one who made David trust in him even at his mother's breast (Psalm 22:9; 71:6), who called Jeremiah to be a prophet while he was still in his mother's womb (Jeremiah 1:5), and who made John the Baptist to leap with joy in response to the good news of salvation while yet in his mother's womb (Luke 1:41). Jesus regenerated this child without the child's saying a word. Therefore, you have chosen the perfect name for your baby boy, who is now in the arms of Christ—Joshua, "the LORD saves."

---

8. Gerhard Kittel, ed., *Theological Dictionary of the New Testament* (Grand Rapids: Eerdmans, 1964), 2:755.

9. See Genesis 17:7–9; Exodus 20:6; Deuteronomy 4:37–40; Psalms 100:5; 102:28; 103:17–18; Isaiah 44:3; 54:13; 59:21; 65:23; Jeremiah 32:28–29; 35:19; Ezekiel 37:25; Zechariah 10:6–7; Acts 2:38, 39; 16:14–15, 31.

In September 1542, Magdalene, one of Martin Luther's daughters, lay dying. In tears, the German Reformer asked, "Magdalene, my dear little daughter, would you like to stay here with your father, or would you willingly go to your Father yonder?" She answered, "Darling father, as God wills." Though Luther prayed for God to preserve her life, she died in her daddy's arms. As she was placed in her coffin, Luther declared, "Darling Lena, you will rise and shine like a star, yea, like the sun. I am happy in spirit, but the flesh is sorrowful and will not be content, the parting grieves me beyond measure. I have sent a saint to heaven."[10]

I know your pain is great, Mary and Daniel. We have wept together over the loss of your son and the death of your dreams for a little boy. Though your pain is unspeakably great, your comfort is not merely that of lay astronomers who know that the moon is round when they can only see a sliver. Your comfort is that your son shines like a star, yea, like the sun itself, with Jesus in heaven. And because Jesus is your faithful Savior too, your assurance is the same as David's; though Joshua cannot return to you, someday you will go to him. In the meantime, the Father of mercies and the God of comfort knows how to love you. Above all others he knows how to care for you empathetically because he, too, knows the pain of losing his Son — another Joshua.

The Lord has given — though it does not seem to us for long enough. And the Lord has taken him away from you in order to keep him safely with himself until you can join him. In the gap between what we know by revelation and what we cannot understand in our humanity, let us declare with Job, "Blessed be the name of the LORD," who does all things well. Mary and Daniel, I love you, and so does your church family.

---

10. Preserved Smith, *The Life and Letters of Martin Luther* (New York: Houghton Mifflin, 1911), 353–54.

Chapter Eight

NEWBORN LOSS

SITUATION

Dustin, the father of this newborn child, movingly describes the situation that Pastor John Piper[1] faced in preparing this funeral message:

> In 2002, my wife, Kellie, and I left for the Middle East to work as cross-cultural peacemakers. We had been members at Bethlehem Baptist Church, and I had graduated from The Bethlehem Institute. The grand theology of John Piper and Bethlehem was (and is) part of our DNA. In 2003, Kellie became pregnant with Owen. Kellie began to go into labor at only twenty-four weeks. In our city, there was no chance of survival for a baby born that prematurely, so we were medically evacuated to Istanbul, Turkey, where the chance of survival was better, but still only 10 percent (it is about 50 percent in the United States).
>
> Owen was born by C-section shortly after we arrived in Istanbul and lived for only twenty minutes. Other than the doctors and nurses, I was the only one who saw him alive (Kellie had been given general anesthesia). Because of the surgery, we had to stay in Istanbul for ten days before we could return to the States. Owen actually arrived before us.
>
> John had written us a very encouraging and helpful e-mail while we were in Turkey. I called him right after getting home to ask him to preach the funeral sermon. He graciously agreed. We are very glad. This sermon has been a great blessing to us and to many others who have lost babies. May the truth here continue to speak grace and comfort from our good and kind Father.

1. Well-known for his preaching and writing ministry, Dr. John Piper is Pastor for Preaching and Vision at Bethlehem Baptist Church (Baptist General Conference) in Minneapolis, Minnesota. His many books include *Desiring God*, *The Supremacy of God in Preaching*, *Let the Nations be Glad*, and *The Future of Justification*. Many helpful resources from Dr. Piper are available at www.desiringgod.org.

CONCERNS

Pastor Piper states his concerns clearly in the headings of the main points of this short sermon. He wants a young couple who just lost a newborn to know that their child is precious to and safe with God, that God is yet trustworthy because he is sovereign and good, and that this awful loss is not without purpose in the lives of the family and in the lives of others. In short, as we would expect from John Piper, he wants to make it clear that God's glory is yet being made known—even in the face of pain and suffering—for those with the eyes to see eternity through the truths of Scripture.

APPROACH

Pastor Piper assumes two critical burdens in this message: (1) proving from Scripture that a newborn incapable of expressing faith can, nonetheless, be eternally safe and uncondemned, and (2) proving from Scripture that the short life of a newborn can bring glory to God and change the world.

These are heavy burdens, and this caring pastor lifts them with an intellectual rigor atypical of most funeral services. But his willingness to wrestle with Scripture in such a time reflects his awareness that he must deal with such questions in order for this spiritually mature and scripturally sophisticated couple to find rest for their souls. Piper goes before them, asking and answering the hard questions these parents will surely have, in order to enable them to grieve with the assurances of Scripture and without the additional burden of having to wrestle their answers from Scripture without his help.

Earlier messages dealing with child death in this book have reflected the covenantal perspectives of Presbyterian preachers. The Baptist convictions of Dr. Piper cause him to approach Scripture somewhat differently and yet come to wonderfully similar conclusions about the spiritual security of the children of believing parents.

THE PRECIOUS LIFE AND POWERFUL LEGACY OF A CHILD OF GOD

John Piper

> So God created man in his own image,
>> in the image of God he created him;
>> male and female he created them.

— Genesis 1:27 ESV[2]

Owen Shramek Was and Is a Human Being Created in God's Image

To show that subsequent generations of humans bear this same image of God with which Adam and Eve were created, the Bible tells us in Genesis 5:1–3:

> This is the book of the generations of Adam. When God created man, he made him in the likeness of God. Male and female he created them, and he blessed them and named them Man when they were created. When Adam had lived 130 years, he fathered a son in his own likeness, after his image, and named him Seth.

Millions of people don't believe this. They would say that Owen was just an evolutionary product of time, energy, and matter. Their hearts know better. Others would say that Owen was not human because he had not reached viability. The Bible has a different view. When Mary, pregnant with Jesus, approaches Elizabeth, who is pregnant with John the Baptist, the word used

---

2. All Scripture quotations in this chapter, unless otherwise indicated, are taken from the English Standard Version (ESV).

to designate John in the womb is the same word as that used for babies outside the womb. Elizabeth says to Mary: "Behold, when the sound of your greeting came to my ears, the baby in my womb leaped for joy" (Luke 1:44).

Owen was a *baby*—a *human being* created in the image of God.

Owen Shramek Was and Is Your Son

Some day when you have other sons and daughters, perhaps four, people will ask you, "How many children do you have?" And you will say, "We have five children. One is in heaven, and four are still with us." Owen is your son. He will always be your son. And you may say, with David in 2 Samuel 12:23, when his baby died, "Now he is dead. Why should I fast? Can I bring him back again? I shall go to him, but he will not return to me."

Owen Shramek Is Safe and Uncondemned in the Presence of Jesus Christ

I want you to be sure that Owen is safe and uncondemned, but there is something more important to be sure of than that, namely, that God is sovereign and wise and good and trustworthy. The Bible assures us of this in many places:

> "Shall not the Judge of all the earth do what is just" (Genesis 18:25).
> "Good and upright is the LORD" (Psalm 25:8).
> "Oh give thanks to the LORD, for he is good, for his steadfast love endures forever!" (Psalm 107:1).
> "Praise the LORD, for the LORD is good; sing to his name, for he is gracious" (Psalm 135:3 NRSV).

This assurance of God's good nature is your rock first and foremost; all other comforts are secondary. But I will give you biblical reasons for why I believe that Owen is safe and uncondemned. It is not because he was not sinful by nature, for all of us are.

> "Behold, I was brought forth in iniquity, and in sin did my mother conceive me" (Psalm 51:5).
> "We ... were by nature children of wrath" (Ephesians 2:3).

What we are by nature—not experience—Paul says, is hostile to God (Romans 8:7–8). A child does not learn this nature. A child expresses it.

Our confidence that Owen is safe and uncondemned is not that he was innocent but that he was forgiven and was counted righteous because of Jesus Christ. The Bible is very plain that we are saved from our sin and from God's punishment by grace through faith in Jesus Christ, who died in our place and rose again from the dead.

But what about tiny children who do not yet have the physical ability to even know the basic facts of the gospel or even of any of God's revelation in nature? Does the Bible teach that God will judge them in the same way that he will judge an adult who consciously rejects the truth of God that he knows?

No, there are clues that God does not condemn those who are physically unable to know the truth that God has revealed in nature or in the gospel. I'll mention two of these clues.

One comes from Deuteronomy 1. God is angry because the people would not trust him to help them take the Promised Land. They rebelled against him. So he says, "Not one of these men of this evil generation shall see the good land that I swore to give to your fathers, except Caleb" and Joshua, who had trusted him (verses 35–38). Then he adds a word about the children: "And as for your little ones, who you said would become a prey, and your children, who today have no knowledge of good or evil, they shall go in there. And to them I will give it, and they shall possess it" (verse 39).

Not having the "knowledge of good or evil" takes away the judgment. They were not yet physically able to know what they needed to know, and so God does not sweep them away with the adults who wouldn't trust him.

The second clue, from the New Testament, confirms this principle. It is found in Romans 1:19–21 (RSV). The text is not about children, but the same principles of justice apply. Listen to the relationship between having available knowledge and having accountability:

> For what can be known about God is plain to [men], because
> God has shown it to them. Ever since the creation of the world
> his invisible nature, namely, his eternal power and deity, has been
> clearly perceived in the things that have been made. So they are
> without excuse; for although they knew God they did not honor
> him as God or give thanks to him.

The point is this: to be held accountable at the judgment you need two things: (1) available knowledge of the glory of the God whom you should have adored and thanked; and (2) the physical ability to know that glory, to perceive it. If this knowledge were really not available, then, Paul implies, there really would be an "excuse" at the judgment. No adult, except perhaps profoundly retarded or mentally ill ones, have this excuse. That's Paul's point. We adults are without excuse. But children are in another category. They do have this excuse. They don't have the physical ability to know what God has revealed. Therefore we believe that God will apply to them the blood and righteousness of Christ in a way that we do not know. We adults can have this pardon and righteousness only through faith. That is the clear teaching of Scripture (Romans 3:28; Ephesians 2:8). How are infants united to Christ? We don't know. And speculation would not help us here.

We leave it at this: Owen Shramek will glorify Christ all his everlasting days through salvation by grace on the basis of the death and righteousness of Christ. There is no other name under heaven by which he could be saved. Jesus Christ will get all the honor for Owen's salvation.

Owen Shramek Was Created to Glorify God

"Bring my sons from afar ... everyone who is called by my name, whom I created for my glory, whom I formed and made" (Isaiah 43:6–7).

"Before I formed you in the womb I knew you, and before you were born I consecrated you" (Jeremiah 1:5).

"But when he who had set me apart before I was born, and who called me by his grace ..." (Galatians 1:15).

God's designs for Owen were decided before he was born. He would exist for the glory of God. Twenty minutes of that work was on the earth; the rest will be in heaven. None of us can even begin to estimate the magnitude of either. Who knows what has been set in motion on earth by the birth and death and life of Owen Shramek. It would be wild and unwarranted folly to think he has not changed the world.

His conscious life—his obedience to his Maker—was appointed to be lived out in heaven. That is a good place to live for the glory of God. Woe to us if we think that the only place to glorify God is on this tiny planet!

God glorifies his grace in many people by the pardon and power he exerts to make them in some measure Christlike here. But he glorifies his grace in many others—perhaps more—by the pardon and power to perfect them instantly and put them to work in the realm of just men made perfect (Hebrews 12:23).

Owen was created to glorify God. He did and he is.

The Length of Owen Shramek's Twenty-Minute Life on Earth Was Virtually Indistinguishable from the Length of Ours

Oh, for eyes to see things from the standpoint of eternity!

> "You do not know what tomorrow will bring. What is your life? For you are a mist that appears for a little time and then vanishes" (James 4:14).
> "For this slight momentary affliction is preparing for us an eternal weight of glory beyond all comparison" (2 Corinthians 4:17).

The longest life of any person on earth is like a vapor's breath on a cold winter morning. If the distance between the walls in this room represent eternity, the distance from the wall representing Owen's life and the distance representing ours would be so infinitesimally small that you would not be able to see the difference with the naked eye. We will all be gone very soon. This is one of the great truths Owen was sent to teach us.

Owen Shramek Is Happier Today Than the Happiest Person on Earth Has Ever Been

> My desire is to depart and be with Christ, for that is far better.
> —*Philippians 1:23*

That Owen missed earth's pleasures of marriage and children and food and friends do not cause him the slightest regret. He took a much shorter route to the One in whose presence is fullness of joy and at whose right hand are pleasures forevermore. By comparison, the pleasures that Owen enjoys today make all of ours boring in the extreme.

Owen Shramek Was a Test for Your Faith

> Count it all joy, my brothers, when you meet trials of various kinds, for you know that the testing of your faith produces steadfastness.
> —*James 1:2–3*

Losing Owen was not in itself a joy; it was an agonizing test. If it were not agonizing, it would be no test. But now that it has laid you low, it is a test. And what is being tested is your faith in the goodness and power and the love of God—and his call on your life. Owen has become a test of his parents' faith. I know it seems backward. It is a strange kind of homeschooling. You—the parents—are supposed to be the teachers. You should teach the lessons and give the tests. But God's ways are not our ways. Owen has become the teacher and he has given the test.

Count on my prayers, Dustin and Kellie, that the testing of your faith will produce steadfastness. When it does, Owen will give the grade. And when you come home, he will say with his Master, "Well done, Dad. Well done, Mom."

Owen Shramek Is a Gift to You and to the Middle East

When Job lost his children he said, "Naked I came from my mother's womb, and naked shall I return. The LORD gave, and the LORD has taken away; blessed be the name of the LORD" (Job 1:21).

The Lord *gave*. Owen is a *gift*. Yes, he has been taken away. But that does not change the fact that he was and is a gift. You had him, and *you have him still*—not in your arms but in your memory; not in your home but in your heart; not on earth but in heaven.

And Owen is a gift to the Middle East. It is not an accident in God's design that this is missions week at Bethlehem Baptist Church. In Cedar Falls at the Navigator conference, and here at Bethlehem, Owen has had and will have his ongoing influence for the sake of the nations—already he has had more impact than many adults who throw their lives away on trifles and never give a thought to eternity or to missions.

But Owen is a gift in particular to the Middle East. I don't get to say this very often at funerals. Generally I say it to college students: *Suffering and death in the path of obedience to Christ is not only the price of missions but also the means of missions.* God has ordained that in our own suffering we complete what is lacking in the afflictions of Christ by showing them to the world. The apostle Paul states this: "Now I rejoice in my sufferings for your sake, and in my flesh I am filling up what is lacking in Christ's afflictions for the sake of his body, that is, the church" (Colossians 1:24).

In the path of obedience in the Middle East, you have now suffered much. And Owen has paid with his life. This is the way it will be recorded in heaven.

And it will not be lost on the people you are called to serve. Owen has not died in vain. You have not suffered loss in vain. Be steadfast, immovable, always abounding in the work of the Lord. Our time is very short. We will all be gone quickly. Nothing done for Christ is in vain. No life, no death, no loss is in vain.

Chapter Nine

CRIB DEATH

SITUATION

Our seminary community was rocked by the death of this young child. Wonderful Christian parents with three children and a great zeal to minister the gospel experienced the tragic loss of their three-month-old child. When he did not awaken as usual from a nap, his mother investigated and discovered her child was barely breathing. An emergency ride to a nearby hospital, the finest medical care, and the gathered prayers of pastors, professors, and fellow students did not preserve the life of the child. The couple's local pastor, Dr. Wilson Benton of Kirk of the Hills Presbyterian Church, delivered this funeral message to a combined service of the church and seminary communities.[1]

CONCERNS

In this message, Pastor Benton has the immense task of ministering to young people in a seminary community, few of whom are of an age to have known death intimately. Fewer still have had to face the death of a child. One even asked, "Has any tragedy like this ever happened before at this seminary?" It has, but the question itself indicates the innocence of this generation of students in terms of experiencing such tragedy. Benton knows that he needs to provide comfort as well as answers that a theological community will accept. In such a setting, there is an easy temptation to turn such an experience into a philosophical reflection or a classroom lecture. Instead, Benton provides needed pastoral care by weaving biblical truths into the hospital, church, and

---

1. Dr. W. Wilson Benton Jr. has pastored churches in Mississippi, Missouri, and Tennessee, and taught preaching in a variety of seminaries. He now pastors Christ Presbyterian Church (PCA) in Nashville, Tennessee.

family experiences of the couple. He refuses to abstract the tragedy but deals with it in tender terms by describing the loss and God's promises in the context of the intimate details of the family's life.

APPROACH

Pastor Benton handles the issue of the baby's eternal security by referring to the covenant promises God makes to Christian parents. God's promise to mark as holy the children of believing parents is the basis of covenant baptism and also a great comfort to believing parents when a child dies (Acts 2:39; 1 Corinthians 7:4). In addition to reminding the parents of this covenant promise, Benton brings a sense of wonder to the occasion by delighting in the promises and mysteries of heaven: What will be the age of the child when we see him? What will he wear? How much does he already know? How glorious is it to already be in the arms of Jesus? Answers to these and other questions are given to fulfill the main obligations of all such funerals: to assure parents that a sovereign God has not failed and that a lost child is safe.

THE GLORY THAT IS REVEALED IN US

Wilson Benton

> For I consider that the sufferings of this present time are not
> worthy to be compared with the glory which shall be revealed in us.
> —*Romans 8:18 NKJV*

The Reality of Our Suffering

"And they lived happily ever after." It is a precious and fond American illusion that every story must have a happy ending. In our Disney World environments with our Pollyanna personalities, our Cinderella complexes, our Mary Poppins syndromes, we believe that a spoonful of sugar will make all manner of ills disappear.

Rod and Karen[2] got married and had four wonderful children, and they were to live happily ever after. But it didn't happen that way, and the Bible never said it would.

The apostle Paul writes with all candor—in Romans 8:18—about the sufferings of this present time. Paul was a realist. He was not one to hide his eyes from the tragedies of life and just hope they would go away; nor was he one to explain away his own troubles as if they were but figments of his imagination; nor did he seek to hide his own pain as if it were an embarrassment to his faith. Paul knew the Savior, and Paul knew suffering. He even catalogs for us his catastrophes in 2 Corinthians 11. You remember that list of horrors. He tells us how many times he was beaten, how many times he was shipwrecked, how many times he was stoned, and how many days and nights he spent in the sea, deprived of what you and I would call the necessities of life. And all of these things happened to him *after* he met Jesus Christ on the Damascus Road.

---

2. Individual names and some personal details have been changed as an expression of care for the family.

Paul knew the lives of the patriarchs. He knew that Abraham was the friend of God, the father of the covenant family of God, and yet Abraham suffered. Paul knew Moses was the prophet, the priest, the king (all rolled into one), the meekest man on earth, that particular person with whom God spoke mouth to mouth—whatever that means—and yet Moses suffered. Paul knew David was a man after God's own heart, and David suffered. And Paul knew the Lord Jesus Christ, the Son of God himself, the only perfect man who ever walked this earth, who was also a man of sorrows and acquainted with grief—smitten, stricken, afflicted.

Paul was not one to believe that Christianity immunizes Christians from the problems and pains of this world. He did not believe that being a child of God exempts one from trial and trouble. Because he knew that "God has not promised skies always blue, flower-strewn pathways all our lives through"; God has not promised "sun without rain, joy without sorrow, peace without pain"; God never said that we shall not bear many a burden, many a care; he never said that we shall not know toil and temptation, trouble and woe. Paul was a realist, and so he spoke about the reality of this present grief.

The Sovereignty of His Appointment

Tragedy struck Rod and Karen last Thursday about one o'clock with a vengeful forcefulness that really can't be measured by human standards. They experienced every parent's worst nightmare. William had stopped breathing.

In the waiting area outside the emergency room, we cried. We cried to God, "Please let this little boy live. Please restore his life; let his heart beat again." We cried to each other, and we cried to God. And when news came that they had a pulse, we cheered. We cheered as loudly as we cried. And when, in a few moments that seemed more like days, the report came that William's heart was beating on its own without any external stimulation, we cheered even more. And when he was moved from the emergency room to the pediatric intensive care unit, we formed a parade through the hospital, taking him to that place where he would receive the best possible care in the world.

And then the word came that his little lungs were not functioning; they simply could not sustain his life. He was on the respirator, and without the respirator he could not live. We were crushed, and we cried all the more, "Please, God, let William live. You are the God of life. You're the one in whom we live and move and have our being. We acknowledge you as our Creator. Sustain this little boy whom you have created." Sometimes we couldn't even talk. Sometimes there were just tears streaming down our cheeks, and sometimes there were just moans emanating from within, but we knew that God understood. In fact, the tears running down our cheeks may have been the greatest prayers that we prayed. Paul says here in Romans 8 that, when we don't know how to pray as we should, God's own Spirit intercedes for us with groanings too deep for words, and we experienced the Spirit's intercession.

I heard Karen saying over and over and over, "O God, he's so precious; he's so precious." And he was precious—not just to Rod and Karen, but to all of us who were there, for life is precious. As the immediate shock began to subside, the truth slowly began to surface. We realized that if he is precious to us, he is even more precious to God. This is God's child, not just Karen's and Rod's. This is *God's* little boy. He is precious to God. So we began to sense that God was not far away. God was right there. We didn't need to shout for him to hear us. He could hear thoughts within that we couldn't verbalize or articulate or express in any words. He was there. And we understood that this tragedy was not an accident; this tragedy was not a quirk of circumstances; this tragedy had not struck out of the blue; this tragedy had not just happened. This tragedy was appointed—appointed by God himself.

Isn't it amazing that, in the providence of God, less than ten days ago Rod and Karen attended a conference on the sovereignty of God, along with many of us here, right in this place. And we were reminded of the fact that God is sovereign over all, or God is not sovereign at all. And we knew him to be sovereign in that very situation. This was not outside of his control; this was not beyond the reach of his loving, gracious, strong arm. God was there superintending, governing, controlling all of the affairs in that pediatric intensive care unit.

I heard Karen say somewhere at sometime in the afternoon, "I don't want him to live if it's not best for him." I thought, *God's amazing grace is at work right here*. Do you understand what was happening in her heart? And in Rod's heart? In the midst of all their grief, they acknowledged their God as the sovereign Lord of life, the sovereign Lord of William's life.

All of us should understand what was happening. Karen's bitter disappointment—and it was disappointment when God did not seem to respond to our requests as we registered them with him—was giving way. Even as William's life was slipping away, Karen's own disappointment was giving way to acceptance and understanding of God's divine appointment. Her heart began to adjust to the truths these words of the poet Edith Lillian Young express so well:

"Disappointment—His appointment,"
Change one letter, then I see
That the thwarting of my purpose
Is God's better choice for me.
His appointment must be blessing,
Tho' it may come in disguise,
For the end from the beginning
Open to His wisdom lies.

"Disappointment—His appointment,"
Whose? The Lord, who loves me best,
Understands and knows me fully,
Who my faith and love would test;
For, like a loving earthly parent,
He rejoices when He knows
That His child accepts, unquestioned,
All that from His wisdom flows.

"Disappointment—His appointment,"
"No good thing will He withhold,"
From denials oft we gather
Treasure of His love untold.
Well He knows each broken purpose
Leads to fuller, deeper trust,
And the end of all His dealings
Proves our God is wise and just.

"Disappointment—His disappointment,"
Lord, I take it, then, as such.
Like the Rod in hands of potter,
Yielding wholly to Thy touch.
All my life's plan is Thy moulding,
Not one single choice be mine;
Let me answer, unrepining—
"Father, Not my will, but Thine."[3]

---

3. Edith Lillian Young, "Disappointment—His Appointment," quoted in *Poems That Preach*, comp. John R. Rice (Murfreesboro, Tenn.: Sword of the Lord, 1952).

In the midst of their grief, Rod and Karen expressed such trust in God. They said it: "Lord, we love our little boy. We beg you, let him live; yet not our will, but yours be done."

William was precious. He was precious, not only in his parents' eyes, and precious not only in the eyes of their friends, but precious also in God's eyes. The Bible affirms this: "Precious in the sight of the LORD is the death of His saints" (Psalm 116:15 NKJV). Whether it is a big saint or a tiny baby saint, precious in the eyes of the Lord is the death of one of his saints—one set apart to be used as he chooses for his own glory.

Rod gathered us in the waiting room and gave us the news: no neurological functions. With red and swollen eyes, and yet with calm and steady voice, much calmer than mine on this occasion, he said, "William is in God's hands." What a confession to make, and what comfort was his, and what comfort he ministered to us: *William is in God's hands.* What better place for William could there be?!

The Joy beyond Our Suffering

We don't know exactly when God called William to himself; even with all of our scientific and technological knowledge, the mysteries of life and death are still too deep for us to plumb. But Rod's comment changed the atmosphere of that room. Suddenly we began to think about God's hand, and William in God's hand, and we began to think about heaven itself. Is that surprising? I don't think so. Listen to what the apostle Paul says; he is our theologian on this occasion. He is our teacher instructing us under the inspiration of God's Spirit. Listen: "The sufferings of this present time are not worthy to be compared with the glory which shall be revealed in us."

With Rod's words, we were suddenly transported from an intensive care unit into the very presence of God himself. We began to discuss the last session we had in this sanctuary on the sovereignty of God over eternity. We were reminded of those glorious passages in the book of Revelation that describe the place that God has prepared for us. The Bible says, "Eye has not seen, nor ear heard, nor have entered into the heart of man the things which God has prepared for those who love him" (1 Corinthians 2:9 NKJV). And we remembered standing here, singing at the top of our lungs the "Hallelujah" chorus. Do these circumstances mean we could no longer say, "Hallelujah?" Of course not. In fact, it is precisely because God is sovereign even in the midst of tragedy and suffering and affliction and pain that we can take the greatest joy in saying, "Hallelujah."

We began to talk about William, not lying there on the bed, but William in the presence of God. We talked about his mansion and wondered what it looked like; we talked about the crown he was wearing and the golden streets he was walking, and we wondered how big the robe was that Jesus had put around his shoulders. We wonder about things like that, don't we? Stephen's greatest concern for his baby brother has been just this: *How can he grow in heaven without his mother there to feed him?* We wonder, don't we? *Are babies in heaven?* Children ask me those questions all the time. Adults don't; they're afraid to ask. But children don't mind asking, and we ask *ourselves*, don't we? Is the perfect body an eighteen-year-old human body or a twenty-one-year-old human body or a twenty-five-year-old one or a thirty-year-old one? No one would say a more than forty-year-old one, for sure—and we all know why!

We know that suffering (the wear and tear of life) affects the body, and grief affects the body; but so, too, does the glory that is revealed. We measure our age and health by time-reference statements of years, but when the trumpet of the Lord shall sound, time shall be no more, and William's body will be perfect—perfectly suited for that heavenly environment. His little body was sown in weakness, but it will be raised in power; it was sown in dishonor, but it will be raised in glory; it was sown a natural body, but it will be raised a spiritual body. His mortal will put on immortality; his corruption will put on incorruption (1 Corinthians 15).

As we considered these truths, we also began to think about what was happening to William's mind. You see, glory affects the mind as well as the body—just as grief affects both. We should understand this. Surely the greatest suffering that has come to these parents has been in the mind, not the body. We wonder why, we really do. We have the freedom to ask why. To say that God is sovereign is not the same as saying we know why God sovereignly acts as he does.

Yesterday, as I was considering some of my "why" questions, I was honestly shocked by a thought: William knows more than I do! I've lived fifty-three plus years; he lived three months and three days—and yet he has gained a perspective I've not yet attained, nor has anyone here. Now we see through a glass darkly, but *he sees face-to-face.* Now he knows even as he was known. The scope, the glory that God reveals in us is mind-boggling, isn't it? I trust you understand that this family is not grieving *for* William today. The grief we feel is for ourselves and not for him, for he is better off than any of us. He has entered that realm mentioned in one of our Scripture readings earlier in the service—that realm where there is no more death, no more mourning or crying, no more sorrow or tears, no more pain. Even if we could, would we bring him back from that place to this place? Of course not. We long for him because we love him, but our knowledge that he is secure in the hands of God means we grieve for our loss and rejoice in his gain.

Isn't it amazing that in the providence of God, just one week ago yesterday, Rod and Karen, covenant parents, returned to their home church, this covenant community of God's people, to present their child to receive the sign of the covenant in the sacrament of baptism, committing him into the care and keeping of our covenant God. Can you imagine the comfort that is theirs even now in knowing that God saves according to the promise of his covenant? The Bible says that the promise is to you Christians, covenant people, and *to your children* (Acts 2:39). We have solid cause, biblical assurance, to believe that William is in heaven, and we don't appeal to some syrupy sentimentality that says all babies who die go to heaven. That may be the case, but beyond all conjecture or speculation, we believers rejoice in the security that is ours and our children's because of the covenant faithfulness of a sovereign God.

So as we talked about these things, Rod and Karen began to minister to us. I want you to know they ministered to us more than we ministered to them. Are you surprised? You shouldn't be. Listen to what Paul states: "I consider that the sufferings of this present time are not worthy to be compared with the glory that shall be revealed in us." Paul, as it were, pictures for us a set of scales, and on one side of the scale he places the reality of the present grief, and on the other scale he places the revelation of future glory. He says that the revelation of future glory so outweighs the reality of present grief, as great as that grief may be, that the two are not worthy to be compared. One is earthly, and the other is heavenly; one is transient, and the other is eternal; one is caused by sin, and the other is the fruit of salvation through faith in Jesus Christ.

Now the fullness of that glory will be revealed only in the future, and only then can we really understand what Paul is saying about the relationship between the two. But please understand that we don't have to wait until the end times to know this glory that is revealed in us. I can assure you *it has been revealed in Rod and Karen*. For all the grief that has been theirs has been outweighed by the sufficiency of God's sovereign grace.

The Glory That Is Revealed

I asked Karen if she had anything she wanted me to include in the service by way of hymn or Scripture text or poem or whatever. You know what she gave me? Michael Card's lullaby that he wrote for his child, a lullaby that Karen sang to William: "Sleep sound in Jesus sweetheart of my heart; the dark and the night will not keep us apart. When I lay you down in your bed for the night, He holds you gently till morning is light."[4]

You know the most amazing part about that? The most amazing thing is that Karen wants these lyrics read today. For you see, God's glory has been revealed in her, and she knows it's the truth. William is held gently in the arms of Jesus Christ.

Saturday morning, Rod was reading Scripture to his family, Scripture that God had used to comfort his heart and he was using to comfort his loved ones' hearts. He read these verses from Lamentations 3: "For men are not cast off by the Lord forever. Though he brings grief, he will show compassion, so great is his unfailing love. For he does not willingly bring affliction or grief to the children of men" (Lamentations 3:31–33 NIV [1984 ed.]).

The God who does not willingly bring grief to his children will bring its end to all who trust in him. "Weeping may endure for a night, but joy comes in the morning" (Psalm 30:5 NKJV). If that's true—and you know it is because it is the Word of God—then our grief, as profound as it now is, will not be the most persistent aspect of our present or future lives. *Weeping may endure for a night, but joy comes in the morning*—joy, which is the fruit of the Spirit, that joy in which we are to rejoice always, that joy that came into the world a long time ago when another little baby boy was born. That joy currently envelops William as he rests in the arms of our Savior. And dare I say it? I *must* say it: "And they will live joyfully ever after." So shall we when, in the Lord's timing, we are gathered together into his heavenly family forever.

Rod and Karen, we love you, but God loves you more, and I commend you to the sovereign sustaining love of God. We weep with you as you weep, and we will continue to weep with you as you continue to weep, and yet we will also rejoice with you as you rejoice in the brief but very blessed life of William Arthur Harris, who is already embraced by the same precious Savior who will now carry you until that day when we all rest together in him.

---

4. Michael Card, "Sleep Sound in Jesus," from the album *Sleep Sound in Jesus: Gentle Lullabies for Baby* (Chatsworth, Calif: Sparrow Records, 1989).

Chapter Ten

YOUNG CHILD

SITUATION

Dr. Robert S. Rayburn has pastored one church for his entire pastoral life.[1] An advocate of long pastorates, he has performed the baptisms and marriages of children whose parents he once baptized and married. He has also buried the children of families he has so long pastored. His knowledge of his people is comprehensive and intimate. Their knowledge of him is deep as well. They know that this Aberdeen-trained New Testament scholar loves doctrine, history, and Scripture. To attend his church is to become immersed in the same. For those who are part of this church culture, the historic teachings of the church are not dry insights from dusty documents; they are nutrients of daily life, preparing the mind and heart for our hardest decisions and greatest challenges. True to himself and to his church, Pastor Rayburn here addresses parents who have lost a young child, offering comfort through the doctrines that he and they love dearly. I would not contend that his doctrinal emphasis and language would serve well in all church situations, but the doctrines he so masterfully unfolds are those that in some manner most need to be expressed by all pastors faced with addressing such tragedy.

CONCERNS

Pastor Rayburn's obvious primary concern is to assure Christian parents that their young children who have died are eternally secure in heaven. He also assumes the burden of ignorance, indicating that Scripture does not address the eternal state of unbelieving parents' children. The reason for addressing

---

1. Dr. Robert S. Rayburn is pastor of Faith Presbyterian Church (PCA) in Tacoma, Washington, where he has pastored faithfully for more than thirty years.

this topic is not to stir controversy or introduce speculation but to encourage all parents to affirm faith in Jesus Christ for the sake of their children, as well as for their own sakes.

APPROACH

Pastor Rayburn uses his rich knowledge of doctrine and history to prove that the young children of believing parents are safe in heaven and secure with Jesus. He initially builds his case by quoting doctrines from historic documents. But with tender pastoral instincts, he then moves from the merely cognitive to the personal, using his knowledge of history to give a biographical account of a well-known theologian who also wrote of his experience of the loss of a child.

THE SERMON

HOPE THAT HEALS THE HURTING HEART

Robert S. Rayburn

Pastor Rayburn refers to various texts throughout his sermon, including Ezekiel 16, Revelation 21, and 1 John 5.

The Consoling Power of Biblical Doctrine

From time to time, I hear people say they find doctrine dull and unhelpful. Of course, they would never say that the teaching of the Bible is dull or unhelpful —and that, after all, is what doctrine is: the teaching of the Bible. These people mean, rather, that long-winded explanations of the Bible's teaching on some piece of theology strike them as not very relevant or practical or personally useful. And sometimes, alas, the way doctrine is taught can give people that impression.

But, of course, rightly understood, doctrine is the furthest thing from being dull or uninteresting or irrelevant to daily life. When people think it is, they are usually not in a position at that moment to appreciate how vitally important, how heart stirring, how wonderfully encouraging, that particular truth of Holy Scripture actually is. Doctrine is, after all, what the Lord has taught us about himself and about ourselves and our lives; it is the living God's own instruction to his creatures about how we are to think about what happens to us, how we can escape the tragedy of life, and how we can face its inevitable end. Doctrine is the rope or the life ring thrown to a drowning man; it is the ladder by which he or she can escape a burning house; it is food for the starving, and cold, clear water for those with parched throats.

At a grave such as this one, all we crave to know is whether God has revealed something to us that will help us in our great need. Is there hope left for us in a time of such shattered hopes? Is there some truth to lift our hearts when they have been so terribly dashed to the ground? All we have at such a moment—all we could possibly have—is the teaching of the Word of God, the Bible's doctrine.

So, as your pastor, let me give you some doctrine that, I pray, will be of comfort to all of us in this time of grief. It is the doctrine of our Reformed church because it is first the teaching of Holy Scripture. I am reading from the Canons of Dort, a summary of the Bible's teaching prepared by that august body of Reformed divines or theologians in 1619. It was written in Latin. So what I am about to read to you is old, the kind of thing that theologians write when they get together to formulate theological definitions and repudiate theological errors, and it was written in a language now long dead. We may well wonder what help there is for us in this on such a day. *Until we begin to read!*

> Because we must judge the will of God from his Word, which testifies that the children of believers are holy, not indeed by nature but by the blessing of the covenant of grace in which they are embraced with their parents, pious parents ought not to doubt the election and the salvation of their children whom God calls from this life in infancy.[2]

There it is. The word we need above all words from God as we stand beside this grave. Our theologians, speaking to us across the centuries, are telling us what God is saying to us now, at this moment: "I have taken your children from you; but I have taken them to heaven. I have left you desolate, for reasons you cannot now know, but in doing so I have brought your children to the world of everlasting joy. Your loss has been their indescribably great gain." Is there anything else we could hear that would bring so much comfort, that would help us to come to terms with what God has willed, that would give us back some joy, even if still in the midst of our understandably great grief?

Those old Dutch and German and English divines were not talking off the top of their heads, after all. They were simply summarizing what the Bible teaches those who love God and believe in Jesus to believe about our children. What else could anyone conclude who reads in Holy Scripture that God is our children's God! For God to be our God is, in the Bible, the shortest way of saying everything we mean by salvation. The terrible condition of the unbelieving is that, as Paul puts it, they are "without God" (Ephesians 2:12). Heaven, we read in Revelation 21, is the place where, to the ultimate degree, God is our God, and we are his people. But that can be said already about our children. God is their God! What else, then, could we believe about our little children who have died when we read in Ezekiel 16 that we bore those

---

2. Canons of Dort (1619), chapter 1, article xvii; available online in various formats.

children *to him*, that they are *his* holy seed (verse 20)? What else should we think about our little ones who have died when the Bible says they are holy (1 Corinthians 7:14)? What else when Jesus said, even of nursing infants, that the kingdom of heaven belongs to such as these (Matthew 19:14)? What else when Paul preached the gospel by saying that if we believe in Jesus we will be saved — we *and our household* (Acts 16:31)? What else indeed! And what else ought we to believe when David says of his dead baby boy, "I will go to him …" (2 Samuel 12:23). David was a man with a strong hope of heaven. More than once in the psalms he gave expression to his living hope of the world to come. What else could that good man and loving father have meant when he said, "I will go to my baby boy"? The encouragement that the divines of the Canons of Dort have given to us concerning the salvation of covenant children who die in infancy is neither more nor less than the teaching of the Word of God. It is the Bible's doctrine, and so it is our faith.

And this doctrine has led our Christian ancestors who stood at graves like this one to much happy reflection in the midst of their grief, a grief they knew even better than we, as babies often died in those days. As one old poet has written:

Babes thither caught from womb and breast,
Claim'd right to sing above the rest;
Because they found the happy shore
They never saw nor sought before.[3]

Or this:

Oh! when a mother meets on high
The babe she lost in infancy,
Hath she not then, for pains and fears,
The day of woe, the watchful night,
For all her sorrows, all her tears,
An over-payment of delight![4]

I remember reading Bishop J. C. Ryle's wise response to the question of what happens to the children of *un*believers when they die in infancy. He replied that, in respect to that question, "he had nothing to read." Anglican

3. Ralph Erskine, "The Work and Contention of Heaven," in *The Sermons, and Other Practical Works* (London: R. Baynes, 1821), 249.
4. Robert Southey, "Mount Meru," in *The Curse of Kehama* (London: Longman, Hurst, Reeds, Orme, and Brown, 1811), 108.

priests customarily speak of "reading" their services, including the funeral service or the graveside service. The service is read out of the *Book of Common Prayer*. And what Bishop Ryle meant was that he had been given no service to read at the grave of the infant child of unbelieving people. Why had he no service to read? Because the Bible never addresses the question. It leaves us in the dark. And ministers, in such solemn moments especially, are not to share their own opinions. In the hour of death, people need to hear the sure Word of God. But if the Word is silent on a question, the minister must remain silent as well. He does not know what to say because God has not spoken to the question in his Word. In saying, "I have nothing to read," Bishop Ryle meant that he had nothing to tell unbelieving parents because God had not told him what to say to them.

But that is *not* the case when the little baby of *believing* parents has died. I very definitely have something to read, something to tell such a grieving but believing man or woman: "Your baby is with the Lord in heaven." "Your baby, whom you mourn, has entered the City of God." "Your baby is, as the old song has it, 'safe in the arms of Jesus.'"

The Healing Power of Biblical Promises

All through the long history of the saints, babies have died and parents have been heartbroken over their loss. This is a holy fellowship of sorrow, but it is also a holy fellowship of faith and hope. Let me give you a superb example of this sorrow overcome by faith and hope. Thomas Boston was a faithful Scottish pastor of the late seventeenth and early eighteenth centuries. He was famous in his own day as the author of the spiritual classic *Human Nature in its Fourfold State*. Boston has been loved and admired by generations of Christians who came after him primarily for the impression of his godliness that one receives reading the great man's memoir[5] or autobiography, an account of his life that Boston prepared for the sake of his children.

Boston's wife was not a healthy woman, and each childbirth was for her not only an ordeal but a threat to her life. In April 1707, Boston recorded in his journal that he was praying earnestly for his wife's safety as she was near to delivering a child. He wrote that while he was praying he had an impression that the child would be a boy. At that moment he promised the Lord that if it

---

5. See *Memoirs of the Life, Time, and Writings of the Reverend and Learned Thomas Boston, M.A.* (1776; available in many editions), www.iclnet.org/pub/resources/text/ipb-e/epl-10/web/boston-memoirs-00.html.

were a boy and delivered alive, he would name the child Ebenezer, after the
memorial to God's faithfulness and power that Samuel had set up after Israel's
victory over the Philistines at Mizpah. In his *Memoirs*, Boston recorded that
on the twenty-third of that same month of April his wife safely delivered, and
his heart leaped for joy upon hearing that the baby was a boy. And so Boston
named his son Ebenezer.

But in one of the pastor's journal entries in September of that same year
we read, "It pleased the Lord, for my further trial, to remove by death, on
the 8th of September, my son Ebenezer." Boston goes on: "I had never more
confidence with God in any such case than in that child's being the Lord's. I
had indeed more than ordinary, in giving him away to the Lord, to be saved
by the blood of Christ. But his death was exceeding afflicting to me, and a
matter of sharp exercise. To bury his name was indeed harder than to bury his
body ... but I saw a necessity of allowing a latitude to [God's] sovereignty."

A year later, in August, Mrs. Boston delivered another son, whom, Boston
said, "after no small struggle with myself, I named Ebenezer." But in October
of that same year this son too fell ill with the measles. Boston recorded how
he went out to the barn and there prayed for his son. "I renewed my covenant
with God and did solemnly and explicitly covenant for Ebenezer, and in his
name accept of the covenant, and of Christ offered in the gospel; and gave
him away to the Lord, before angels, and the stones of that house as witnesses.
I cried also for his life, that Ebenezer might live before him, if it were his will.
But when, after that exercise, I came into the house, I found, that instead of
being better, he was worse [and in a few hours he was dead]."

After the funeral of this his second Ebenezer, Boston wrote, "I see most
plainly that ... I must stoop, and be content to follow the Lord in an untrod-
den path." Later we read this: "When the child was laid in the coffin, his
mother kissed his dust. I only lifted the cloth off his face, looked on it, and
covered it again, in confidence of seeing that body rise a glorious body."

Later in his *Memoirs* Boston wrote: "I saw reason to bless the Lord, that
I had been made father of six children, now in the grave, and that were with
me but a very short time; but none of them lost; *I will see them all at the resurrection.* That clause in the covenant, 'and the God of thy seed,' was sweet and
full of sap [emphasis added]."

In Thomas Boston we see a man whose broken heart was healed by doctrine, by the teaching of the Holy Scripture, by one article of the gospel of
Jesus Christ. This salvation, we are taught in the Word of God, is for you
who believe *and for your house, your children, your seed.* And lying behind that

promise is something still more wonderful: God's mighty love. What does he say in his Word? "He who *loves* the father loves his child as well" (paraphrased from 1 John 5:1). If that is true for men, how much more it must be true for God himself, from whom all love comes and who is love itself.

Should not these glorious truths—God's promise to be our children's God, and God's love for our children, who are, finally, *his* children, *his* seed— should they not also heal our hearts here today? It will not take away the pain of the loss, surely. But it will absolutely take away the despair and replace it with a firm confidence that all is well. Ultimately, finally, all is well!

There is a gravestone in the churchyard of Winchester Cathedral. It marks the resting place of one Susannah Taylor, who died at four years of age. It reads simply:

Amicis chara
Parentibus charior
Deo charissima.

"Dear to her friends; dearer to her parents; dearest to God." This is pure biblical doctrine put to the purest human use. It doesn't take the pain away; it doesn't remove the mystery; but it removes all fear and all despair. Our children are "dearest to God." Thus we shall see them all with our Lord at the resurrection. For now, this is all we need to know, all we need to remember, all we must call to mind whenever the doubts rise. "*Dearest to God*. I shall see them at the resurrection!"

Chapter Eleven

CONJOINED TWINS

SITUATION

After multiple tests and trips to experts, Joshua and Sonya Taylor, had to face the reality that their conjoined daughters, Joanna Joy and Hanna Hope, would not survive.[1] Near Christmas, the infant girls entered heaven. Pastor Bob Flayhart[2] delivered the funeral message with reference to a statement in the e-mail notice that Joshua sent to friends announcing the deaths: "Though they were infants, Joanna and Hanna already had what many years of being a Christian has failed to achieve in my own life—an undivided heart." The father's words were indicative of the deep faith of this family that enabled them to endure this trial with joy and hope and that enabled their pastor to preach with the same.

CONCERNS

The concern Pastor Flayhart most wants to address he states at the beginning of his message: "With our God there is no 'oops!'" But the message quickly moves beyond the obvious need to assert the sovereign purposes of God and addresses how God has used—and will continue to use—these infant girls for his glory. As is true of other pastors in this book who deal with infant

---

1. Individual names and some personal details have been changed as an expression of care for the family.

2. Dr. Robert Flayhart is pastor of Oak Mountain Presbyterian Church (PCA) in Birmingham, Alabama. His preaching and teaching ministries take him to numerous international settings, but the gracious heart for which he is best known is most apparent in this difficult funeral message for conjoined twins.

death, Flayhart indicates that the duration of a child's life is no indication of his or her impact on eternity. God uses our trials as well as our triumphs to knit our hearts to his and to each others'. In addition to speaking about the spiritual status of the girls, Flayhart also addresses his community's concern for these beleaguered parents by making special note of how the Lord's care of the mother and father has been present and will continue.

APPROACH

The preliminary comments, opening prayer, and closing benediction of this message each have a role in communicating God's care in the midst of tragedy. The message is really not complete without each piece, as each communicates differing dimensions of God's sovereignty, intimacy, mystery, glory, and love.

The message itself demonstrates the pastor's personal knowledge of the couple's struggles, his presence with them through their trials, and his understanding of how God's Word applies to their pain. In each of these, he understands that he acts as Christ's representative to the couple, and his reference to such things in the sermon is part of the ministry of the Incarnate Word to them and to those gathered for the funeral.

In the message, the necessary references to the sovereignty of God, the eternal safety of the children, and the love of God for them and their parents are tenderly expressed. Unique to this message, and a mark of the pastoral wisdom behind it, is the willingness of the pastor to acknowledge the mystery of God's hand in such difficulties. But with this acknowledgment is also the reminder that there is no other God to whom we can turn, or to whom we want to turn, than the One who gave his Son to save such children eternally.

THE SERMON:

FUNERAL FOR JOANNA JOY AND HANNA HOPE TAYLOR

Bob Flayhart

[10]Behold, the Lord GOD comes with might,
and his arm rules for him;
behold, his reward is with him,
and his recompense before him.
[11]He will tend his flock like a shepherd;
he will gather the lambs in his arms;
he will carry them in his bosom,
and gently lead those that are with young.
—*Isaiah 40:10–11 ESV*[3]

Opening Prayer, Scripture Reading, and Context

Precious Jesus, give us the grace to trust you right now. We have met here to grieve the loss but celebrate the homegoing of Joanna Joy Taylor and Hanna Hope Taylor and to thank God for their lives, brief as they were, trusting that their impact will never be forgotten. As we gather, let us remember that we are here in the presence of God. The words of man are much too weak for a time like this. We need supernatural help in this time, so let's go to the Lord together in prayer.

Father, what a privilege it is to be able to call you Father, particularly in times like this—to know that we have a Father in heaven who cares, a Father in heaven who rules, a Father in heaven who comforts, a Father in heaven who is near. Father, we give you praise that you have sent your son Jesus Christ to live a perfect

---

3. All Scripture quotations in this chapter, unless otherwise indicated, are taken from the English Standard Version (ESV).

life on our behalf, to die a substitutionary death on our behalf, and to send a spirit of adoption to our hearts that cries out, "Abba, Father!"

Spirit of the living God, we would invite you even now into this place and to fall upon us in power, to move in every heart, to open every eye, to unstop every deaf ear, to comfort every broken heart, to give hope to the hopeless, joy to the despairing, peace to the anxious. Holy Spirit, move among us so that we may leave this place knowing that God has been with us. Take these words now, Father, and apply them to our lives. We pray particularly for Joshua and Sonya to be comforted and strengthened. Please confirm and establish them. In Jesus' name, Amen.

In thinking through what to say to Joshua, Sonya, and to the rest of us as well, I asked them if there was any verse, any passage, that they particularly wanted me to use. Fairly quickly, Sonya said, "Isaiah 40:10–11." Let us read it now. This is the Word of God:

[Pastor Flayhart then read the passage as quoted above.]

Now if you will just bear with me for a moment, I need to help us understand the context of these verses. Isaiah was writing to the people of God. Because of their disobedience and sin, they were going to be exiled to Babylon. Isaiah, 150 years before it would be fulfilled, is prophesying to the people of God. Though things look grim now, he tells the people, things will get better because God is on the throne, and God has a plan. God is a good shepherd. Isaiah is to prophesy to the people of Israel that at the end of their exile when things look most grim, they are to step out in faith and trust in the goodness of God. They are to go back to the Promised Land and expect to see the goodness of God in the land of the living.

This passage is filled with the simple message of the sovereign power of God. With our God there is no "oops!" With our God there are no accidents. With our God we are never victims of blind circumstance or unfeeling fate. Notice, Joshua and Sonya, the strength of our God: "The Lord GOD comes with might, and his arm rules for him." There is no wringing of his hands; there is no wiping the sweat off his brow; there is no going on vacation. These truths assure us that there has never been a moment when you have been outside the will of God.

Because of that encompassing will of our sovereign God, you know that everything is ordained and has purpose. Everything is ordained for his glory. Everything is ordained for your growth in Christ and your ministry in the gospel. God has infinite power. But if all we knew was God's power, we might fear him, but we would never love him, and we could never trust him. So we need to understand not only that our God is a God of power, but also that he is a God of mercy. He is a God of compassion; he is a God of goodness and grace. His will isn't like castor oil—tasting awful despite assurances that it is probably good for you. No, his purposes are really and truly good. Sometimes we don't see God's purposes, and often times we don't understand them. Like the people of Israel, we are required to exercise faith in the goodness and power of God.

What God declares in these verses is that, regardless of how our circumstances appear to human sight, the kingdom of God is advancing. I want to remind us all that through these two young lives the kingdom of God has been advanced. I also want you to know that because of these two brief lives, the kingdom of God will continue to be advanced. I'll give you several ways I have seen the kingdom of God advance through Joanna Joy and Hanna Hope.

The Kingdom of God Has Been Advanced in Heaven

First of all, the kingdom of God has been advanced in heaven because right now these two young lives—two souls—are in heaven. As a Presbyterian minister, I think one of the beauties of the Reformed faith is that we believe that God is a covenant-keeping God. We believe God is so gracious that not only has he promised to be a God to us as we trust in Jesus Christ, but he also has promised to be a God to the children in our household. In Genesis 17, when God gives Abraham a promise of the Messiah who would come to save his people from their sins, the Lord says, "I will be a God to you and to your children."

God then instructs Abraham to administer the sign of circumcision to those within his household. The mark becomes a lifelong reminder for all in Abraham's family of their identity with the God who provides righteousness to those who put their faith in him. Children who could not yet believe— eight-day-old male infants who couldn't possibly understand the gospel— were given this sign of the righteousness that is by faith. All throughout the Old Testament, the people of Israel believed the promise that not only were they God's children, but also that their children were blessed by inclusion in a holy covenant relationship with God.

In the New Testament, during Peter's first sermon at Pentecost, he echoes the language of God's promise to Abraham. Speaking of the salvation now available through Christ Jesus, Peter says to all the people gathered: "the promise is for you and for your children" (Acts 2:39). In 1 Corinthians 7:14, Paul says that the children of at least one believing parent are holy to the

Lord. This is a covenantal language. This isn't cold, abstract doctrinal musing. This is warm, living, practical truth. Unless you have been where Joshua and Sonya are right now, you will never know how warm and real these covenant promises are. There is no doubt in my mind that Joanna and Hanna are in the arms of Jesus because these parents trust in the heart of Jesus. My confidence is based not on their goodness but on the covenant mercy of their God.

King David committed an immoral act and consequently a child was born (see 2 Samuel 11–12). The child became sick, and while the child lived, David pleaded with God in prayer to save the child. For reasons known only in heaven, God chose not to. But after the child died, David arose from his prayers and said of his child, "I shall go to him, but he will not return to me" (12:23). David understood the covenant promises. He understood that the child was already in the presence of God—a presence David himself would experience after his own death. In the Bible, parents who believed in God also believed that the souls of their children who died were also with God. With their faith as our example, we also believe that Joanna and Hanna are in heaven. Heaven has been expanded and the kingdom of God advanced simply because they were born.

The Kingdom of God Has Been Advanced on This Planet in the Church of Jesus Christ

Not only has the kingdom of God been advanced in heaven, but I want us also to realize that the kingdom of heaven has been advanced on this planet in the church of Jesus Christ through the lives of these two little girls. Joshua and Sonya have repeatedly shared their amazement at how the body of the Christ has come together through this trial. Joanna and Hanna have been used to bring the body of Christ together—churches, Christian schools, students, teachers, pastors, and friends. Their very birth was a symbol of the unity of the body of Christ. I will never forget the e-mail message I got from Joshua in which he said that in the twenty weeks of life in Sonya's womb, his daughters had achieved what many years of being a Christian had failed to achieve in his own life: *they had an undivided heart.*

And what a picture of the body of Christ you have been! Your hearts have been united to Joshua's and Sonya's. I say to you as the body, "Well done. Well done." The grace of God has been on this group. Joshua and Sonya want you to know that they know this! They have experienced the awesome presence of

Christ. Jesus chooses to work, lead, and gently care for those who are young, and he does it through the body of Christ. Let me exhort this group. It is not over. Joshua and Sonya are still going to need us, and I am convinced by God's Spirit and his grace, we will be there.

Another unique aspect of this situation—and how Christ cares for us, as well as how Christ will care for Joshua and Sonya—is that we will continue to love one another, as the Scriptures tell us. We will "rejoice with those who rejoice, weep with those who weep" (Romans 12:15). In doing this, we are expanding the presence and ministry of Christ on earth. We rejoice and weep as Christ himself does. I can't quite comprehend how this is true. Though God ordains everything, he can still be touched and grieve over that which he ordains.

Think of the death of Lazarus. Jesus, the Son of God, knows what he is going to do. He knows he is going to raise Lazarus from the dead, and yet, when he is in front of the tomb with the people who are grieving, what does he do? He weeps. We do not have a high priest who is unable to sympathize with our weakness, but One who has been touched in every way by what touches us (see Hebrews 4:15). Joshua and Sonya, as you grieve, as you weep, I want you to know that our God weeps with you. If you don't believe, look at the body of Christ right here. The tears of the church are his tears. By these tears we know his care, and we also know by this expression of his heart that it is OK for us to grieve—but we grieve as those who have hope because of our faith in this God who cares now and provides eternally!

The Kingdom of God Will Be Advanced in Your Lives

Finally, I want you to know, Joshua and Sonya, that God is going to use Joanna and Hanna so that the kingdom of heaven will be advanced in your lives. He is already doing this, but I want you to know that he is going to continue to do this. I want you to know that everything is more dependent on his grace and his goodness than it is on your faith. There are going to be days when you seem to be hanging on by your fingernails. There are going to be days when you want to let go. Already, there have been days of living moment to moment, when you just wanted to chuck the whole thing. I want you to know that it is not you who hold the hand of God; it is your Father in heaven who holds your hand—and he won't let go!

John 10:27–29 reads, "My sheep hear my voice, and I know them, and they follow me. I give them eternal life, and they will never perish, and no one will snatch them out of my hand. My Father, who has given them to me, is greater than all, and no one is able to snatch them out of the Father's hand." Philippians 1:6 reads, "And I am sure of this, that he who began a good work in you will bring it to completion at the day of Jesus Christ." And in 1 Peter 5:6–10, we read:

> Humble yourselves, therefore, under the mighty hand of God so that at the proper time he may exalt you, casting all your anxieties on him, because he cares for you. Be sober-minded; be watchful. Your adversary the devil prowls around like a roaring lion, seeking someone to devour. Resist him, firm in your faith, knowing that the same kinds of suffering are being experienced by your brotherhood throughout the world. And after you have suffered a little while, the God of all grace, who has called you to his eternal glory in Christ, will himself restore, confirm, strengthen, and establish you.

Your Father will not let you go! Though times get rough and you may be filled with doubt and anxiety or even despair, I want you to know that it is going to be OK because the future doesn't depend on you.

What a picture of the gospel we had the other night at the baptism of your daughters! We looked at those helpless, dying daughters of yours, who were unable to lift a finger to feed themselves spiritually or to give themselves any kind of spiritual medication that might heal our broken hearts. Yet, we rejoiced in God's blessing of them in their helplessness. The vision of the gospel seen through baptism is that *help comes from above*. As the water was poured over their heads, we were reminded yet again that help has to come from above, deliverance has to come from above—and that is the message of the gospel. Your daughters have brought to our lives a clear picture of the gospel of Jesus Christ.

Unless we recognize that we are as helpless and as in need as Joanna and Hanna were, we will not understand the goodness of Christ. It has been said that the Westminster Catechism was the head or the brain of the Reformation. It has also been said that the Heidelberg Catechism was the heart, the beating pulse, and the passion of the Reformation. Question 1 of the Heidelberg Catechism asks, "What is your only comfort in life and in death?" The answer is:

> That I am not my own, but belong—body and soul, in life and in death—
> to my faithful Savior Jesus Christ. He has fully paid for all my sins with
> his precious blood and has set me free from the tyranny of the devil. He

also watches over me in such a way that not a hair can fall from my head without the will of my Father in heaven. In fact all things must work together for my salvation. Because I belong to him, Christ, by his Holy Spirit, assures me of eternal life and makes me wholeheartedly willing and ready from now on to live for him.

At times like these, our hearts can get pretty thirsty—thirsty for hope, thirsty for joy, thirsty for relief—and that is OK, as long as we are going to the right well. Joshua and Sonya have heard me talk many times about C. S. Lewis and his famous children's series The Chronicles of Narnia. Narnia is a make-believe world where the animals talk and it is always winter, but never Christmas. Spring never comes because of the controlling power of the wicked White Witch. Still, a few lost children are able to find their way to Narnia. Then they are able to summon Aslan, a great lion. Aslan is the ruler, the Son of the Emperor beyond the Sea. Aslan is the Christ figure in these stories.

In one of the accounts, there is a little girl named Jill. Jill is thirsty. Jill is dying of thirst! Jill wants some water to refresh her, and she sees a stream—the cleanest and clearest stream she has ever seen. She approaches it to take a drink, and as she does, she sees this great reflection in this stream. It is the lion, Aslan. Jill backs up, and she is frightened and says, "Would you mind going away while I take a drink?"

The lion lets out a low growl that might seem as if he is angry or is trying to scare the girl. But the growl is just a way of letting her know that in asking him to go away, the girl might as well have asked the whole mountain to move.

Then she says, "Will you promise not to do anything to me if I come to drink?"

And Aslan says, "I make no promises like that."

Jill says, "Well, do you eat little girls?"

Aslan says, "I have swallowed up girls and boys, women and men, kings, emperors, cities, and entire realms."

Jill says, "I dare not come for a drink."

The lion says, "Then you will die of thirst."

Jill says, "Oh dear, what shall I do? I know; I'll go and look for another stream."

Aslan looks at her and says, "My dear girl, there is no other stream."[4]

---

4. This episode is paraphrased from chapter 2 of C. S. Lewis's *The Silver Chair* (New York: Macmillan, 1953).

154 · PREACHING AFTER THE LOSS OF A CHILD

There are going to be times when we will have no idea what to say to you, Joshua and Sonya. One thing I do know, however, is this: *there is no other stream*. There is nowhere else to turn. There is no other place to drink and no one else who will ever care as much as our Aslan will!

As I close, I believe the greatest impact that Joanna and Hanna will ever have is the impact they have had by bringing together this group. There may be people here who think this Christmas that, in fact, there can be no God if things like these losses of little girls occur. Let me tell you what Joanna and Hanna would say if they were here now and could talk. They, who have now experienced heaven, would say, "It's all true! It's not a fairy tale. It's not a fable. There really is a God. Christ is truly his Son. He makes all things right in his heaven, and the only way to get there is through acknowledging your sins and your helplessness and fleeing desperately to the cross of Christ."

On Saturday evening at six o'clock, we sat together and were told that the girls were on their way to heaven. Sonya and I looked at each other, and I said, "You know, I hope this is not inappropriate, but it's almost making me a bit envious, because they are in a place where we most long to be."

I know Joshua and Sonya wouldn't want anything more than my being clear about these gospel truths on the day they celebrate the homegoing of Joanna and Hanna. These dear parents want the people they love the most to understand deeply the goodness of the gospel of the grace of Jesus Christ that eternally claims their hearts and their daughters' hearts too!

Closing Prayer and Benediction

Let's pray: *Father, there are times when we are fearful to approach you, just like Jill was at the stream. Sometimes, Father, it doesn't seem like you are very safe. We pray for things, and our prayers don't get answered the way we would like them to. Circumstances we would never dream up seem to find their way into our lives. Father, would you remind us that there is no other stream; there is no other place to drink; there is nowhere else we can go. Father, remind us that you do come with light to our darkness. You do feed us; you do care for us; you do carry us in your arms; and you do gently lead each one of us.*

Father, thank you for Joshua and Sonya, and, yes, Father, we give you praise for Joanna and Hanna. Father, we pray that the Taylor home — even though these girls are gone for a time — may be filled with joy and hope. We ask this in Jesus' name. Amen.

And now, receive the benediction from God:

May the Lord bless you and keep you. May the Lord make his face to shine upon you and be gracious to you. May the Lord lift up his countenance upon you and give you peace, both now and all your days. Amen.

Part Three

PREACHING FUNERALS
WITH ESPECIALLY DIFFICULT
CAUSES OR CIRCUMSTANCES

Chapter Twelve

"LIFESTYLE" CONSEQUENCES

SITUATION

One of my dearest friends and most troubled parishioners, Paul, died at an early age. Complications of bad habits, family genetics, and a past lifestyle took him.[1] Further complicating his passing was the complexity of his artistic temperament. He was at the same moment one of the most profound spokesman for the grace of God and one of the most doubtful of its application to himself. He produced beautiful music but refused to write or record it; loved literature but detested intellectuals; loved people but lived alone; made his home interior a designer's dream but rarely let anyone enter; was a snob about art but made his own gloriously accessible; dressed with panache but struggled with his sexual identity. He was sensitive and stubborn, caring and exasperating, funny and full of despair. He taught me more about worship than anyone else. He argued with me more about worship than anyone else. No one I have ever known could make me feel better about myself or madder at him. I loved him dearly. Preaching his funeral with full knowledge of his faults and a heart full of love for him was one of the most difficult things I have ever done.

CONCERNS

Simply holding myself together during this funeral was one of my major concerns. My grief over the passing of this dear and influential friend was very

---

1. The causes of my friend's early death make this message applicable to those situations where sad lifestyle choices result in life-shortening consequences (e.g. alcoholism, AIDS, tobacco illnesses, drug addiction, anorexia) that must be addressed in order to demonstrate and exalt the greater grace of our Savior.

intense. I needed to make sure that I and others not only heard the comfort of the resurrection promises that assure us of reunion with loved ones, but also were reminded of the grace of God that is greater than all our sin. My friend's past struggles would not have been known by all in attendance and did not need to be mentioned directly. Still, it was important for those who knew his situation to know that I knew and to hear me say clearly that the *grace of Jesus was more than sufficient* for this Paul too.

APPROACH

My intention was to represent God's love for a troubled soul by expressing my love in the context of honest reflections on his life. My hope was to reflect Paul's personality and interests by humor, artistic references, and personal reminiscences. I wanted it to be apparent by these comments that neither ignorance nor a decision to ignore truth was the reason that I would speak with such confidence about God's grace toward my friend. I chose to speak on a text from Isaiah 6 because it so clearly tells of God's atoning and cleansing work that makes us fit for God's service. Despite his struggles, my friend had been blessed to see much of the glory of God that was revealed to the ancient prophet. No aspect of that glory was more radiant than the grace that accompanied it. I believed that making this grace plain toward the soul of my friend would make the glory of God bright for those who gathered to mourn Paul's too-soon loss—even if his own struggles had hastened that day.

THE SERMON
HEAVEN'S SONG
Bryan Chapell

[1]In the year that King Uzziah died, I saw the Lord, high and exalted, seated on a throne; and the train of his robe filled the temple. [2]Above him were seraphim, each with six wings: With two wings they covered their faces, with two they covered their feet, and with two they were flying. [3]And they were calling to one another:

> "Holy, holy, holy is the LORD Almighty;
>   the whole earth is full of his glory."

[4]At the sound of their voices the doorposts and thresholds shook and the temple was filled with smoke.

[5]"Woe to me!" I cried. "I am ruined! For I am a man of unclean lips, and I live among a people of unclean lips, and my eyes have seen the King, the LORD Almighty."

[6]Then one of the seraphim flew to me with a live coal in his hand, which he had taken with tongs from the altar. [7]With it he touched my mouth and said, "See, this has touched your lips; your guilt is taken away and your sin atoned for."

[8]Then I heard the voice of the Lord saying, "Whom shall I send? And who will go for us?"

And I said, "Here am I. Send me!"

—Isaiah 6:1–8

AS WE WERE GETTING DETAILS for this service my wife, Kathy, said, "Doesn't it seem unreal that we are talking about getting ready for Paul's funeral? We should be talking about getting ready for Paul's recital or Paul's rehearsal—not his funeral."

A Taste of Heaven

This does not seem possible. His slow-growing lung disease turned to an aggressive and deadly carcinoma with almost unbelievable speed. Though I saw him on his hospital bed struggling for air and comfort, even that does not seem real. The reality of Paul Ester is that of someone always ready to chuckle at your jokes and then add a word that made them funnier and smarter than you could have. To think of Paul is to remember one full of life, full of laughter, full of iced tea, full of anxiety, full of *maximum* expressiveness. Everything was said in hyperbole—it was either the best movie ever made or the worst movie ever made; nothing was ever mediocre, unless, of course, it was the *most* mediocre movie ever made.

There is no adult in my life who has encouraged me more or worried me more, inspired me more or exasperated me more than Paul. I could have both hugged him and strangled him many times, and if that sounds irreverent or inappropriate, then you did not know him well. But while I could go on at length about the mixture of music and mirth and misery that was Paul, what I can tell you without any qualification is that I loved him deeply, and this was not hard to do at all.

Paul was my brother in Christ; he was my comrade in Christian service; and he is my forever friend.

When I first came to the farming/mining community of Woods, Illinois, as a freshman preacher, Paul was already well entrenched as a pianist, organist, choir director, custodian, lawn mower, and country farmer—a most unlikely combination. But that unlikely combination became one of the most formative influences in my ministry. Paul already knew far more about music and worship than I did. And as he informed me and stretched me, and occasionally chided me to stretch me, we put together worship services in that small-town church that were as near to expressing the heavenly glories of our faith as any worship I have ever been a part of. It is *rare* these days that I participate in worship that brings tears to my eyes with the realization that I am tasting the first-fruits of heaven, but that was my *regular* experience when working with Paul.

His musical creativity, spiritual sensitivity, and love of the gospel gave *maximum* expression to what was deepest in our heart.

The services were deeply mindful of the glory of God, deeply respectful of the saints who had gone before us, deeply committed to expressing our faith in authentic terms, remarkably aware of what touched the soul, and profoundly scriptural. Only after I left Woods, Illinois, did I learn the depth and divisiveness of the worship wars that were enveloping our church culture, and only afterward was I appropriately grateful for what the godly church folk in Woods, and the genius of Paul, allowed us to express for the glory of our Savior and the good of his people. Those were heavenly days!

A Life of Separation

But many of you know that I would be less than honest if I implied that the heaven for us was also the heaven Paul experienced. Though he was always a wonderful musician (and actually was the featured musician for our church's national assembly as a very young man), his concerns about separation from farm and family and his own self-doubt about his gifts kept him from finishing formal education in music. Though we visited college campuses together, I could not encourage him or scold him or push him (as he was able to push me) enough to get him to commit to further study. Thus, when opportunities to be a church musician opened up here in Chicago, these opportunities were truly a blessing of the Lord that allowed Paul to express his music and lead others in worship in ways that caused him less anxiety.

Being anxious was a large part of Paul's life. More than once I wished I could quiet his heart and help him as much as he helped me. Daniel [here I was addressing Paul's brother in the service], what a dear brother you have been to keep the family ties so close with him all of these years. As different as you two were, your and your family's faithfulness to him have been a stabilizing anchor of love in his life. He needed such anchors.

Paul truly had an artist's temperament. A biographer of Handel and Bach once described them as prone to "dramatic fits of agitation" and I thought to myself, "That's Paul." But though I could laugh about his temperament at times, I also grieved for him. Paul, as any true artist, had the perspective of one who lives apart from us. The reason I think he was such a good adviser and encourager for me was that, though he was physically enmeshed in all aspects of the church, the poetic works in which his heart and thoughts stirred were always some distance away.

The separation allowed him an objective distance for amazing insight into others' motives and needs, but always it was the insight of one whose heart was a half step removed from us. He could see right through most of us, but he used that vision to help us. He was often able and willing to correct me in my perspectives, but if anyone critiqued me in unfair ways (ways I was tempted to accept), none would be more ready to defend me *to me* with the actual realities than Paul.

The separation of the artistic spirit gave Paul perspective and poetic insight but also loneliness, great storms of self-doubt, and even self-destructive isolation. When he was with us, he interacted so adeptly and gregariously that it was easy to forget how he held himself apart and was well acquainted with the darkness of the world that he closed in around himself. For that I grieved, and still do. I do not know if he ever really found a kindred spirit with whom he could share all of himself. I often thought of the great poet and hymn writer William Cowper when Paul came to mind. A biographer wrote of the gifted Cowper, "His life seemed strangely addicted to sorrow." Wrote Elizabeth Barrett Browning in her poem "Cowper's Grave":

> O men! this man, in brotherhood, your weary paths beguiling,
> Groaned inly while he taught you peace, and died while ye were smiling.

The Joy He Shared

It was hard not to smile often when you were around Paul. His ready laugh, frequent compliments, wry humor, and willingness to let us smile at his latest outlandish fretting about some silly nothing just made us feel good. No matter how bad we felt, we at least had the sense that our lives were not as twisted as his — and he wanted us to feel that way. Daniel, when you and your family were with me at his bedside while he was dying, we often smiled and laughed as we remembered old times, and also as we remembered the joy that Paul brought us.

For every Christian there is the calling of bringing Christ's joy to one another. Paul not only helped us to sing of the glories of our Savior; he also shared with us the joy and peace of our Savior by being so open about his own maladjustments and frequent worries. Somehow we knew that regardless of how greatly the anxieties loomed in Paul's life, he still trusted in a Savior who suffered more to embrace him and to love him forever.

Paul could so easily have let his anxieties rob us of the Savior's music; Paul could so easily have let his self-doubt blind him to the Savior's beauty, but he did not. The world that Paul clearly and rightly perceived to be full of dangers and darkness and loneliness was not able to blind him to the greater reality of the Savior, who picks us up when we fall, holds us when we weep, and cleanses us from the filth of our sin by mercy more vast than this world can contain.

Paul saw the reality of both worlds, but the reality of the heavenly world was the one that he most shared with us and that most sustained him. That is why he had the choir's recording of "It Is Well with My Soul" played to him again and again in the hospital. When the song would end, he would turn his head as the signal to start it again. And when he could no longer turn his head, he simply caught his breath to signal. So that when he drew his last breath, he was hearing the joy of the greatest of eternal realities: *It is well with my soul.*

The Song He Sings

This past Sunday, I preached on Isaiah 6 in which the prophet sees into heaven, but his heavenly vision initially is not one of comfort. The holiness of God not only causes the angels who are singing around the throne to shield themselves from the searing radiance of God's glory but also causes the prophet himself to tremble and fall to the ground with the moan *Woe is me! I am ruined because I am a man of unclean lips, and I live among a people of unclean lips, and my eyes have seen the Lord* (verse 5). The holiness of God by itself does not comfort; it convicts — and the prophet characterizes the effect in his heart by saying that his lips are unclean. He is so stricken by his sin in the light of God's holiness that the prophet acknowledges that his lips are not worthy to sing with the angels.

But then an angel takes a coal from the altar of atonement on which God will provide the sacrifices that signal how he will ultimately take away the sin of the world by the sacrifice of his Son. With that coal, the angel touches the lips of the prophet. It is the sweet burning of a divine kiss, for by that kiss the prophet's lips are made pure (as a sign of what is now true of his heart), and he can join the angels' song, as can all who trust in God's provision for them.

We wondered how much of Paul's ability to sense was still operating the other night when we gathered around his bed in the hospital. But he let us know. As we prayed for him and then sang "All for Jesus," Paul, who had been so miserable and unresponsive, sat up in bed and smiled directly at us. He was sharing his vision again. In all of the darkness he was experiencing, he knew that the light of his Savior was very near. And when Paul smiled, it was with lips that would soon sing with the angels.

And now he sings with the angels and plays cantatas and races between pianos and organs without back or hip pain, and he knows the embrace of the most kindred of spirits, his Lord Jesus. I think that in some ways Paul has waited for that embrace all of his life, and now he will know it forever.

So I will grieve this passing of a dear friend and a very special man, but I will not grieve as one who has no hope. Rather, my song with the angels and with Paul, who taught me how to worship, will be "It Is Well with My Soul."

Thanks be to God, who gives us the victory through our Lord Jesus Christ (1 Corinthians 15:57 ESV).

Chapter Thirteen

DRUNKEN DRIVER

SITUATION

The daughter and only child of a middle-aged couple was driving home from a friend's house at night when a teenaged drunken driver crossed the center line. The drunk boy survived; the young woman was killed instantly.

The tragedy seemed especially sad because the young woman, Joni, was well-known for her joy. This is not said with the euphemistic emphasis of a funeral message that polishes the positives of the deceased. In our church and community, everyone knew Joni's bubbly voice, beaming smile, and wide eyes that glistened with approval for whomever she was addressing. Although she was recently divorced from an unfaithful husband, her faith and bright spirit had remained undiminished. In fact, her prayers for her former husband and her continued affirmations of confidence in the Lord's provision for her life had led a number of her coworkers to consider the claims of Christ. They were attending our church and brought their unbelieving friends to her funeral in great numbers.

CONCERNS

There were three sets of persons whom I was most concerned to address in this message. I needed first to address the parents, whose grief seemed so overwhelmingly tragic in light of the loss of an only child. Having so recently experienced the grief of their daughter's divorce from the son of their best friends, this mountainous tragedy added pain that seemed beyond bearing. Out of love and respect for this dear couple, I considered it vital not to try to offer explanations for why such a tragedy had occurred, but rather to offer the comfort of key gospel promises: we will see believing loved ones again in eternity; even tragic events are not beyond God's use for eternal purposes; gospel hope will give us strength for tomorrow.

For these mature believers, it was especially important that their daughter's funeral be an opportunity for the gospel to be presented to her unbelieving friends. This was the second set of persons for whom I was most concerned. Some of Joni's unbelieving friends had been exploring her faith in our church in the weeks prior to her death. Many of their friends came to her funeral. Without turning the funeral into an evangelism crusade and without using the friends' grief to manipulate them into faith commitments, it was important to make sure these friends understood that Joni's death made plain the eternal consequences of their spiritual decisions. I especially wanted these young people to know that Joni's spiritual concern for them (which she had regularly expressed to them) was a reflection of God's love and evidence of his willingness to show mercy to those who received him.

The message of mercy was also central to the last set of persons I was most concerned to address: Joni's former husband and his mistress. I did not expect the mistress to come to the funeral, but I expected her former husband to accompany his parents. Joni's parents and I loved this young man, and we were very hopeful that her death would shock him into consideration of his spiritual peril. If the Holy Spirit were so to work in his heart (and through him in his mistress's heart), then it was important that both the need to repent and the willingness of God to extend mercy to the repentant had to be evident in the message.

A dimension of mercy not directly mentioned in the message related to God's readiness also to forgive the young man who caused the accident that took Joni's life. He was in the hospital recuperating from injuries at the time of the funeral. I do not recall if that is the reason I did not then address matters relating to him. Still, in hindsight, I believe not speaking of concern for him was a mistake. Even if he were not personally present to hear of how the gospel could apply to his heart, the church and community were largely present. It would have been good to remind everyone of our shared need of forgiveness and of the pardon God offers to all who trust in Jesus. Addressing this concern may have better equipped all to deal with anger and bitterness toward this young man, as well as prepared him to hear the gospel, should he have gotten word of how he was treated at the funeral. An important footnote to this account is an encounter Joni's parents had with the young man in a store weeks after the funeral. Though he looked at his feet to avoid facing them, they offered him their forgiveness. And months later, he committed his life to Jesus Christ.

APPROACH

My goal was to offer comfort to Joni's parents and loved ones with the security and purpose the gospel promises each believer. I also wanted to remind them that, despite the tragic death of their loved one, the deceased knows the joy of being in the Lord's presence. In addition, her life and its end are fulfilling purposes of God's design, even if we cannot discern them in this life. I had to be careful not to imply that God was the author of the tragedy but at the same time to make it clear that he can use all things for the good of those who love him. I wanted to offer the gospel hope, forgiveness, and security affirmed by the deceased to the many unbelieving and spiritually rebellious persons in attendance at the funeral. I chose a text that emphasizes the comfort we have because of the eternal security our loved ones have in him. Because Joni's testimony was so exemplary, I was also able to use her character and demeanor to help demonstrate the reality of the gospel truths taught in the scriptural text.

THE SERMON

THE GIFTS OF A GIFT OF GOD

Bryan Chapell

[13]Brothers and sisters, we do not want you to be uninformed about those who sleep in death, so that you do not grieve like the rest of mankind, who have no hope. [14]For we believe that Jesus died and rose again, and so we believe that God will bring with Jesus those who have fallen asleep in him. [15]According to the Lord's word, we tell you that we who are still alive, who are left until the coming of the Lord, will certainly not precede those who have fallen asleep. [16]For the Lord himself will come down from heaven, with a loud command, with the voice of the archangel and with the trumpet call of God, and the dead in Christ will rise first. [17]After that, we who are still alive and are left will be caught up together with them in the clouds to meet the Lord in the air. And so we will be with the Lord forever. [18]Therefore encourage one another with these words.

— 1 Thessalonians 4:13–18

JOHN AND SUE,[1] you named your daughter Joan, we called her Joni — each name is special. The name *Joan* means "God's gift." How appropriate for the child who brought such joy and love into our lives to be named "God's gift." She was a gift to us. Her joy was such a gift that I miss her now being able to reassure and comfort me in my pain over her loss. Still, her joyous testimony was so vibrant and so evident that I think I know what she would say and how she would say it.

United to Him

If I were able to talk to her now, I would say, "Joni, I am so sorry. I hurt so much for your loss. Tell me how not to worry and hurt so much." Then she

---

1. Individual names and some personal details have been changed as an expression of care for the family.

would smile, and her eyes would glisten as she bubbled, "Oh, it's all right. I'm OK."

And she would be right, because she *is* OK. More than that, she is with the Lord she loved, the One who filled her with such joy. For the Scriptures say that those who trust in Jesus are God's own children, and he takes them to be with himself. What a beautiful picture, for even as I think of how full of joy Joni always was, I know that she, like us, could see her Lord only as through a glass darkly while she was clothed in this earthly body. But now Joni sees her Lord face-to-face, and those eyes of hers—always so bright and glowing—are now gleaming even brighter. Those eyes are filled with the face of Jesus, whom she sees more clearly and loves more deeply. That's why she would say, "It's all right. I'm OK."

"Oh, but Joni," I would want to say, "Why? Why now? Why this way? Why you?" I don't think she would smile quite so broadly at those questions. She would furrow her brow and say, "Oh, I don't know that I can say, but I know it's gonna be all right." And she would be right again. She would be right in not answering what we cannot answer, but claiming by faith the truths our Lord gives in his Word that his love continues, even where our eyes cannot see.

We so appreciated her that we cannot understand why we had to lose Joni, but perhaps by meditating more on the love of the Lord we can be comforted. Joni's aunt, Christine, helped lead me through an appreciation of Joni to a greater understanding of the Lord's comfort with these words said a couple of days ago: "The Lord must have loved her very much to want her home so soon."

I am not going to try to figure out why the Lord wanted her in his home so soon, but the Scripture we read does say that she is already "in Christ" and will come "with Jesus." She is united to him forever, and she will come with him when he returns. These truths affirm with Aunt Christine that the Lord loved Joni so much that he took her to himself now. She is OK because she already rests in his arms.

Forgiven of Sin

This promise that she is already in Jesus' presence helps to comfort us, but we may look for more—something to make sense of it all. We look for purpose. And I believe we may even now be able to glimpse that. Because Joni is united to Jesus, we also look forward to being with him and, consequently, with her again. This is one way that Joni was God's gift to us. God's gifts always lead us to himself, and because Joni is now with him, we long to be with him too. Her presence with him leads us to seek him too.

But though we long to be with our Lord, we know that our faults and frailties keep us from him. That's why the gift that Joni also appreciated so much was the Lord's provision of his own Son, who made a way for us to be with God. In order for us to be united to a holy God, he had to deal with our unholiness. He did that by allowing his sinless Son, Jesus, to take the weight of all of our wrongdoing on himself. On the cross Jesus suffered the penalty we all deserved for our sin and, by doing so, conquered sin's guilt and greatest consequence — death itself. The evidence of his victory for us is his resurrection and his coming again to claim those who love him. Now if we believe that and ask him to forgive us, God says that his love for us will never go away, even after we die.

Joni was so captivated by this love of her heavenly Father that she ordered her life so as to reflect him. She wanted the joy she felt in his love and forgiveness to be known and shared by all those she loved. If she had a wish for us today, I know it would be that her testimony would not be in vain. She would want us all to know the joy she had in the Lord, and she would want that blessing to be so evident in us, despite these horrible events, that our joy in the midst of pain would defy any earthly explanation. As a consequence, the only way people could make sense of us was if we possessed transcendent hope, a confidence in a love that was more powerful than death and that extended beyond this life. If those wonders could be made more plain by their contrast with the tragic events of Joni's passing, then even these events might be used as a gift to help others understand the greatness and goodness of our God. Since he is so great that he can use even tragedy to turn hearts to himself, we can trust he is so good that he loves despite past fault, forgives past failures, and embraces us beyond this life.

Reunited Again

The greatness and goodness that provide God's continuing care beyond the limits of this life would have to be the source of Joni's final comfort for me. For even if I understood that she was OK, and even if I could glimpse some purpose in this tragedy, I would still say, "But Joni, I miss you so much."

At that comment I know she would flash a wide smile, and her eyes would dance, and she would say, "Oh, I know, but it's gonna be all right. I'll see you again later."

There were few "good-byes" for Joni. Like most of us when we're young, she did not use these words. Instead, she usually said, "I'll see ya later." And she would be right yet again. For she would be comforting us with the Scriptures stating that we who remain here will one day go to meet those who have gone to be with the Lord.

What joy Joni would still share with us because of the homecoming she knows the Lord is preparing—a time when we will all gather together with our Lord!

How can we be so sad and still share her joy? By remembering that she is God's gift and remembering the gifts she has already shared. Two weeks ago, for instance, some of you remember we had a prayer meeting at Joni's house. She showed us a Christmas gift she was making for a friend. The gift was a quilted star made into a wall hanging—strips of cloth intricately woven into a beautiful tapestry. That gift was so like her and her life, a tapestry made of many different elements, including this tragedy, that have been interwoven into a tapestry bound together by her love and joy. Still, some of you know there was a problem with that tapestry Joni showed us: Christmas is still some time away, and she hadn't finished putting on the border of lace.

The tapestry of Joni's life also will miss the lace of years. But the tapestry will be even dearer to the friend for whom it was intended because of the special memories of Joni that its uniqueness will symbolize. May Joni's life tapestry be as meaningful to many of us, and may our lives be even more beautiful as we remember how much one life could do to beautify so many others.

Joni's ultimate gift was the joy she shared with so many of us. May we all continue to partake of that joy, as we remember that *Joan* means "God's gift," but *Joni*, which we all called her, means "my gift from God." She was a personal gift to each of us. And to each who called her Joni, she still offers you this personal gift: her joy in the Lord. By faith you may share it with her. As you trust in the Lord, who enables us to be with him, forgives our sin, and reunites us in him, may you also experience the gift of his eternal joy.

Chapter Fourteen

CANCER: LONG-SUFFERING

SITUATION

Betty Marcus was a middle-aged woman with adult children who gave herself with great zeal to Christian service. For many years, she led an interdenominational Bible study attended by hundreds of women weekly. She was on the boards of numerous Christian organizations. She and her husband sacrificially, prayerfully, and with personal encouragement supported key Christian organizations in our town and nationally. A voracious reader, Betty was a tireless student of God's Word, yet remained humble in learning from others. A courageous evangelist, she invited friends, neighbors, family, and strangers to explore the Christian faith with her. When she was diagnosed with a particularly virulent and painful cancer, the entire Christian community of our city grieved. But Betty, with characteristic fervor, picked the text for her funeral, insisted on a full sermon, and urged a message that would reach nonbelievers as well as comfort her family.

CONCERNS

Betty's main concern for her funeral was making sure that the gospel would be made plain to her nonbelieving friends. At the same time, she wanted nothing that could be regarded as milquetoast. "They need to understand the meat of the gospel, Bryan," she said. "Don't let them off the hook with a simple message. They have brains that need to be challenged."

While that was Betty's concern, and it was my desire to honor her wishes, I also needed to comfort her family. Her son, daughters, and husband, Bill, are among the dearest believers I know, and they were deeply affected by the passing and suffering of Betty. Her cancer was very painful. Her struggle against the disease left us marveling at her courage but also grieving that her testimony had to be sustained through such challenging final days.

Approach

The text selection was easy because Betty requested a specific passage of Scripture. The teaching difficulty of the text and the depth of theology she desired for her funeral would not have been my choice, but all who knew her understood her choice. My task was to take the theological truths and wed them to the reality of her pain. While I usually try to focus on some career or personal aspect of the person's life to illustrate the spiritual truths I emphasize in a funeral message, it would have been uncaring and lacking in credibility to talk about Betty's life without addressing the pain of her final days. In essence, her pain became the lens through which to discuss the hope of the gospel—the provision of God to deliver us from all pain, both physical and spiritual. In this way, Betty's evangelistic goals were met as I sought to help her family faithfully process the difficulties of her illness as well.

ALL FOR THE GLORY OF GOD

Bryan Chapell

[1]Therefore, since we have been justified through faith, we have peace with God through our Lord Jesus Christ, [2]through whom we have gained access by faith into this grace in which we now stand. And we rejoice in the hope of the glory of God. [3]Not only so, but we also rejoice in our sufferings, because we know that suffering produces perseverance; [4]perseverance, character; and character, hope. [5]And hope does not disappoint us, because God has poured out his love into our hearts by the Holy Spirit, whom he has given us.

[6]You see, at just the right time, when we were still powerless, Christ died for the ungodly. [7]Very rarely will anyone die for a righteous man, though for a good man someone might possibly dare to die. [8]But God demonstrates his own love for us in this: While we were still sinners, Christ died for us.

[9]Since we have now been justified by his blood, how much more shall we be saved from God's wrath through him!

—*Romans 5:1–9 NIV [1984 ed.]*

BILL, I DO NOT REMEMBER who told me—I think it was one of your daughters—of the experience of a couple of weeks ago when you were trying to ease Betty's pain.[1] It had been a terrible weekend of trying to find the balance she wanted of not hurting too much and being lucid enough to talk to and enjoy the family. Somehow the balance got off, and she was in a degree of pain that made her almost begin to panic. It was hard on her, hard on you, hard on everyone. Finally she took a medicine that allowed her to relax, and though the pain didn't disappear, she was able to recline in your arms. The pain was still there, but in your arms she was at peace.

---

1. Individual names and some personal details have been changed as an expression of care for the family.

That picture of Betty in her husband's arms, finding peace from her pain, expresses the truth I want to communicate to you today from this Scripture that Betty chose for her funeral. I do not promise that what I will say will take away your pain — in fact, it would be wrong not to feel pain over the loss of one so dear. Rather, my intention is to place you in the embrace of the Savior, so that in his arms you might find peace in your pain.

The Explanation of our Peace

The peace that the Savior wants for us he explains in words rich in the promises of God that Betty was so anxious for everyone around her to know. With each promise God enfolds us deeper in his embrace.

We Are Justified through Faith (verse 1)

In the first verse of Romans 5, the apostle says that we have peace with God, "since we have been justified through faith." The word *justified* means that we have been made right with God, no longer facing guilt for our sin, punishment for our wrong, or fear of his wrath. Why do we have these beautiful blessings? Not because of our earning or deserving, but because of our faith in what Jesus Christ did (verses 6–9).

God is not waiting for us to get good enough to love us. He is not measuring how much he will care for us by how righteous we will become. Rather, the guilt that was ours, he has taken away and replaced with the righteousness that is not ours. We do not have to get as good or as knowledgeable or as zealous as Betty in order to be at peace with God. He rather tells us to believe that Jesus died for our sins and that such faith makes us right with God.

We Are Standing in Grace (verse 2a)

Now, almost all who call themselves Christians acknowledge that it is Christ's work in our behalf rather than earning or deserving that lifts us from the guilt and shame of our past sin to a loving relationship with God. But Paul goes on to tell us of something that was the zeal of Betty's life in the past few years, and the reason she was so anxious for you to hear this text. The apostle states not only that we are justified by faith but that "through [Jesus] . . . we have gained access by faith into this grace in which we now stand." God did not lift me to his love through faith for just a brief moment; he *keeps* me in his love. I am standing in grace. Once any of us truly places our faith in him, our souls are eternally secure.

The reason this is so important is that so many Christians view their relationship with God as the equivalent of the experience of my daughter and me as we walked across a creek on a log. She wanted to do it herself and fell into the water. The log was too high for her to get up to it again by herself, so I reached down and lifted her out of her misery. This is what God has done on our behalf. He has lifted us from our misery by his mercy—and not through any accomplishment of our own. Virtually everyone understands this, but many think that God's love is such that we are still on that narrow, shaky log, always in danger of slipping off by our failure to walk as carefully as God requires. Instead, the apostle declares that once God has rescued us, we are standing in grace. We have been lifted to the eternal plane of God's love. The safe place on which I walk is as broad as eternity, as high as heaven, as secure as is God in heaven.

I may not do everything right. I may not say all the right things, think all the right thoughts, or have patience even for the religious things that I am supposed to say and think at the time of death, but I am still secure in the Savior's love. My works did not earn my salvation, and my weaknesses will not jeopardize my salvation, because I am standing on the ground that God provides by his grace.

What is the result of my knowing that God is waiting for me neither to get good enough for him to love me nor to step out of line enough for him to reject me? What is the result of being totally secure in the arms of a God who is eternal? The simple answer is *joy*.

We Are Rejoicing in Hope (verse 2b)

Paul states, "We rejoice in the hope of the glory of God." Hope here is not hope against hope or optimistic wishing, but is rather a future confidence that because we have been justified through faith and because we stand in grace, our eternal relationship with God is secure. When this mortal reality with all of its weakness, frailty, and sin falls away, we will be with our God in glory—in the arms of Jesus, secure in his love for all eternity.

Several of us got a glimpse of that glory over the last few days as we gathered around Betty in her bed and as hour after hour the Scriptures were read, hymns were sung, and prayers were offered. Betty's life at those moments was very tenuous, but our hope was so secure that the experience was undeniably glorious. We had a hope so sure that it filled us with a deep sense of rejoicing.

Of course, we needed such a profound cause for joy because our pain was also so piercing. It is a pain of which Paul speaks here too. For having described so beautifully and powerfully the loving embrace of our God, he speaks just as plainly of the pain that makes us long for those arms. We should be grateful that the apostle does speak so plainly of this pain. The Bible is not an unrealistic book that veils its view of misery or sugarcoats our problems as though they do not exist. Having so beautifully pictured the source of our peace, the apostle now addresses our pain.

The Explanation of Our Pain

How can we have peace in a fallen world where disease, disappointment, and disaster are still so prevalent? By recognizing the purpose of our suffering.

The Purpose of Our Suffering (verses 3 – 4)

Paul says that just as "we rejoice in the hope of the glory of God," so "we also rejoice in our sufferings" (Romans 5:3). Rejoice in suffering?! How can this make sense? The answer is that suffering in this world produces aspects of heaven's greater realities in those who are eternally secure (verse 4). Since neither our suffering nor our handling (or mishandling) of it can separate us from God, life's challenges produce *perseverance*. Such perseverance is long-term confidence that God will perform his ultimate purposes in this world and in our lives, resulting in faithfulness in the face of challenge. That's why Paul also states that such confidence in God produces *character*, a greater light of Christ in us in the face of the darkness of this world. And as a light shining in darkness gives *hope*, so the apostle says suffering ultimately gives us greater hope in the glory that will be revealed in us (verses 4–5).

Suffering eases our grasp on the things of this world. It makes us less willing to die for the things that do not last and more willing to live for the things that are eternal. We watched these truths burst into reality in Betty as her suffering made the joys of heaven all the more precious to her and all the more important for her to share.

Last week some of us powerfully witnessed these dynamics of suffering and joy in Betty. We went over to her house in the afternoon, and Betty was able to get up and go outside to enjoy the afternoon sun. As if on cue, though it was only a wonderful providence, as she went out into the sun, friends and family began to drop by. The crowd grew, and as the nurses adjusted her tubes, we had a party around her. Everyone enjoyed her company, and she enjoyed ours.

As I left that impromptu party, I embraced Betty and repeated Psalm

100 to her. As I got to the words "enter his gates with thanksgiving and his courts with praise," Betty gazed at her family and friends gathered around and framed by the colors of the fall leaves made brilliant by the sun. The picture was as heavenly as I can imagine, and Betty said to me with a smile of profound peace, "Entering his gates with thanksgiving and his courts with praise has never meant so much as it does now." Her suffering had produced such an appreciation for the things God provides, such a hope of glory, that it gave her peace even in the midst of her pain.

But more than peace was produced. The reason Betty wanted to be so lucid in her pain was that she wanted the heaven that had become so dear to her to become the hope of all whom she loved as well. Even in her pain, love was pouring out of her, as it has so consistently in her testimony of many years. This is part of the explanation of how we have peace in our pain too. Pain strips away many of the distractions of the world that parade as important, making us all the more conscious of the importance of the work of the Spirit in us and others. Pain is handled not just by sensing the purpose of our suffering but also by signaling the importance of the promise of God's Spirit.

The Promise of God's Spirit (verse 5)

Paul writes, "Hope does not disappoint us, because God has poured out his love into our hearts by the Holy Spirit, whom he has given us" (Romans 5:5). What Betty exhibited in that time of basking in the glow of the sun and her family and in her fight to remain a testimony to her family was the evidence of the Spirit of God in her. All her zeal, her energy, her exuberance for others to know the Lord, which even made her willing to face pain rather than lose one moment of opportunity to share the love of her Savior, were the evidences of that love of God poured out into our hearts by his Spirit.

Many of you remember the birthday party that Jackie Simpson gave for Betty a few months ago. I remember it well because another pastor and I were the only men present. But what I remember more vividly was the description of Betty that her daughter Sandy wrote and that was included in the book of remembrances given to Betty. Sandy wrote:

You taught us to ...
Love passionately,
Forgive completely,
Pray fervently,
Work happily,

Worship reverently,
Serve sacrificially,
Eat healthily,
Laugh heartily,
Live fully.

What a wonderful tribute to Betty! What a wonderful eulogy these words could be! Yet for those of you who know Betty well, you know how angry she would be if I used these words that way. Betty would say, "All those things are not a tribute to me. They are a testimony to the Holy Spirit in me. God saved me and kept me by his grace, through no merit of my own. I am only living out the beauty of the Spirit of love that God has poured into my heart, and this is available to all who will put their faith in him, regardless of their weakness, sin, or failings."

Thus, these attributes of Betty are evidences not merely of God's Spirit in her but of the expression of God's Spirit through her. Bill, I began by speaking of Betty finding peace in your arms. But there have been moments when you have been in her arms too. And when you realize that these arms are, in fact, the Lord's own expression of his love, then you recognize how precious is his eternal care that will yet reunite her with you in his care when he takes all his loved ones to himself.

Therefore, I will grieve for Betty's present loss and separation from us, but not as one who has no hope. Rather, I will say, "Thanks be to God, who gives us the victory through our Lord Jesus Christ" (1 Corinthians 15:57 ESV). We rest in his grace that embraces us with such security that we can know peace in our pain, joy in our sorrow, and hope that perseveres until the One who loves us beyond all our weakness and suffering and sin unites us with himself in glory.

Chapter Fifteen

MURDER

SITUATION

Early on a sunny morning, our family breakfast was interrupted by a student knocking on the back door of our home on the Covenant Seminary campus. "Dr. Chapell, you need to come," he said frantically. "Someone has been hurt." I quickly followed him up the path through our suburban campus to one of our academic buildings. As we walked, he told me more. "Dr. Chapell, I think someone has killed herself." By the time we got to the building, many police officers were present. But the conclusion of the student was wrong. Though arranged to look like a suicide, the death was actually a murder. An international student named Ellen, who had been doing custodial work in the early morning hours, had been killed. Although this incident happened more than two decades ago and thousands of students have come and gone at the seminary, neither the murderer nor motive has ever been identified. Ellen's family traveled from England for the funeral that was held on the seminary campus with our entire staff and student body present.

CONCERNS

A chief concern was not to soft-pedal the horror of the event, but rather to declare the necessity and hope of the gospel in its wake. All kinds of questions arise in the face of such tragedy: Why did God allow it? Why hasn't the murderer been found? Was he/she a stranger, or could he/she still be among us? Did Ellen do something wrong to deserve this? Has the seminary done something wrong to deserve this? Is the seminary succeeding so wonderfully that Satan is making a special effort to stop us? Will there be more attacks? My concern was not to try to answer any of these questions, but rather to confess the darkness of our understanding and situation so that the light of the gospel would shine all the more brightly and clearly.

Because the murder was unsolved, a great deal of fear pervaded the campus. Rumors abounded. Police officers blanketed the campus repeatedly. Our world was turned upside down every day. Our stomachs were in knots all day. The funeral message provided an opportunity not only to calm emotions but to remind everyone of our deepest beliefs and most profound commitments: this world is miserably fallen and in desperate need of our proclamation of the Savior. Rather than making us flee from our purpose, the horror of a murder should make it all the more plain how much our world needs the message of Jesus.

The darkness of our lives in those days was an opportunity to consider anew how important the gospel was, not just for lost people somewhere in the world, but for a seminary community needing to respond to the harshest realities of the world. We could either faint before the challenge or meet it with the strength of our scriptural convictions.

Approach

Providing a strong and comforting reminder of gospel truths for our students and staff in such a painful and fearful situation was my main goal. The message preached was meant not to expound on a lengthy text but to offer an expanded thought on a simple claim of Jesus: *He is our Morning Star.* I confess that my concern was more to inspire than exegete; to rally us with a fresh sense of purpose rather than allowing us to wallow in dread. The message was designed both to calm and to instill courage. Other believers throughout history had faced danger without lessening their gospel resolve. Now it was our turn.

This desire to inspire had to be tempered with the need to minister to those grieving Ellen's loss—including roommates, fellow students, her family (who had traveled internationally to be with us for a funeral service), and my family, because Ellen had lived in our home for a time.

Ellen's extended family was comprised of mature believers and others who were struggling. My own family, still living on campus with young children, was experiencing both grief and fear. We also needed to remember and claim eternal truths for the questions our own hearts shared. Thus, the message had the twin goals of providing both courage and comfort.

The Sermon

What's in a Name?

Bryan Chapell

"I, Jesus, have sent my angel to give you this testimony for
the churches. I am the Root and the Offspring of David, and the
bright Morning Star."

—Revelation 22:16

"WHAT'S THE LAST NAME?" We ask this question when we want to
distinguish one person of common name from another. "Which Bill or Jane
or Mary are you talking about? What is the last name?" The last name sets a
person apart with that which is special or unique about him or her. And here
in this text is Jesus' last name. It is not Smith or Jones—nothing quite so
common. No, here as we close the canon of Scripture, the Lord Jesus, through
his prophet speaks a last time, and in doing so he tells us his last name. Previously he has been called by others the Christ, the Anointed One, the Rose of
Sharon, the Prince of Peace, the Lion of Judah, the Root of Jesse. Previously
he has called himself the Son of Man, and in this last chapter of the Bible
he calls himself the Alpha and the Omega. But what is *the last name he calls
himself* as a special distinctive to echo through the centuries? The last name
by which Jesus identifies himself is "Morning Star."

The name with which he leaves us is so important because it now beacons
through the ages—which often seem so dark—to represent Jesus' own testimony of what is distinctive about himself. His final name tells us what is
precious and what is promised.

What Is Precious

What is precious about a morning star? Darkness sets it off, but darkness cannot conquer it. We have a saying that "it is always darkest before the dawn." I
don't know if this is so. I do know that the darker the night, the brighter the
morning star appears. And the night can get very dark.

Even in this passage we learn that in the darkness come evildoers, immoral people, murderers, liars. Such is the world around us, characterized by its sin and its fall. It is so dark. This world is especially dark in this time of great evil, when senseless, horrible violence has destroyed precious life. In this time, the darkness deepens and seems to close in on us. It may seem to have won the day. But the darkness never wins over the morning star; the darkness only shows the star more clearly.

Darkness does that. When evil descends so overwhelmingly, its darkness reveals both how necessary light is and how precious such light is. The darkness cannot win; it only shows how much more precious is the light. As black velvet reveals the beauty of a diamond, so this darkness makes our Morning Star shine brighter. Precious is the light of that Star!

Consider for a moment the reasons we loved Ellen: her compassion, her zeal for the Lord, her accent, her directness, her bright spirit.[1] But as much as we loved her, the Lord loved her more. The evidence of his love is in the coming of our Morning Star. Ellen came here and lost her life; the Lord came to earth to give his life.

This truth of the Morning Star is what Ellen wanted so desperately for others to know and is why she studied here. In her death, her ministry and message shine even brighter. "Look!" her death says. "There is desperate need for light. Look at sin unrestrained, look at the heinousness of evil, and look at the darkness of the night. Then look at the preciousness of the light, the Morning Star that breaks this darkness. How precious to have this Morning Star!"

What Is Promised

With any morning star there is more than precious light. There is also promise. With the morning star there is the promise of dawn—a new day, a new beginning that cannot be stopped. The darkness cannot stay the dawn; the sun rises. So too, Jesus arose, and now the spirits of those he loves rise too. Their lives are like the dawning light, always shining brighter. For when this life of shadows passes, we are in the full presence of the *Son*. Ellen is there now. Hers was a deep darkness before her dawn, but now she is the light that is brighter than midday, basking in the warmth of the Son, held in the arms of the Savior. He rises with healing in his wings. "Look," our Morning Star promises, "the Son of righteousness appears. This night, too, shall pass."

---

1. Individual names and some personal details have been changed as an expression of care for the family.

The poet tells us to "rage, rage against the dying of the light." Our Morning Star promises that the light will not die. The night may rage for a time. But for believers, our journey is not into darkness, but we are on the path to dawn.

For the moment the darkness rages, but the Morning Star rises. The dawn is coming for all who see and claim the Morning Star. The darkness cannot hold back this light.

Therefore, though we sorrow because we are separated for a time from one we love, we will not grieve as those who have no hope. She is safe in the arms of Jesus. The darkness of the grave cannot claim her. The Son drives its shadows away. "Look," the Morning Star says, "this night will not win." With Paul, we declare, "We are more than conquerors through him who loved us. For I am convinced that neither death nor life, neither angels nor demons, neither the present nor the future, nor any powers, neither height nor depth, nor anything else in all creation, will be able to separate us from the love of God that is in Christ Jesus our Lord" (Romans 8:37–39). Thanks be to God, who in our darkness sends us the light of his Morning Star.

Chapter Sixteen

ACCIDENTAL
DEATH

SITUATION

Dr. Robert S. Rayburn[1] was asked to speak at the funeral of a young man who was killed in a climbing accident. He did not know the young man well, but the man's friends and family wanted Rayburn to deliver the funeral message. Thus, he quickly acknowledged his lack of deep acquaintance as a way of underscoring the significance of the testimony of others who had related so powerfully the faith and character of Joel McLin.

CONCERNS

Was this death as senseless as it seemed? The youthfulness of the one who had died and his zeal for his Savior made his untimely death seem all the more impossible to explain. Had God fallen asleep, lost touch, or made a mistake? Rayburn takes on the hard questions in a manner that is at first unflinching and seemingly insensitive—"It was God's will"—in order to lead to powerfully comforting conclusions: God's ways are always loving, and the young man's heaven is far better than anything we can experience here.

APPROACH

Pastor Rayburn's message follows a pattern familiar to those who know him. He begins with doctrinal truths and historical allusions that are dear to him.

---

1. Dr. Robert S. Rayburn is pastor of Faith Presbyterian Church (PCA) in Tacoma, Washington, where he has pastored faithfully for more than thirty years.

These establish the biblical basis for hope in the midst of tragedy. Then the pastor draws from his extensive knowledge of historical figures to relate intimate details from the biography of someone who has faced great difficulty with deep faith. The combination takes facts that could be doctrinally abstract or historically distant and makes them powerful expressions of pastoral care.

SEEING THE TRIUMPH IN THE TRAGEDY

Robert S. Rayburn

Pastor Rayburn refers to a variety of biblical texts throughout his sermon.

I met Joel McLin only once, in the narthex of the church I pastor, after a Sunday morning service. He struck me as a bright, personable, and interested young man. But I had little acquaintance with his virtues until hearing so many speak of them over these past days. Shortly before his death, Joel had begun a new pocket journal. The first and only entry is dated April 19, 2003. The entry reads:

> This great land of Kentucky, where Daniel Boone trudged his happy days through its wilderness, has graciously offered us a high cliff hollow of the most premium quality for our night's stay. Spring has finally triumphed over winter's ruthless pursuit, and the fragrance of new birth fills the woods. Each infant leaf has burst from its casing and spread its arms in the strength of the season — exalting the Creator from its proper post. The voice of the birds contains the very substance of joy, and the ancient cliffs echo God's pleasure. My soul is awakened and stretches in the space of such newness and promise. My Lord is faithful to work the same miracle of renewal of my soul as overcomes all creation in the new season. The impact of God's testimony of life all around me charges my smile so that it cannot reach a happier expression. I praise God that I am welcome among his works, and I desire to live as naturally in the spirit of worship as the rest of creation.

Such was and is the young man whom we are remembering today and for whom we are giving thanks to God.

Now what are Christians to think and what are they to do in the face of such a tragedy as the death of this young man whose life held such extraordinary promise? Well, we are to do what we are always to do: we are to believe; we are to exercise our faith; we are to put our faith to work in bringing home to our hearts the things we know to be true, no matter that we cannot see the truth with our eye or touch it with our hand.

Let me remind you of three extraordinary and wonderful things that we are to believe, that we are to be sure of on this day and in coming days; sure of because God has told us that these things are true—absolutely and unqualifiedly true.

This Death Was Not outside God's Will

The first is that, with respect to Joel's death—sudden, unexpected, tragic as it was—it was God's will. As we stand before this great deep, it is our Christian duty to say that God did not falter in this. "All our days," the Bible declares, "were ordered for us before there was a one of them" (see, for example, Psalm 139). There was never going to be another outcome for Joel's life than this one. His life was always going to end when it did and how it did.

"The LORD does whatever pleases him, in the heavens and on the earth" (Psalm 135:6). With respect to life and death in particular the Bible teaches us to say, "The LORD gave, and the LORD has taken away; blessed be the name of the LORD" (Job 1:21 NKJV). We may not understand God's ways—we often do not understand them—but that they are God's ways we cannot doubt. The Almighty God—he who inhabits eternity and who dwells in unapproachable light, whom no man has seen or can see—the living God holds to himself the right of an absolute dominion over our lives.

One of America's greatest theologians put this understanding of God's dominion over all in this memorable but entirely biblical way:

> When we speak of the sovereignty of God, we mean his right to work all things after the counsel of his will; to do what he wills with his own; that he has in reference to the whole universe the most absolute dominion and right to deal with his creatures just as seems good in his sight; to allow them to sin or to prevent their sinning; and when they have sinned, to allow them to perish or to provide salvation; and, if salvation be provided, to reveal it to one nation and not to another; to apply it to one person and not to another. Of course he has an equal right to determine their destiny on earth, whether it shall be civilized or savage, rich or poor, learned or ignorant, healthy or infirm, happy or miserable.
>
> The sovereignty of God supposes that the whole plan of creation, providence and redemption, was adopted on the ground of God's good pleasure; that the carrying out of that plan in all its infinitude of details is determined by his absolute will. So that if it be asked why Adam fell; why salvation was provided for man and not angels; why that salvation was

revealed at first to Jews and not to Gentiles; why now it is made known to us and not to [others]; ... why one man is a noble and another a peasant; one sick and another well; one happy and another miserable; we have nothing to say but: "Even so, Father, for so it seemed good in thy sight."[2]

That the sovereign will of God is a great deep and far beyond our finding out we cannot doubt. But that not a sparrow falls to the ground apart from the will of our heavenly Father we cannot doubt either. So we are today face-to-face with the inscrutable but perfect, wise, and holy will of the living God. The Lord has done this, and this must have the effect of causing us to place our hands over our mouths and to submit to his will in the confidence that the Judge of all the earth does right. His ways are far above our ways and past finding out.

This Death Was Not outside God's Love

Second, we must remember that all of God's ways toward his people, no matter how difficult, are the ways of holy love. No one knew the consequences of Joel's death in the hearts and lives of his family and his loved ones nearly so well as did the Lord himself. No one felt more keenly the pain of the loss, the mother's and father's broken hearts, the brother's desolation, than did the One who shared in our humanity and is able to sympathize with our weaknesses in every way.

The Lord himself apparently lost his earthly father when he was still a boy or very young man. Jesus lost his father, Joseph, when his father was, apparently, still a young man. And from what we know of Joseph and what we know of Jesus, we cannot but believe that theirs was an especially close and affectionate relationship. Jesus knows the desolation of unexpected death and of an unwelcome and unexpected separation between loved ones.

And so he assures us that *in all of our afflictions, he will be afflicted too* (see Isaiah 63:9). We will bear nothing that is not first a weight and burden and sorrow in his own heart. If afflictions, the terrible troubles of life, are absolutely necessary—as the Bible says they are—they will, at least, be his afflictions as well as our own, so perfect is his sympathy. *That* is the love of God and of Christ.

But to God's love there is more than that. When I went to see the McLins the other day, I brought along the volume of Samuel Rutherford's famous

---

2. Charles Hodge, *Princeton Sermons* (1879; repr, Edinburgh: Banner of Truth, 1979), 4–5.

letters. Rutherford was a seventeenth-century Scottish pastor whose collected letters to other Christians, containing spiritual counsel and his own inimitable presentation of the Christian faith, are one of the literary treasures of Christendom. Charles Spurgeon, the great nineteenth-century Baptist preacher, said that he thought those letters the nearest thing to inspiration in all of Christian literature. Rutherford, who had uncanny insight into the ways of the Lord, argued that the trials and tribulations of life were *absolutely* necessary. That is, God ordered them because they were essential to our salvation. We couldn't get to heaven in any other way but by that difficult path that our Father and our Savior have ordered for us. In other words, the tribulations themselves are an instrument of divine love—a tool of a Father's care and a Savior's devotion to his people.

In one of those letters, Rutherford wrote to a much-afflicted woman these glorious words:

> Madam, when ye are come to the other side of the water, and have set down your foot on the shore of glorious eternity, and look back again to the waters and to your wearisome journey, and shall see, in that clear glass of endless glory, nearer to the bottom of God's wisdom, ye shall then be forced to say, "If God had done otherwise with me than He hath done, I had never come to the enjoying of this crown of glory."[3]

When I read that God loves us with an everlasting love, that his people are always on his heart, that he weeps with those who weep, that we never pass through a trial but that he passes through it with us, I am persuaded that Rutherford must be right. We cannot know why it had to be, but it was divine love that knew it had to be! That, too, we must believe about Joel's death.

This Death Was Not outside God's Love for Joel

Third, we must believe that Joel's death, however bitter, hard, and tragic it may be to us, is not so to him. Our entire faith teaches us that to be in heaven, even to be suddenly and unexpectedly there, is, as Paul wrote to the Philippians, "better by far" (1:23). He is, as Paul said in another place, "at home with the Lord" because he is absent from his body (2 Corinthians 5:8).

To be at home with the Lord is the fulfillment of every longing of the human heart. "Today you will be with me in paradise," the Lord told the thief

---

3. Samuel Rutherford, Letter XI, *The Letters of Samuel Rutherford* (1783), available in a variety of easily accessible print and online editions; see Rutherford, *Selections from His Letters*, 16–17, www.apuritansmind.com/SamuelRutherford/SamuelRutherfordLetters.htm.

on the cross, just a few hours perhaps before they were there together (Luke 23:43). *Paradise* is a Persian word taken over into Hebrew. It originally meant "garden" or "park" and came to stand for everything beautiful. Joel was climbing in part because he loved the beauty of the mountains. He spoke of the beauty of spring in the extract from his journal that I read to you. The beauty he is beholding now throws all of the beauty he had ever seen or previously experienced into the shade.

I tell you in the name of the Lord Jesus Christ, if somehow you could go up to Joel in heaven and offer him the choice, he would not come down with you again. And if you love him and saw him with such everlasting joy on his head, you would not ask him to come down.

I took Rutherford to the McLins because I wanted to read to them one of his letters. It seemed so appropriate and so true to our faith and so almost impossibly beautiful in light of the circumstances of Joel's death. I close with what I read to them from the great Scot and the great Christian and the great lover of Jesus Christ. He was writing to a Christian mother who had just lost her young adult son.

> It is true, he died before he did ... much service to Christ on earth. But that were a matter of sorrow if this were not to counterbalance it, that he hath changed service-houses, but hath not changed services or Master ... What he could have done in this lower house, he is now upon that same service in the higher house; and it is all one: it is the same service and the same Master, only there is a change in conditions. And ye are not to think it a bad bargain for your beloved son, where he hath gold for copper and brass, eternity for time.
>
> I believe that Christ hath taught you ... not to sorrow because he died. All the knot must be, "He died too soon, he died too young, he died in the morning of his life." This is all; but sovereignty must silence your thoughts. I was in your condition; I had but two children, and both are dead ... The supreme and absolute Former of all things giveth not an account of any of His matters. The good Husbandman may pluck His roses, and gather in His lilies at mid-summer, and, for aught I dare say, in the beginning of the first summer month; and He may transplant young trees out of the lower ground to the higher, where they may have more of the sun, and a more free air, at any season of the year. What is that to you or me? The goods are His own. The Creator of time and winds did a merciful injury ... to nature, in landing the passenger so early. They love the sea too well who complain of a fair wind, and a desirable tide, and a

speedy coming ashore, especially a coming ashore in that land where all the inhabitants have everlasting joy upon their heads. He cannot be too early in heaven. His twelve hours were not short hours. And withal if you consider this; had ye been at his ... side, and should have seen Christ coming to him, ye would not, ye could not, have adjourned Christ's free love, who would [do without] him no longer.

And dying in another land, where his mother could not close his eyes, is not much. Who closed Moses' eyes? And who put on his winding sheet? For aught I know, neither father, nor mother, nor friend, but God only. And there is as expeditious, fair, and easy a way betwixt Scotland and heaven, as if he had died in the very bed he was born in. The whole earth is his Father's; any corner of his Father's house is good enough to die in.[4]

---

4. Rutherford, Letter CCCX, *The Letters of Samuel Rutherford*; see Rutherford, *Selections from His Letters*, 119–20, www.apuritansmind.com//SamuelRutherford/SamuelRutherfordLetters.htm.

Chapter Seventeen

NEW PARENT

SITUATION

John Terry's fifth child was born days before Christmas, and days before the heart attack that ended the father's life. While John's wife and new baby were still in the hospital, the duty of telling his children what had happened to their father fell to me. A well-meaning grandmother gathered the older children in the living room of the family's home and, with an expression mixing bewilderment, exasperation, and grit said, "OK, Pastor, explain it to them." The stern grandmother was determined to make it through the crisis, but the children did not share her resolve. They ranged in age from four to fourteen, and I did not finish explaining their father's passing before the oldest left the room in tears and with curses. The youngest were too young for explanations and just needed to be held. We held the funeral on the mother's and baby's first day out of the hospital.

CONCERNS

Although the family attended church occasionally, their faith was nominal and their understanding of biblical truth elementary. My greatest concern was to give the family hope for the future. The mother needed comfort for her loss. The grandmother needed to trust in something (Someone) beyond her own resolve. Smothering her grief in a stoic determination to rescue the family was actually hardening a teenaged son against the faith. The younger children needed to know that God would love them and take care of them. They also needed their mother to be back in the home with some semblance of a normal routine restored. The key to the well-being of all was the mother truly embracing her faith, trusting the Lord to provide for her family and to give her the strength to support her children.

Approach

Because the funeral took place near Christmas, I chose to emphasize aspects of a nativity narrative that deals with birth and death in close order. Since the mother was experiencing the consequences of both, I hoped the biblical account would help her understand that God could identify with her pain, and that he had a record of rescuing his people from desperate circumstances. My goal was not only to share traditional promises of God's comfort in the face of death but also to show how God's purposes are not thwarted by tragedy. I hoped to show that God's fulfillment of prophecy demonstrates that he has purpose beyond the immediate so as to provide for renewed hope in the future.

A BIRTH, A DEATH, AND LIFE ETERNAL

Bryan Chapell

[25]Now there was a man in Jerusalem called Simeon, who was righteous and devout. He was waiting for the consolation of Israel, and the Holy Spirit was on him. [26]It had been revealed to him by the Holy Spirit that he would not die before he had seen the Lord's Messiah. [27]Moved by the Spirit, he went into the temple courts. When the parents brought in the child Jesus to do for him what the custom of the Law required, [28]Simeon took him in his arms and praised God, saying:

[29]"Sovereign Lord, as you have promised,
   you now dismiss your servant in peace.
[30]For my eyes have seen your salvation,
[31]   which you have prepared in the sight of all nations,
[32]a light for revelation to the Gentiles
   and the glory of your people Israel."

—*Luke 2:25–32*

Though I have frequently read this selection from the account of Jesus' birth at Christmastime, I have never used the passage as a guide through grief. It never seemed an appropriate choice until now. And now, I can scarcely imagine how the Lord could speak to the sorrow we are facing more clearly.

The Christmas account is apt because again it is Christmastime. Even more important, in this Christmas text there is an account of the passing of one life joined with an account of the beginning of a new life. We have witnessed the joining of these two life polarities also—in the death of John Terry during the week of the birth of his son, Michael.[1] And even more striking

---

1. Individual names and some personal details have been changed as an expression of care for the family.

and poignant is the fact that, in this biblical passage, the life of the one passing is preserved just long enough for him to experience the joy of the birth of a long-expected child. We witnessed this sequence of events, too, in John's passing and Michael's birth.

The parallels of the old story with our recent experience are so striking that they draw our attention. But, more importantly, the account of an unlikely union of death's sadness and birth's joy directs our attention to the message and ministry of our Lord.

The passing of life in the passage and in our experience forces us to recognize our transience. Although we may plan the details of our future years with little thought given to interruption or detour, yet the tragedy of a passing life reminds us of the overwhelming power of the unexpected. We are as the Lord says we are—so subject to the trials and circumstances of this world that, despite apparent vigor and strength, we are as vulnerable as the grass of the field, growing today and gone tomorrow.

The evidence of our frailty is all too evident to many of us here. We have gathered here recently to mark the passing of other family and friends. None of us would have predicted we would be here again so soon. It seems so impossible.

In such times, we search for understanding. There should be no shame or blame in this search. There is much to question in these events, but we will probably not have many answers in this life. For now, we are left to say that, in a fallen world, joy and pain will enter every family's experience. So we must remember to "number our days" and prepare our hearts for what we do not expect and cannot anticipate.

But to say that we live in a fallen world where each of us will face sin, disease, and hardship is not to imply that we are in the throes of fate and have no option other than fearful desperation. The events of this Christmas account in Scripture make us aware not just of our frailty but also of God's provision. Along with the passing of Simeon's life is the birth of the Christ child. The child symbolizes new hope. He was the most gracious provision that our Lord could make for his people. Simeon, in looking at the child, said, "My eyes have seen your salvation."

What Simeon knew then, and what we know now, is that this child named Jesus was God's own Son and our Savior, Christ the Lord. This baby Jesus would in his sinless life and sacrificial death pay the penalty for the sins of those who trust in him and turn their lives over to him. This small child, so protected by his mother at this time in his life, now protects us as we are wrapped in his holiness through faith in him. Though he came in the last days of Simeon, this child Jesus is the greatest symbol of hope to all who trust that he came, died, and rose again as the victor over sin and death. Because of the life of this child, our sins can be covered, our guilt relieved, and our lives made whole.

Those who witnessed the birth of this child would face more trials on this earth, but because of the child they would also be prepared for eternity with the Father, when there will be "no more death or mourning or crying or pain" (Revelation 21:4). These future assurances gave God's people strength for the daily difficulties that were still to come.

If the blessings were only for the far-distant future, then God's people might still despair in the face of today's challenges were it not for one last aspect of the story of Simeon. God's present and special care for his people becomes obvious in a very special way in this account. We should remember that there was not just the close proximity of the passing of life and the birth of new life in this text. In addition, there was the special preservation of Simeon's life until he could see the new life of Jesus. In that preservation is the evidence of God's present care. He is not only waiting until some future day to provide what we most need. God is active today, providing what his people most need to get through these days before eternity.

God does not promise that we will never face hardship, difficulty, or tragedy, but he does promise his people this: he will provide what we need and will allow no more than we can bear.

Simeon was an old man. He could have died at any moment, but the Lord knew he needed to see the face of the Christ child. John was not old, yet we know now that, because of his hidden heart condition, he could have passed away at any moment. But the Lord knew that John needed to see the face of his child, and God provided that present care for this family. No, I can't answer all your questions about why there was not a longer life for John or what the future holds for his child. I cannot see what God sees. But I can see God's hand today in this: John lived to see Michael.

I can see that while this family has been hurt deeply, yet the Lord has at a very special time provided a special child as a reminder of his provision. Whenever we see this new child, we will remember how God provided a final but precious joy to his father: he saw his son before he went to his Lord. When I think on that gift, I will also remember the loving God who provided his own Son for me, and I will trust him with my eternity, even when I cannot make sense of many earthly things.

I will grieve today for the passing of a life, but I will also remember the joy of the coming of a child. And though the passing of a life reminds me that I must "number my days" and prepare my heart for the tragedies of this world, the coming of a child reminds me of the God who provided for endless days with the birth of the Christ child. Because he loves us enough to rescue us from this world of tragedies, our God provided the Christ child, Jesus—my Savior, my Redeemer, and my Lord. And this same God continues to care for his people. The way that he puts his hand into history (ancient and present) to highlight special moments of providential care assures me of his love and care today. The greatest evidence of this present care is the preservation of life, not just until one man could see a new child, but until all of us could see again how great is the God who would send his Son to rescue us from this world's sadness. We have been preserved for this moment of testimony from God; the One who holds the keys of life and death wants you to know his care. Knowing it—claiming it and trusting it—you can face the tragedies of this life and claim the blessings of eternity.

Chapter Eighteen

SPECIAL
NEEDS ADULT

SITUATION

For fifteen years the family of Old Testament scholar Jack Collins[1] had been neighbors with a family that included a special needs adult (mentally and physically disabled from birth). The Collins family sought to provide friendship, care, and Christian witness to their neighbors. A special bond developed, and though the neighbors have yet to acknowledge faith, when the special needs adult died unexpectedly, his parents asked Professor Collins to conduct the funeral. The service was attended by neighbors, friends, and family members who predominantly were unfamiliar with Christian truths. This brief but caring message is a remarkable exhibition of a scholar wrestling to put his faith in the simplest terms in order to care for his neighbors in Jesus' name.

CONCERNS

Collins has to balance expression of truth with the need to offer comfort. He knows that a funeral message is not primarily an evangelistic message, but he wants the hope of the gospel to be plain. He needs to make this hope apparent by presenting the eternal promises of the gospel without guaranteeing them

---

1. Dr. C. John Collins planted and pastored Faith Presbyterian Church (PCA) in Spokane, Washington before devoting his life to Old Testament scholarship at Covenant Theological Seminary. A Massachusetts Institute of Technology graduate, his works on science and faith have also made significant contributions to evangelical confidence in Scripture. Still, the pastoral heart that was foundational to Collins's academic ministry continues to shine in this message for neighbors without biblical background, who must bury a special needs child.

to those who have not acknowledged faith in Jesus Christ. Thus, he follows the wise and standard course of Christian preachers through the ages: state the truths of the gospel without promising that they apply to unbelievers. He does *not* say the promises do *not* apply to those present or to the deceased. He has neither the right nor the insight to judge souls. Rather, he states the comforts of the gospel that would be especially important to the parents of special needs children—ultimate redemption of body, mind, and soul in eternity—and encourages all those present at the funeral to believe these things so that they may share in the joys of the gospel.

APPROACH

Speaking directly to the family in order to offer the greatest comfort and not make the gospel abstract, Collins first speaks of his personal affection for the family. He then uses his own care and the care of the parents for their special needs child as a reflection of God's care for his children. Jesus feels the pain we do. The message uses Jesus' tears in John 11 to show how the grief that we feel is also experienced by Jesus, who cares enough to provide profound reasons for comfort even in the midst of suffering. Further, Collins shows how the care that the parents and neighbors have shown for this special needs adult is a gift of God, demonstrating the nature of his love for his children. True to his own theology, this Bible professor unfolds the story of redemption to validate the rightness of our grief over the intrusion of death into God's perfect creation and to press the necessity of faith in the Savior, who will make all perfect again for those who trust in him.

THE SERMON

TRUSTING IN THE GOD WHO CARES FOR HIS PEOPLE

C. John "Jack" Collins

"I am the resurrection and the life. Whoever believes in me, though he die, yet shall he live."

—*John 11:25 ESV*[2]

Jim and Jackie, I am deeply honored that you would ask me to conduct this service today. We have been neighbors these fifteen years, and you have shown so much love to my children.

Let me take you back to some words of Jesus that we read earlier in this service. In John 11, we read about how Jesus' friend Lazarus died from some illness. When Jesus arrived at Lazarus's house, the man's sister, Martha, ran to Jesus and said, "Lord, if you had been here, my brother would not have died." Jesus said to Martha, "I am the resurrection and the life. Whoever believes in me, though he die, yet shall he live."

A little later, the man's other sister, Mary, said the same thing to Jesus. As Jesus saw the sisters' grief and their tears, we read that he wept. He was deeply moved by the pain of others and by the awfulness of death. As a result, Jesus raised Lazarus from the dead—as a kind of foretaste of the way he will raise from the dead on the last day all those who believe in him.

For my words of comfort, I want to help us think about the Lord Jesus, who felt the grief of these people and who was deeply moved at their sense of loss. On Saturday, I heard Jackie say, "No parent should ever have to outlive their own child." I heard the same words from my father's mother when my father died; my wife and I said the same thing when we lost our first child. The pain is horrible; the loss is beyond our ability to describe.

---

2. All Scripture quotations in this chapter, unless otherwise indicated, are taken from the English Standard Version (ESV).

When we feel this grief, we are feeling that it is just not right for this to happen. We don't want our loved ones to suffer; we don't want to be separated from them by death. We want to be sure they are happy, and we want to be able to enjoy their company always.

The Bible tells us that these feelings are *right*. Death and suffering are intruders in God's good world; they don't belong here. The story of Adam and Eve, the first human beings, tells us how these evil things came in: When these, the parents of us all, disobeyed God, they opened the door to all manner of sin and evil, not only for themselves, but also for us.

You don't need me to prove that sin and evil entered our world. The things that are not as they should be are all around us. Such things are why we are here today.

But the Bible story doesn't end with how the hard things entered our world; instead, Scripture tells us about how God wants to help us, to heal us of what is wrong with us. We can see this here in the passage we read. Jesus wept with his friends in their sorrow; he was deeply moved. He also did something about the sorrow. He went on to raise Lazarus from the dead.

When Jesus raised Lazarus from the dead, that was pretty special, of course; but poor Lazarus would still have to die all over again later in his life. But something even more special would happen before that second earthly death of Lazarus: Jesus died—and he rose from the dead himself. He did this to be the firstfruits of a harvest of people that God promises will occur. For that harvest at the end of all time, Jesus' resurrection was the firstfruits— God's guarantee that all who believe will have their sin and sorrow taken away, will one day rise from the dead, and will never again die. Instead, they will enjoy happiness with God and with one another forever. That's why Jesus said to Martha, "Whoever believes in me, though he die, yet shall he live, and everyone who lives and believes in me shall never die."

Jim and Jackie, there were many things that your son, Jimmy, could not do. That was sad; we do not know why God allowed this in his life. At the same time, we can be grateful to God for Jimmy. Through him, we all got to learn how to love without reward and to give ourselves unselfishly to another. We all learned more about being compassionate in caring for him.

Jim and Jackie, I saw you give amazing love and compassion to Jimmy. You are just awesome. And that awesomeness that you displayed was a gift from God, who is the source of all awesomeness.

The God who made the world is big enough to care for Jimmy. The God who sent the Lord Jesus to be our Savior is also good enough and kind enough to take Jimmy to himself. I believe that; I want you to believe that and to be comforted. God gave you your kindness as a gift, and in your kindness toward Jimmy, God has shown you what his own heart is like.

God reveals most about his heart in the person of Jesus, God's own Son, who came to suffer for our sin and save us from the pain and evil of this world. I believe in Jesus, and so I look forward to one day seeing what he promised come to pass. Jesus said that he will return to us and make everything right. We will see Jimmy again with a new body, healed of all his disabilities. I can hardly wait; I *want* to see that! And my friends, you who are so dear to Jim and Jackie and their extended family, I want *you* to see that too. I want you to be able to live in hope and gladness, even in your pain. You can trust the same Jesus who wept with Martha and Mary to care for you too. You express this trust when you tell God that you want and need his unearned care as much as Jimmy did. May God help us all to find our peace and comfort by believing in the care he offers through his Son, Jesus Christ.

On behalf of Jim and Jackie, I thank you for being a part of Jimmy's life. Thanks especially to the caregivers for all the wonderful ways you have cared for Jimmy over the years. Through Jimmy, we have had the chance to learn to value everyone — whole or damaged, healed or hurting — and we can thank God for teaching us this.

We can entrust Jimmy's soul to a God who is full of such grace. Let us be thankful for what we have learned through God's provision of Jimmy and also trust that same God with our eternity.

Part Four

PREACHING
FUNERALS
FOR
PUBLIC
FIGURES

Chapter 19

NATIONAL BUSINESS LEADER: CANCER

SITUATION

Ben Edwards headed one of America's most prestigious businesses. In that position he knew wealth, power, and honor. But he also knew trial, temptation, and heartache that challenged his dearly held Christian faith. He was a major supporter of church efforts and one who was zealous to conduct his business with Christian principles. He never pressured his thousands of employees to accept his religious convictions, but he sought to demonstrate his faith to them by treating them with Christlike fairness and respect. They responded with tremendous loyalty and love. The thousands who worked for A. G. Edwards, Ben's brokerage firm, often referred to their employment as working more in a family than a company. Although he had been retired for a decade, Ben's funeral was attended by the business and political luminaries of the nation and also by company employees, who came in large numbers to St. Louis's largest concert hall. Despite the classy venue, Ben and his family requested "putting on no airs" and wanted a simple message that would speak of his faith and minister to the company "family" that he loved.

CONCERNS

The two major concerns of the family were to honor a great man (recognizing that he would not have been enthusiastic about eulogies) and to tell others why he trusted Jesus Christ. This meant speaking respectfully to many persons of different degrees and varieties of faith. Among those who gathered, many were Christians, but many were not.

As a pastor, my concerns were similar: I wanted to honor the man and preach the resurrection hope of Jesus Christ. My primary concern was the latter, but I knew that not to give clear honor to Ben Edwards would have seemed odd or disrespectful and would not have lent credence to the Christian message that Ben and I wanted his colleagues, family, and friends to hear. Thus, I wanted to intermingle words that honored Ben with the message of the gospel. My intention was to use aspects of his business life to introduce gospel concepts in terms that would be familiar and unintimidating to his business associates.

A last concern that should be confessed was to do a good job. Ben's life not only brought the nation's business elite to his funeral; it also brought many Christians who were praying for a message that would adequately express their (and Ben's) faith to their nonbelieving friends. Here was a clear opportunity for a significant gospel witness, and I didn't want to blow it. Readers will have to judge whether these goals were accomplished, but for reasons both noble and vain, such thoughts inescapably meshed in my mind as I prepared.

APPROACH

As a public figure, Ben Edwards's interests, hobbies, and eccentricities were as well-known as his business and community leadership. Knowing this, my initial approach was not different from what it has been with many other funerals. I sought to tie some aspects of Ben's personal life to gospel concepts that were evident in the text chosen for the message. What differed for me in this message was the sense of an enlarged family to address. Ordinarily I would speak directly to the family at a funeral and allow others to "listen in" as I explained our Christian hope. Due to the nature of Ben's character and company, I felt the need to address not only his immediate family but also his colleagues and employees as an extended family. In doing so I wanted to "humanize" Ben, knowing that his great wealth and power could make his faith seem unreal or removed from common experience. In order to put his faith within reach of both ordinary and celebrity listeners, I chose to mention his struggles and disappointments, as well as his accomplishments and success. I did not want the Christian hope to be shoehorned into a scheme for material gain, but rather to use Ben's life of both success and struggle to point to the need for all present to consider the priority of spiritual and eternal matters.

THE SERMON

WHERE YOUR TREASURE IS

Bryan Chapell

[19]"Do not store up for yourselves treasure on earth, where
moth and rust destroy, and where thieves break in and steal. [20]But
store up for yourselves treasures in heaven, where moth and rust
do not destroy, and where thieves do not break in and steal. [21]For
where your treasure is, there your heart will be also."
                                    —*Matthew 6:19–21 NIV [1984 ed.]*

WHERE WAS BEN EDWARDS'S treasure? It is natural to assume that
with a life of great success in business, brokerage, and finance, his treasure was
at his company address—One North Jefferson Avenue. But what is natural
to assume would be quite mistaken in assessing the treasure of Ben Edwards.

He both understood and charted the course of his life by what his Savior
said in the passage we read from the Sermon on the Mount.

If anyone could attest the truth of these words of Jesus about where your
treasure is, it would be Ben Edwards. He certainly knew the treasures of this
earth. In three decades he took A. G. Edwards from 300 brokers in 44 offices
to more than 7,000 brokers in 700 branches. He loved antiques, relishing a
strange red and blue Chinese porcelain. He delighted in travel, taking many of
you to the wonders of this world; and he knew the halls of privilege and power.

But Ben Edwards also knew what it was to lose much of this world's
resources, rewards, and regard. These last years of business transition in a
troubled economy were challenging and disappointing—even heartbreaking.

The successes could have made him overbearing, and the losses could have
made him bitter, but neither occurred because his real treasure was never in
such accounting. He well knew that the difference between great success and
great loss is in *timing* beyond any man's measure, *events* beyond any man's
control, and *perceptions* beyond any man's management.

Those who tie their heart's happiness to what we can accumulate in this world are only building mountains with marbles and have not yet discovered that success and happiness often do not reside at the same address.

A Life of Great Blessing

Ben Edwards was turned neither haughty by success nor hard by loss because his happiness was not based on things bought and sold. The evidence of "where his heart was" I discerned in conversation with him more than a year ago, a conversation quite alarming in its initial stages. He had received the cancer diagnosis and knew it was dire. I called to encourage and comfort him. Ben said to me, quite uncharacteristically, "I find that I cannot pray."

Ben was *not* a man who paraded his faith, but he was a man of deep faith. And it was quite unusual for this Sunday school teacher, hymn lover, regular church attender, generous benefactor, and genuine lover of Jesus to say that he could not pray. I assumed that the diagnosis had discouraged and depressed Ben. These are natural human responses, and pastors are prepared for such understandable reactions to bad news. But I soon discovered that I did not need those preparations for Ben. I asked, "Why can't you pray?"

He said, "The Lord has been so good to me that I don't feel it's right to ask for anything more. I have already been blessed beyond what anyone has a right to expect."

In this last year, he had time to think about that positive reaction to bad news, but he did not change his mind. In an interview in the *St. Louis Business Journal* some months later, he summarized his thoughts this way: "There isn't a mortal who could have had a better life and career than I had. I was *blessed in every way.* Now that I have cancer that won't get better, I have zero regrets. If anybody needs a break or a benefit, it's not me."

Now you may think, "That's right. He sure *was* blessed in every way. He certainly *did* get more than most people in this world." But before you too readily reach this conclusion about what Ben Edwards "got," remember that when he said these things about being so blessed, he had just "gotten" a terminal disease diagnosis, had experienced great disappointment in the company his family had built over generations, and had seen the erosion of much of his own personal wealth. I am not speaking out of turn here; he said all of this and more in last December's *St. Louis Business Journal* interview.

I love this line from Ben in that interview: "My whole estate was in Edwards stock, which became Wachovia at $55 a share and now is at $5 a share ... So I'm not tempted with the pridefulness of wealth."

A Faith of Great Power

Why did Ben not lose his humility, his hope, his humor in the hour of so much distress? The answer is because he was a good businessman. He had counted the costs of his commitments *and had invested in the long term*. And he knew the long-term gain was still secure.

There is a line from the martyred missionary Jim Elliot that a lot of us in this room know: "He is no fool who gives what he cannot keep to gain what he cannot lose." Ben gained and lost some things in this life, but he knew that the most important things — the eternal things — were never in jeopardy.

Ben enjoyed making money, enjoyed doing well in business, and took pride in the company's expansion — but these were *not* the most important things to him. More important were family, fidelity, and fun. That's why he treated people like *family*, ignoring his private entrance to walk into the front of the building like everyone else and greet receptionists, always answering his own phone — wasn't *that* a surprise when you called him? — and fighting to keep everyone employed in hard times. He made "putting the client first, the employee second, and the shareholder third" an unlikely slogan for an investment company because he believed *fidelity* to the Golden Rule ("Do to others as you would have them do to you") was more important than profit and in the long term would bring and retain more customers. And Ben Edwards made "having *fun*" a corporate goal because he believed that when people were treated right and enjoyed their work, they would work better together and for others.

But as important as were family, fidelity, and fun, these were still not the most valued investment of Ben Edwards's life. Each of these actually had their root in another investment of even greater worth. That stock on which he banked everything was *faith*. It was never paraded, never pushed in your face, but neither was it ever left behind. Most of us here know that. I clipped from the Internet (not Ben's favorite medium) quotes from some of you.

First from an employee who had experienced difficulty in the company:

> In … 1997, I felt my manager had … infringed on my … beliefs. Not wanting my complaint swept under the carpet, I made an appointment with Mr. Edwards, and he spent 30 minutes of his time listening to my concerns. He set up a meeting with management, and the way things were handled changed … I will always cherish the memory of how he put God and the Golden Rule first in all his business dealings.

Next, a note from an employee who is the spouse of someone who works with me:

> Two phrases for Ben Edwards's company: (1) "It was like a family," and (2) "one always had the sense that the company was about *something more* than what it looked like to the world."

What was that "something more?" A family member replies:

> By putting God first, he ... paved [the] path of family, friends, and business.

"Putting God first"—that was the prime investment. What did this mean? I came to understand what Ben meant in a conversation early in my presidency at Covenant Seminary. I was supposed to raise money for the school. I wasn't very good at it—in fact, didn't know how to do it. I visited Ben. He took me into his office, sat me by the desk, and said, "Just tell God's work to God's people and let God take care of the rest." Putting God first wasn't about manipulating or cajoling or worrying; it was just about acting faithfully and trusting God to take care of the rest.

It meant every day reflecting the confidence that God would provide what is best for us eternally. It meant—whether God is providing much or little, sun or rain, an up market or a down market—self-consciously acting with the faith that the Lord is always taking care of those who love him. It meant that when people fail us, when prosperity fails us, and when we fail ourselves, we still live the truth that *our Lord never fails us.*

A Lasting Legacy of True Wealth

The great evidence of God's abiding care is the presence of the One who spoke these words about not getting too attached to the treasures of this world. His name was Jesus. He was the Son of God. Though deserving heaven's acclaim, he, too, would face great earthly loss, but Jesus was God's provision for our eternity. By his life of righteousness, we learn what it means to live as God wants. By his sacrifice for our sin, we learn what it means to love as God loves. And by his resurrection from the dead, we understand that sin and death do not have the final word. This is not the final world. Heaven without shame, pain, or loss awaits all those who confess their need of him and trust him to take care of the rest.

Ben Edwards deeply, deeply believed these things, invested in them, and now treasures the eternal gains. But you know that one of the great things about some kinds of stock is that you don't have to wait a long time to reap some of the gains. Some stock pays dividends *while you wait*.

Ben's life was evidence that he was already enjoying the dividends of his heavenly investment. Do any of you remember the movie *Big Fish* from a few years ago? It's the story of a son who struggles with his father's tall tales of amazing successes and exploits. Such things could not possibly have fit into a normal man's life. The son thinks it is all exaggeration and eccentricity. But what the son does not know is that early in life his father had a vision revealing how he would die. The father knows that until that end comes, he is immortal. He can live with wild abandon, attempting the impossible, living without fear and in larger-than-life ways because he is entirely secure until the envisioned end.

Ben Edwards had something of a similar vision. It was a vision not of his final end but of his future. Early in Ben's life, the Lord opened Ben's heart to see the empty tomb of Jesus. Because the tomb of his Lord was empty, Ben knew that this *life is not the end; death does not have the victory; sin does not win; disease does not last*. Heaven is the future of all who trust in the resurrected Lord Jesus to take care of them.

Knowledge of these eternal truths enabled Ben to do business with a certain unconventional, wild abandon. It enabled him:

to put others ahead of himself
to be gentle in spirit and generous in care
to *not* make the bottom line his master (or his people's fate)
to *not* take himself, his successes, or his setbacks too seriously
to have *fun*

He could do all this because he knew that the most important things, the eternal ones, were entirely secure in heaven, where neither moth nor rust nor thieves can hurt us.

The *St. Louis Post-Dispatch* called Ben Edwards a "gentle titan." I think that description would have embarrassed him, but I like it! He was bigger than life, and still gentle. Do you know how that happened? He invested in the long term (eternity) but spent the dividends every year—on family, fidelity, and fun. He had a knack for business because he kept an eye on the empty tomb. By Jesus Christ's resurrection, Ben Edwards knew that he was so *eternally secure in heaven* that he could live an *extraordinary life on earth*.

One aspect of that extraordinary life was great generosity. And the opportunity we have today to tell you about his faith (not his perfections or saintliness, for he was as human as the rest of us) is his last great gift to us all—family, friends, former employees, and colleagues. His faith was simply in the amazing grace of God, who provides *eternity* for the *earthly* who trust in him. The insider information on that faith investment Ben gladly shared with us all, and his greatest gift is his lasting prayer that we would all share the peace of being full partners with him in that investment of faith in Jesus Christ.

Chapter 20

CELEBRITY: UNEXPLAINED CAUSES

SITUATION

The young woman whose untimely death was the cause for this sermon grew up in South Florida but settled with her husband in New York City. Their careers there flourished, and they had a child. Then the woman died suddenly and without explanation, at the age of forty-one, leaving all who knew her in shock. Her network of relationships was vast and extended from her national media presence to a tight circle of friends, from unbelievers to fellow Christians, and from antagonistic associates who challenged her faith to a family that continues to find hope in the resurrection of Jesus.

CONCERNS

While this young woman socialized with friends from a well-known church, the greater extent of her relationships were on Wall Street and in the national broadcast community. This meant two things: First, any undefined Christian vocabulary used in her funeral sermon would not be "heard" or well received by many of her friends and working associates; and, second, the belief spectrum of those attending her funeral meant that merely gathering together to mark her passing would not truly honor her convictions or share the love of Christ that she wanted others to know. Her pastor later wrote, "It would not be enough to have a Christian burial and to speak assurances to people who did not share her hope in the gospel."

APPROACH

Pastor Mike Khandjian[1] knew that this message would need to offer its comfort with a defense (or at least an explanation) of his friend's Christian convictions. Because this woman was a believer, he needed to communicate that while her life was full of success and extraordinary experiences, for her there was a greater fulfillment than could be seen in her most meaningful accomplishments. This fulfillment that she longed for and claimed couldn't possibly have been fully grasped in a broken world that brings suffering, sorrow, and pain—a world that takes young women in death.

Khandjian's first challenge would be to acknowledge our inability to explain away the death of a believer—acknowledging the *reality of loss*. Then his intention "was to weave in the dynamic of her faith journey in such a way that others could identify and follow." Finally, his desire was to offer a glimpse of the renewal of all things and explain "its vital connection to Jesus, who entered into our pain by his death and offers us hope and healing in his resurrection."

---

1. Pastor Michael Khandjian has pastored influential churches in Florida and Maryland. These ministry settings have put Khandjian in contact with some of the nation's most affluent and powerful individuals, whose life situations often turn out remarkably similar in terms of suffering and spiritual need. Ministering to such with wisdom and grace is Khandjian's calling and gift in this funeral message for a young woman whose light burned brightly and briefly.

THE SERMON

WAITING FOR THE DAY OF NO MORE TEARS

Mike Khandjian

¹Then I saw "a new heaven and a new earth," for the first heaven and the first earth had passed away, and there was no longer any sea. ²I saw the Holy City, the new Jerusalem, coming down out of heaven from God, prepared as a bride beautifully dressed for her husband. ³And I heard a loud voice from the throne saying, "Look! God's dwelling place is now among the people, and he will dwell with them. They will be his people, and God himself will be with them and be their God. ⁴He will wipe every tear from their eyes. There will be no more death or mourning or crying or pain, for the old order of things has passed away."

⁵He who was seated on the throne said, "I am making everything new!"

—Revelation 21:1–5

YEARS AGO, A THEOLOGIAN named Nicholas Wolterstorff lost his twenty-five-year-old son. The young man died in a mountain-climbing accident. Wolterstorff is one of those theologians whose writings are deeper than I can really grasp. But here was a man who studied the things of God and who knew how to parse the faith, yet he was without answers. He later wrote what I consider to be a landmark book, *Lament for a Son*. The book differs from his other works in that it is not the writing of a theologian so much as it is a collection of reflections on sorrow from the perspective of a father. Wolterstorff captures what I think we are feeling here today when he writes, "There's a hole in the world now."

Never is the painful brokenness of our world more obvious than when someone as young as Sara dies. The world wasn't created to bring such sorrow.

Quite the opposite—it was intended to be a place of delight and peace where all people were always living and never dying. Something in us still deeply and residually longs for the original Eden that was the world as God intended.

But things aren't as they were in that original world, and from time to time, people like us find ourselves grieving as we do today. This experience of grief is part of a journey we take together—a journey called life. I look out there and see familiar faces—family, friends, people who attended weddings and baptisms—we are bound together by more than this moment. We are bound together in a shared journey of mutual experience. And walking that journey in love demands that we walk together in the painful moments as well as the sweet ones.

Part of our pain is the recognition that Sara was an extraordinary human being. She embraced us in many ways as a daughter, sister, wife, mother, and friend. And in so embracing us, we learned more about ourselves and became more of ourselves. In his book *The Four Loves*, C. S. Lewis explores this dynamic by telling of three friends who all bring something out in one another. But, more importantly, each brings something out that could not otherwise be seen or known if the other individual was not there. Sara was such a loved one and friend to many of us, making us more able to know and be ourselves by her love.

We know we have lost something special in Sara's passing, but it is more than her beauty or talent. We also know that what she brought out in each of us can never be recovered. You could sense this as her friends spoke today. They remembered the last time they spoke with Sara, or the last time they saw her. Each experience was something added to their lives, and intuitively each feels some loss of themselves in not having her love anymore to enrich their future experiences.

Sara has always been an exceptional woman. I had the privilege of knowing her when she was a girl. Then, as always, she was beautiful both inwardly and as well in outward appearance. She had a great love for life, great passion, energy, excellence, creativity, and an infectious laugh. Her list of accomplishments is long. She served as a reporter for a major news network. She once worked for Martha Stewart as a cook. She co-authored a cookbook. She was on the foundation board of a college here in New York. She was an accomplished pianist, as some of you know well. It is stunning, really, when you think of all of Sara's activities and achievements. She squeezed more life into her forty-one years than many people who live to be ninety.

She had a rare combination of raw power of personality and natural instinct for creativity. She understood enterprise, yet appreciated beauty. She knew when to "go for it," but she also knew when to stop and take in what was lovely. She was a woman of deep emotion and passion. There was nothing shallow in Sara. Her passions ran deep to her very core. What she took on, she took on with the full force of her zeal and abilities. She adored her family. She was amazed with her husband and smitten with her daughter.

And yet, despite all of this goodness so tightly wound into her life, her passing is no less painful. In fact, the fact that her life was so extraordinary makes her passing in early years seem all the more untimely and unfair. We want an explanation. We want comfort. We want answers. Such quests are true of all of us on this life's journey, and we do not need to be ashamed to admit it.

As that theologian I mentioned earlier began to consider the loss of his son and the answers that might be in the gospel, he found himself desperately searching for a comfort he couldn't neatly package for himself and his family. But in his *Lament for a Son,* Nicholas Wolterstorff finds that God never intended for him to have an answer for every question. Every cry cannot be answered with some formulaic platitude or cold proposition. And even the theologian began to realize that what he needed he could not package and that his pain could not be answered away.

Instead, Wolterstorff discovered this:

> [It is a] great mystery: to redeem our brokenness and lovelessness the God who suffers with us did not strike some mighty blow of power but sent his beloved Son to suffer like us, through his suffering to redeem us from suffering and evil. Instead of explaining our suffering, God shares it.[2]

Jesus, the Son of God, came in human skin, lived with the broken things of this world, suffered all that we do. And then, in the presence of his mother on earth and his Father in heaven, at the young age of thirty-three, he died. Three days later, he conquered sin's most chilling consequence — the grave. He did all this to fulfill the hope and the promise that all creation would once again become as it was intended to be.

So in Revelation 21, the passage I quoted at the beginning of this message, John, the disciple of Jesus, inspired by Jesus himself, paints a picture of a new day. In this day to come, there will be no more suffering and no more death,

---

2. Nicholas Wolterstorff, *Lament for a Son* (Grand Rapids: Eerdmans, 1987), 81.

but the renewal of all things. All that has been damaged and mauled by sin in this broken world will be renewed and repaired. And in the new day, we will be reunited with those we love who have gone to be with Jesus. I know this all sounds like a fantasy of the future, but surprisingly this new day is not entirely in the future. Because its coming is so sure, anyone can begin to enjoy the comforts of this new day the moment he or she flees to Jesus in faith. All who believe that Jesus will relieve them of the sin and hurts of this world find that his magnificent kingdom enters them. And his reality enters them, convincing them the world that will one day be theirs, with no vestiges of the fall, is *already theirs* — in Jesus.

Put another way, through Jesus, God has entered our broken world to redeem every bit of our suffering — even the tragic deaths of young, lovely, gifted, powerful, and beautiful people like Sara. This means that Sara's life, though by our standards not a long one, was not a wasted one. She is home with Christ, and she has left behind a legacy of love and friendship that helps draw us to the comfort of his new and eternal world. Sara has left a foundation that will aid young people through many generations. She has left memories of creativity and passion. She has left a husband who will always carry her in his heart. And she has left a little girl who already reflects her mother's beauty. And she has left us the knowledge of a path that leads to her Savior and, through him, to the peace that can be ours now and at the end of our journeys.

Later today, if you come to the reception following the burial, you will taste some of the recipes from Sara's cookbook. In a sense, this book is symbolic of what heaven promises — a feast that forever satisfies, with a Redeemer who has once, for all, and forever paid for our sins to redeem our world. His name is Jesus, and his feast does not need to be in some abstract and remote future. For those who believe in the reality of his promises, the taste of the wonders of his provision begins today.

Part Five

PREACHING
AFTER
SUICIDE

Chapter Twenty-One

SUICIDE OF A PASTOR

SITUATION

After years of cycling in and out of depression, a dear friend and pastor named Petros took his own life. He left two adopted children who were near adulthood, a wife debilitated by many years of struggle with multiple sclerosis, and a church who loved its pastor. Petros was raised in Greece and carried an endearing Greek accent into the pulpit. He was an extraordinary preacher, but the congregation's bond with him was exceptionally intense because he was so sympathetic to hurting people. His own emotional struggles had made him void of judgmentalism and the willing bearer of many others' burdens. His personal insight into others' pain made this pastor's counsel especially wise and, for those he helped, made his self-inflicted death terribly difficult to understand.

CONCERNS

The array of emotions that suicide elicits among loved ones is as understandable as it is impossible to avoid. Accompanying the grief at the loss of the loved one is incredible sadness, dizzying confusion, and even anger at his willingness to inflict hurt on himself and those who loved him. Intensifying these emotions is a sense of betrayal of commitments, family, and faith. And behind all can also be a wondering guilt: Did I or we not care enough, do enough, help enough, listen enough, or perceive enough to stop this? Are we in some measure to blame for this tragedy? And this sense of shared guilt further intensifies grief.

In addition to dealing with the pain of loved ones, the suicide of a pastor creates extraordinary concerns for parishioners. Immature believers who have based their faith on the testimony of such a pastor will wonder if anything he said is valid and if the gospel he professed is real. If it could not help *him*, then what good is it? Those long in the church may too readily look for a scapegoat: Did his family not care deeply enough? Did the church's leaders put too much pressure on the pastor? Was his brand of theology so flawed as to be incapable of supporting him in time of trial? Or was he a just a skilled hypocrite whose empty faith finally caught up with him?

Those whose marriages or psyches have been helped by the counsel of the pastor suddenly question his advice and wonder how valid or fragile is the progress they have made in their relationships or thinking. Along with the intensity and confusion of grief that a spiritual leader's suicide causes, there also exists (often for many years following) an underlying fear that the faith that wasn't adequate to help him will not support us either. The suicide of a Christian leader is often contagious, as those who have been strengthened by that individual's wisdom and example lose hope of emotional health and begin to consider his path as a potential solution to their own pain. Though it was not applicable in this situation, children of suicide victims often wonder if they have inherited the same emotional makeup or carry the same depressive gene that will also make them suicide victims in the future.

Finally, suicide forces us to consider certain theological issues that are not present during most funerals. Some Christian traditions teach that suicide is an unforgivable sin. The assumption is that one who takes his own life is not able to repent of this sin, and so it condemns him to eternity without God's forgiveness. This kind of thinking seems obviously flawed because it assumes that all other sins left unrepented due to some other cause of untimely death (not to mention neglect, forgetfulness, or misunderstanding) don't condemn, even though they have not made it into a prayer of repentance. Further, such thinking wrongly presumes that adequate repentance rather than divine mercy is the cause of our salvation. And finally, a person thinking this way must assert that God will not show mercy to those who, through a tortured psyche or deranged thought, make an awful choice that clearly demonstrates they are most in need of divine grace.

Despite such inconsistent thought about the consequences of suicide, the teaching persists that there is no redemption for those who take their own lives. And even in traditions that do not officially teach the certainty of hell for suicide, many persons share the view that suicide denies the possibility of heaven. The view is widely held because of the perceived need to maintain a deterrent for acts of ultimate despair. Supposedly the threat of heavenly rejection will make the desperate think twice about taking their lives, even though those truly suicidal are likely to be beyond logic and more prone to despair when convinced that God's love has limits.

The last theological concern is the opposite of the one just discussed. Because we do not believe that suicide is an unforgivable sin, we should not imply that suicide is no sin. The damage such an act does to one's body (the temple of the Holy Spirit), family, friends, church, and testimony is incalculable. The modern tendency to dismiss all moral failing as the unavoidable and blameless consequence of circumstances, background, or genetics ultimately declares the gospel powerless. Faithful pastors must resist such tendencies, even when tempted to follow them for the sake of seeming kind. To identify suicide as a sin does not deny the power of Christ's blood to atone for it, but rather makes the preaching of grace more necessary for the one deceased and more strengthening for those who must carry on.

APPROACH

Particularly because there was Internet speculation from aberrant websites about the validity of Petros's faith and the care his church was expressing for him, I wanted to make it clear that I would refuse rejection. First, I wanted to reflect God's love by compassionate references to relationships with the deceased. I also picked a Scripture text that speaks plainly of God's care for hurting people and explained that his love is not dependent on human perfection. It was important to remind those present that Jesus took the penalty for our sin and that his grace is greater than all our sin—even the sin of suicide.

I believed that the integrity of the message also required that I identify the conflicting emotions brought about by such a death and tell how the gospel addresses them. I tried to name the obvious questions that suicide raises about the spiritual status of the deceased and answer with declarations of the sufficiency of God's grace. Then I sought to answer what could be answered and to acknowledge what could not be answered, with the reminder that God has demonstrated infinite mercy in the cross of Jesus Christ.

FUNERAL MESSAGE FOR PASTOR PETROS ROUKAS

Bryan Chapell

[1]Now when Jesus saw the crowds, he went on a mountainside and sat down. His disciples came to him, [2]and he began to teach them. He said:

[3]"Blessed are the poor in spirit,
    for theirs is the kingdom of heaven."

—*Matthew 5:1–3*

THIS IS MY WEDDING ALBUM. This picture in the album shows the preacher who performed the ceremony, Addison Soltau. He is here today. This next picture is of my grandparents. They are not here today but with the Lord. In this final picture are Petros and Jan. And only one of them is here today. We would never have pictured it this way.

Jan, though we have lived hundreds of miles apart, it is interesting—a blessing—to consider how our lives have intersected. Petros and I only got to know each other as we entered seminary together. We even took New Testament Greek together, although, as he who was raised in Greece was fond of saying, I suffered there alone. Petros had an unfair advantage with all matters Greek. Of course, that's why he also became my favorite travel consultant when Covenant Seminary led a tour that traced the path of the apostle Paul in Greece.

Petros and I also invited one another to each other's places of ministry—for special services, for anniversaries, for support in times of crisis, for family camps, and for dodgeball—which, as I recall, was played without Petros's legendary compassion for others. We even shared vacations and congregations together at the Horn Creek Camp in Colorado, in the shadow of the Rocky Mountains.

The reason I refer to these lighter moments in our lives is, of course, because I feel the need for light amidst the darker shadows in which we now find ourselves without Petros. I need the light from memories of his smile and his chuckle and his accent and his hugs to help me find my way from the shadow that has fallen over my heart—a shadow that looms from mountains of pain dredged up from my sense of loss and grief and anger and betrayal and confusion and fear. The mountain of fear probably looms largest over my heart because it forces me to question that if one who was so reflective of the light of the gospel of my Savior could not escape this dark valley, then how can I be sure no such valley of shadows awaits me also?

The questions that I dread to ask and at the same moment find that I must dare to ask, the Word of God answers in this sermon of my Savior. Jesus says, "Blessed are the poor in spirit, for theirs is the kingdom of heaven." With these simple words Jesus assures us that being poor in spirit does not disqualify from the kingdom of heaven.

But how can this assurance be true if such poverty of spirit, when it advances unchecked, can lead to such awful and sinful consequences?

The Pervasiveness of Spiritual Poverty

The first reason that poverty of spirit does not disqualify from the kingdom of heaven is that spiritual poverty is so pervasive. If the poor in spirit did not qualify for the kingdom, then the kingdom would be empty.

What does it mean to be poor in spirit? Even if your mind does not have a ready definition, your heart knows. To be poor in spirit is to be empty inside; to know the anguish and heartache of not having what seems to be necessary for spiritual survival; to feel keenly the bankruptcy of our answers and our adequacy; to feel helpless before the wrong in our world and in our hearts.

Petros knew what it was to be poor in spirit. But he was not alone. Jesus said these words to a crowd gathered on a mountain. If you have been there, you know that it is one of the most beautiful places on earth, a sloping field of grass and flowers overlooking the deep blue of the Sea of Galilee. But somehow, the natural beauty was not enough to counter the spiritual poverty of those Jesus addressed. When he spoke of the poor in spirit, he knew he was not speaking of hypothetical persons somewhere in the world. Jesus was speaking to many right there in his presence for whom the beauty did not bring adequate solace. The crowds gathered and listened because they knew they were the poor in spirit. And the reason we come here today in numbers is because *we* are the poor in spirit—we know emptiness, the bankruptcy of our answers and adequacy, our helplessness before the wrong in our world and hearts.

Are there any poor in spirit here today? You need to be able to answer yes, because your blessing, according to Jesus, depends on your poverty. We have trouble expressing or confessing such poverty because it seems improper for those who know God to acknowledge their struggles, their emptiness. Perhaps that is why the Bible shows us not only the crowds who knew spiritual poverty but the saints too.

One of the times that Jan and I talked in recent days—I do not remember which time—she said that she had just read Psalm 88 to her children. In a gift of providence that we both instantly recognized, I told her that I had turned to this psalm that same day. Do you know why we both did? Because we both know it is the only psalm in the Bible where there is no way out. Oh, yes, there are many lament psalms in the Bible, but they all end with some chord of confidence in God, some hint of salvation hope, some indication of the light at the end of the tunnel. Psalm 88 is the only psalm that gives no such crack of light, and in a strange way this is its blessing. It reminds us that even an inspired writer—a saint so great that his words are forever recorded in the Bible—even such a spiritual giant can come under the shadow of a mountain that for a time seems to obscure the light of the gospel. And yet, this time in the shadow does not mean that the man is apart from the kingdom of heaven. The kingdom of heaven is populated with those who are poor in spirit.

The Power of Spiritual Poverty

The second reason that poverty of spirit does not disqualify from the kingdom of heaven is because our merciful God knows that spiritual poverty is so powerful.

If only those who could entirely overcome poverty of spirit were qualified for the kingdom of heaven, then we would all be overwhelmed. What Petros was entirely wrong and sinful in doing must still be seen in the context of the weakness we all share.

I speak now to those of you who have a worldview derived from Scripture and not from popular philosophy or blind optimism. The Bible declares that we live in a fallen world where every aspect of the created order is fallen and damaged. The effects of human sin have corrupted every aspect of creation.

Thorns encroach on our paths; weeds invade our fields; cracks disturb our sidewalks; disease infects our bodies; hurricanes pound our shores—and we can be plagued by storms of mind as well.

The corruption of our entire nature includes our physical world and the world of our emotions and thoughts. We damage ourselves and others if we do not consider the full extent of this entirely corrupted nature. Disease may come not only to our bodies as a consequence of our fallen world; disease may come to our minds as well. And sometimes it does. As Christians, this aspect of fallen creation most challenges us because we want to believe that our minds, where affirmations of faith dwell, are somehow beyond the reach of this world's corruption. Yet the corruption of our entire nature means that the effects of the fall are entwined around every dimension of our being— physical, mental, and spiritual.

Willingly succumbing to these entanglements of our corrupted nature is not excusable for the Christian, but it is understandable—and forgivable. We do not excuse the sin that is a consequence of yielding to the corruptions of our nature because the Bible states, "Greater is he that is in you, than he that is in the world" (1 John 4:4 KJV). Our spiritual resources through Christ are sufficient to resist the temptations of our corrupted nature. And yet, at the same time, anyone who has ever snapped at his spouse when he is tired or been cranky because a meal was late, or been blue because the day was rainy, or thought he would never get well again because a cold lasted for more than two weeks—such a person can begin to understand how one who, after months and months of mental anguish that he could not explain or escape, could have let down his guard and plummeted into the shadows that obscured the light of God for a time. And when you begin to understand this, then you know that what is still not excusable can be—*must be*—forgivable.

I do not know why Petros could not pull out of the crash dive that spiraled him downward in recent months. I do not know why he was not able to cling to the gospel truths that he so ably preached for so long. But I do know that Jesus says that though we may lose our grip on him, he never loses his grip on us. In our fallen world, these corruptible bodies and minds can go awry in ways that cause us temporarily to lose our grip on the better part of ourselves, and in those moments to do terrible things. But never do these things of earth pry God's children from the hand or heart of their heavenly Father.

Last year, my son was diagnosed with a chronic and debilitating disease that required him to take powerful medications. He needed the drugs to heal his body, but they also affected his emotions and brought on a depression such as he had never before experienced. Something was misfiring in his brain as well as in his body. The worst episode came when on one occasion I reached to help him, and in frustration with all he was experiencing, he slapped my hands away. Never in his life has he done such a thing or come close to it. The reaction not only startled me; it also sent him deeper into despondency. He could not believe he was capable of such an act, and the realization only made his depression more acute. We have never prayed harder for our son, and we praised God when the medications were no longer necessary. But that was then, and in the last few weeks we have learned that he may need medications again. Because of where they took him emotionally and spiritually last time, my son does not want to take the medications again. But he *must* take them, and I pray that what will enable and encourage him to take what will heal him is the assurance that though he may slap away my hands, I will never stop extending them to him. Such is the love of our heavenly Father for Petros and for you. No one and no thing can pluck us from his hand, says our Savior.

Until we are with the Lord, we will probably not understand why Petros slapped away all the hands that reached out to him and resisted the assurance that the Lord held him. But if we do not allow ourselves to understand how one can fail to live fully in accord with what he believes, then we will not only blame Petros; we also will have no choice but to blame each other for other failures. Part of our corrupted nature is to search for those to blame. Whose fault was it, after all, that Petros did not hold on to the hands extended to him? Was it merely Petros who did not believe enough? Or did his church not do enough? Did the leadership not do enough? Did his family not do enough? Did his friends not do enough? Did some of us expect too much and in doing so put the pressures on him of our own idolatry of a person, because he knew he could not live up to our worship of him?

The answer to all these questions is, "Of course we did not do enough, and of course we expected too much." We live in a fallen world, and our entire nature has been so corrupted that each of us who is responsible for one another in the body of Christ has in some measure failed to be all that we should be. We are, after all, the poor in spirit. We gather here today mutually bankrupt in spirit and drained of excuses. The reason that we should and can acknowledge our universal failure is because we know that being poor in spirit does not disqualify from the kingdom of heaven. Even though we lost our grip on Petros, God does not lose his grip on us, and *he will not*. That knowledge should keep us from looking for others to blame for our hurt or insisting that all heal at the same rate and in the same way, instead of confessing in mutual humility our need—now more than ever—of both the love of our Savior and the understanding of each other.

My friends and family in Christ, it is far more important now to be driven to Christ than to be driven to find explanations. We will not fix this, but Jesus will not fail us. He tells us this when he assures people like us that the poor in spirit are not disqualified from the kingdom of heaven because our God recognizes how pervasive and powerful is our poverty.

The Blessedness of Spiritual Poverty

The final and most important reason that poverty of spirit does not disqualify from the kingdom of heaven is that God's riches are so much greater than our poverty.

Jesus says, "Blessed are those who are poor in spirit." What does the word *blessed* mean to you? Those who are blessed are those who receive what they do not deserve and could never earn. Jesus does *not* say, "Rewarded are those who earn their way," or "Compensated are those who measure up to my standards." To the contrary, he promises the kingdom to those who cannot pay the fare and have nothing that they can claim.

When Petros stands before the throne of judgment, he will have nothing of his own that he can claim as his ticket to heaven. All he has preached and lived and shared will not make up for the wrong of what he has done. But *someone else* can make it up—the One who promises the kingdom to those who are too poor in spirit to make any claim for themselves.

This past summer, I had the opportunity to meet a missionary family in Africa. As their older children got to be the ages of Lizzy and Nikos (Petros's children), the father and mother decided to adopt another child. He was from the poorest of urban streets, the child of an absent father and an addicted and abusive mother. The child's new family tried to show him love, but he had trouble receiving it. His obedience had too long simply been a means of avoiding abuse. He had grown accustomed to pleasing so as not to be rejected. The new family was not sure he was capable of doing anything simply out of love. They were not even sure that his smile was more than a means to manipulate. Then one day all came undone. The boy could not find his comb, so he took his new father's comb and forgot to return it. When he was asked if he had taken it, the boy said he had not. But that did not explain why the comb was in his pocket. When his lie was discovered, the child ran—as he had always done to escape his biological mother's abuse. He ran to his room and crawled into the darkness underneath the bed.

The child was not prepared for what happened next. The bedspread lifted, and the boy's new mother crawled into the darkness with him. She took his face in her hands, put her head next to him, and said these words: "What you have done did not get you into this family; and what you do will not get you out of this family."

Listen to me: What Petros did was wrong. But what he did for the last twenty-five years did not get him into the kingdom of heaven, and what he did almost two weeks ago will not take him from the kingdom of heaven. The kingdom of heaven is secured by another—the One who came into the darkness of this world to give himself for those who are poor in Spirit. This is the gospel. He who was rich made himself poor so that through his poverty we might inherit the kingdom of heaven. This same Jesus who came preaching the kingdom of heaven is the One who came to die in our behalf to pay the debt for our sins. He emptied himself of the privileges and glory of heaven, so that through his poverty, the heavenly riches of his righteousness would be ours. The reason those who are so corrupted that they can be guilty of selfishness, cowardice, insensitivity, and sin—even the murder of themselves—and can yet inherit the kingdom of heaven is that Jesus Christ died to pay the penalty for our sins, and he rose to intercede for us before the Father on the basis of *his* righteousness rather than our accomplishments. When we depend on what he provides by acknowledging our poverty and trusting in his provision, then *ours* is the kingdom of heaven. The Bible reminds us that heaven is not too high for God to bend to our lowliness:

Isaiah, the prophet, writes:

For thus says the high and exalted One
Who lives forever, whose name is Holy,
"I dwell on a high and holy place,
And also with the contrite and lowly of spirit
In order to revive the spirit of the lowly
And to revive the heart of the contrite."

Isaiah 57:15 NASB

Facing Hard Questions

Now I know the questions you are still asking yourselves. I have asked these questions of myself also. "Yes, God can save sinners of all sorts—those who falter and fall and even kill. But the ones he saves are those who repent. And since Petros took his own life, and there was no opportunity to repent from that sin, then can he still be eligible for the kingdom of heaven?" I acknowledge to you that, despite the depth of remorse that Petros expressed for his actions in the letter read to this congregation, his repentance is inadequate. But whose repentance is *ever* adequate? God forgives us not because we adequately confess our sin but because Jesus fully covers our sin when we trust in him.

But you are also thinking, "Did Petros really trust in Jesus?" *Yes*, you will acknowledge that Petros certainly was poor in spirit. But did he really trust in Jesus? If he had, could he have done this thing? Ultimately these questions will be answered in the halls of heaven, but I will tell you what I think. Petros did not preach the gospel all those years or love us so well falsely. We would have known it. Instead, he got sick in mind and heart for reasons I do not fully understand. That sickness made him very poor in spirit, and he lost his hold on what was best in him and for him. But I do not think that the strength of his grasp is what counts, but rather the strength of the One who grasps him. The love of Jesus Christ is more than strong enough to compensate for any weakness of faith in us.

Ringing in my mind yet are the words from the note that was read to the church when your questions and concerns needed some explanation. In that note, Petros said, "I still believe the [gospel] truths that I have preached, I think." What was this "I think" about? Was it an affirmation of truth, or was dear Petros, despite all his years in America, still missing the nuances of American speech, as he occasionally did? Did he not realize that when you add "I think" at the end of a phrase, you are casting doubt on what you have previously said? I think that Petros did recognize the doubt in his wording—so that what he was really saying was, "I believe, but I recognize that I do not believe enough." Does this remind you of anything? I pray that it reminds you of the father who needed help for his ailing child and came to Jesus. Our Savior told him, "Everything is possible for one who believes." The man responded, "I do believe; help me overcome my unbelief" (Mark 9:24). Then Jesus healed the child. When a man confessed the poverty of his faith, Jesus supplied what was lacking there also. Even faith as small as a mustard seed God uses to lay claim to his kingdom blessings.

I know some will fear that if I do not shut the door to heaven to Petros for this particular sin, I may open the door for others to consider doing what he did. I know this is a great danger, but the greater danger is to portray my God as One who does not understand human weakness and who draws a line beyond which his love will not go. I fear more the daily and eternal despair of belief in such a god. The God we need is the one Scripture displays: the One who loves you so much that he gave his Son for you so that you need not fear that even your greatest failures will deny you his eternal kingdom or his heart. Love for this God of grace will do more to hold you to life than all threats of hell from a god you dread and wish to flee. The Bible declares that the kindness of God leads us to repentance and draws us to life with cords of divine affection that nothing can sever (Romans 2:4; 8:39). In this assurance there is love that is more powerful than death.

One last question: If our God is so good, why did he let this happen? I do not know. But this I do know. Our tendency in the time of trial and misery is to look at earthly circumstances to judge the character of God. Our God will not be so confined. Always he is dealing on an eternal plane. Even the evil of Petros's untimely, unjustifiable death God can use to remind us of our need for the eternal justification that can only be found in him. If we have been forced to consider our spiritual poverty and need of divine redemption by these events, then even this evil can be used for good by a divine hand. And should you doubt that our circumstances warrant such trust in God, then recognize that his Word points not to our circumstances to define his character but to his cross. There where my Savior hung in suffering to provide for our eternal pardon, our God proves that he is good. And he demonstrates by that same cross that we can always trust that his hand will turn to good even the evil for which our hands are responsible.

Jan, in a book that I just completed this summer, I tell the account of being lost on a mountain, and how you and Petros prayed me down. The fog closed in, along with snow and cold, so that my climbing partner and I were shrouded in darkness and lost for hours. Fearing the dark that was fast descending, we set a time that we would stop trying to find the path leading off the mountain and would instead try to make shelter to survive the night. That time never arrived. Unbeknownst to us, the watch we were using to determine when we had to stop climbing had stopped ticking. As a consequence we kept climbing far past our deadline and eventually found the path that led back to the camp and to you. I will never forget what Petros said when we got back. "Jan even prayed for time to stand still so that you could get down." Little did he know that time really *had* stood still so that we could get home.

I imagine that in these past few months you have prayed more than once that time would stand still again so that Petros would have the rest he needed to stop pressing downward and be able to find his way home from the darkness in which he seemed to be climbing an insurmountable mountain of pain.

Ultimately he did not find his way home to you and his family, but he is off that mountain of pain and, we pray, home—where time is no more, and there are no more tears, and there is no night there.

How can such a prayer be valid or possible? Because the gospel is true and therefore "I am persuaded, that neither death, nor life, nor angels, nor principalities, nor powers, nor things present, nor things to come, nor height, nor depth, nor any other creature, shall be able to separate us from the love of God, which is in Christ Jesus our Lord" (Romans 8:38–39 KJV). Thus, I will grieve, but not as one who has no hope, but rather as one who can say in the face of dark valleys, "Thanks be to God, who gives us the victory through our Lord Jesus Christ."

Chapter 22

SUICIDE OF
A CHRISTIAN
LEADER

SITUATION

Dr. Wilson Benton[1] describes his own reaction and his listeners' obvious questions in this sermon that followed news of the suicide of a noted Christian leader in our community. This is not a funeral sermon, but a Sunday morning message necessitated by the shock of those in a daughter church hearing news about the death of a leader in their mother church. The leader was the father of a special needs child and was facing significant career challenges. He was on heavy medication for depression following an amputation caused by a freak hiking injury. Benton expresses his own shock upon hearing the news of the suicide and addresses questions he knows those in his congregation must have.

CONCERNS

Pastor Benton needs to answer basic questions that every suicide raises: How could a Christian do this? Is suicide a sin? Is it possible for one who takes his own life to enter heaven? If so, what is the basis of that person's salvation? Benton walks the tightrope of offering biblical answers to these questions without being accusing or excusing. He seeks to show compassion toward

---

1. Dr. W. Wilson Benton Jr. has pastored churches in Mississippi, Missouri, and Tennessee and taught preaching in a variety of seminaries. He now pastors Christ Presbyterian Church (PCA) in Nashville, Tennessee.

the one who took his own life and yet maintain the Bible's strong prohibition against self-"murder." The main concern is to make sure he warns against the sin of suicide while demonstrating that the grace of God is greater than all our sin—including the sin of suicide.

APPROACH

Pastor Benton moves from personal reaction to the obvious questions he and others ask at such times. The sermon is noteworthy both for the honesty of the questions and the clarity of the answers. Biblical proofs supporting the answers are also thoughtfully supplied. It is important to note, however, that this message was preached more to a questioning congregation than a grieving one. The person who took his life did not have close relationships with those within Benton's church. Had the death been one of the congregation's own, the pastor's expressions would undoubtedly have been more tender and personal. Here he offers a message to help a congregation think biblically about such crises rather than to comfort persons in the midst of grief. The goal is more preparatory than healing and demonstrates the wisdom of a pastor who knows that waiting until crises come to form biblical perspectives is waiting too long.

THINKING BIBLICALLY ABOUT THE TRAGEDY OF SUICIDE

Wilson Benton

¹The LORD is my shepherd; I shall not want.

²He maketh me to lie down in green pastures: he leadeth me beside the still waters.

³He restoreth my soul: he leadeth me in the paths of righteousness for his name's sake.

⁴Yea, though I walk through the valley of the shadow of death, I will fear no evil: for thou art with me; thy rod and thy staff they comfort me.

⁵Thou preparest a table before me in the presence of mine enemies: thou anointest my head with oil; my cup runneth over.

⁶Surely goodness and mercy shall follow me all the days of my life: and I will dwell in the house of the LORD for ever.

—Psalm 23 KJV

I was in Atlanta to lead a Bible conference at a church. I was alone in the pastor's home, sitting on the couch in the den working on my sermon for the morning. The phone call startled me; the phone caller stunned me. "Bryce did *what*?" I sank back into the couch. Our Christian leader, friend, and brother Bryce Teller had committed suicide.²

This morning I put aside the sermon I had planned to deliver to deal with the issue of Bryce's death. It seems appropriate to do so, for we are shocked and saddened; we are concerned and confused; we are bewildered, not knowing what to believe. So many questions are being asked that should be addressed and answered.

---

2. Individual names and some personal details have been changed as an expression of care for the family.

Is Suicide a Sin?

The first question: *Is suicide a sin?* And the answer is yes. The dictionary defines suicide as "the taking of one's life voluntarily and intentionally." It is the taking of a life in a manner forbidden by God. It is murder—self-inflicted murder, but murder nonetheless—and God's Word states, "You shall not murder" (Exodus 20:13).

God forbids taking another's life, and God forbids taking one's own life for the same reason. Human life is made in the image of God. Every human being bears God's image, so the destruction of a human life is the destruction of God's image bearer, an act that he prohibits.

Furthermore, life—all life—belongs to God. "In him we live and move and have our being" (Acts 17:28). We don't own life. God owns life, and he lends it to us at his pleasure to be lived for our pleasure and his glory. Life is not our own to destroy, so the destruction of life by suicide is a sin.

But suicide is *not* the unforgivable sin. Some have taught that suicide is unforgivable, but such teaching is wrong. Homicide is not the unforgivable sin. If that were the case, the apostle Paul would not be forgiven, for by his own testimony he informs us that he was guilty of murder (Acts 26:11; see Acts 9:1; 10:21). Homicide is not the unforgivable sin; nor is suicide the unforgivable sin. The senseless taking of human life is wrong, but it is not unforgivable, even if the life taken is one's own.

If a person is not forgiven by God, then the effect is the same as if none of his sins are forgiven. But if a person is identified as one forgiven by God, then all of his sins, including the sin of suicide, are forgiven. And suicide is forgiven, just as all other sins are forgiven, for the sake of and by the work of Jesus Christ. When Jesus died, he paid the penalty in full for all of our sins—past, present, and future. In him our sins are removed from us as far as the east is from the west. God did *not* say, "I will forgive you as long as your sins are not too great or as long as you get around to confessing everything you did that was wrong." If that were the case, we would all be condemned. But the Bible declares, "Therefore, there is now no condemnation for those who are in Christ Jesus" (Romans 8:1).

Can a Christian Commit Suicide?

The second question: *Can a Christian commit suicide?* And the answer is yes. Christians can commit all kinds of sins. Christians are not perfect. In this life, we have not been fully sanctified, finally glorified. We still possess remnants of our old sinful nature, and in this nature resides the potential for every kind of sin. We have the capacity to contemplate crimes that we never commit. But even the contemplation is itself a sin.

Do you remember how our Lord Jesus expanded the meaning of the Ten Commandments with his own interpretation? For instance, the seventh commandment: "You shall not commit adultery." Jesus said that if you lust after a woman in your heart, if in your own mind you commit adultery, you are guilty of breaking that commandment (Matthew 5:27–28). The sixth commandment: "You shall not murder." Jesus said that if you are so angry you want to kill, if you cry to your brother, "You fool!" and you desire to destroy his life, then by that very desire you have broken the commandment (Matthew 5:21–22).

It is wrong for one to take his own life, but it is also wrong for one to *contemplate* taking his own life. And who of us has not in a moment of despair or frustration or self-pity contemplated, at least momentarily, the taking of his or her own life?

Sometimes these evil intentions become evil deeds. How does it happen? How does it happen that one takes his own life? I am not a psychologist, but in laymen's language it happens when one focuses on the problems rather than on the solution. The problems loom so large that there seems to be no relief, no escape, no means of bearing the burden.

If you've ever heard theologian Jerram Barrs give his testimony, then you've heard him say that before he became a Christian he seriously contemplated suicide. He said that, to his mind, it was the only logical response to life as he was experiencing it as an unbeliever. But that's not the case for the believer. God's Word states, "No temptation has overtaken you [even the temptation to destroy your own life] except such as is common to man; but God is faithful, who will not allow you to be tempted beyond what you are able, but with the temptation will also make the way of escape, that you may be able to bear it" (1 Corinthians 10:13 NKJV).

We are reminded of how crucial it is that we keep our faith focused on Jesus Christ in the midst of all of our problems.

> Turn your eyes upon Jesus,
> Look full in His wonderful face,
> And the things of earth will grow strangely dim
> In the light of His glory and grace.[3]

---

3. Helen H. Lemmel, "Turn Your Eyes upon Jesus" (1922).

The apostle Peter walked on water, and as long as he kept his eyes focused on the Lord Jesus Christ, he continued to walk on the water. But when he took his eyes away from the Lord and began to look at the treacherous waves around him, he began to sink (Matthew 14:29–30).

> When through the deep waters I call thee to go,
> The rivers of sorrow shall not overflow;
> For I will be with thee thy trials to bless
> And sanctify to thee thy deepest distress.[4]

And yet sometimes in those deep waters we forget. Our faith, which is real, is nonetheless really weak. And the fogs of despair, discouragement, and depression become so thick that we cannot see the face of the Lord Jesus. So we need to pray with the man at the foot of the Mount of Transfiguration, "I do believe; help me overcome my unbelief!" (Mark 9:24).

Actually, it's not so strange that Bryce wanted to die. When we remember his situation, when we recall some of the recent struggles in his life, when we remember that he lost a foot just a few months ago, it's not so strange that Bryce wanted to die and go to heaven because those problems don't exist in heaven. And Bryce is in good company. The apostle Paul said he would rather be "away from the body and at home with the Lord" (2 Corinthians 5:8) and that he had a "desire to depart and be with Christ, which is better by far" (Philippians 1:23). Bryce's desire for an end to his struggles was not wrong; however, the way in which he fulfilled that desire was wrong. We are not to take matters into our own hands. We must say to our God with the psalmist, "My times are in your hands" (Psalm 31:15), and, "in Your book they all were written, the days fashioned for me" (Psalm 139:16 NKJV).

What Happens to the Person Who Commits Suicide?

The third question: *What happens to the person who commits suicide?* Well, that depends. What happens to any person who dies, regardless of how he dies? If that person is an unbeliever, that person goes to hell. If that person is a believer, that person goes to heaven. If the person who commits suicide is not a Christian, that person goes to hell. If the person who commits suicide is a Christian, that person goes to heaven.

Our catechism says, "The souls of believers are at their death" — *whatever*

---

4. "K" in John Rippon's *Selections of Hymns*, "How Firm a Foundation" (1787).

the manner of their death, you see—"the souls of believers are at their death made perfect in holiness and do immediately pass into glory."[5] I hope you have no doubt about the fact this morning that Bryce Teller is in heaven!

Are Others to Blame When One Commits Suicide?

The fourth question: *Are others to blame when one commits suicide?* The answer is no. No doubt many will feel guilty in this situation, as many always do. Why were we not more sensitive? Why were we not more caring? Why did we not encourage him more? What should I have done? It's all my fault. *No, it's not.* God makes each of us responsible moral agents, and each of us is accountable to him for our decisions and the actions that flow from those decisions. This does not mean, however, that others are without blame and without guilt. Yes, we ought to be more sensitive and more caring and more supportive and certainly more prayerful. There is much blame to bear, and we ought to confess our failures before God, but we are not responsible for another's decision. There is a big difference between failing to support some-one who is suffering and the decision of the sufferer to take his own life; and while we may be guilty of one, we are not guilty of the other.

Just as God in his grace deals with the guilt of the victim, so this morning we should pray that God in his grace will deal with our real guilt. You see, we have enough real guilt to face without heaping false guilt on our heads; and besides, if we do heap more guilt on ourselves, we cannot function as the channels of grace that God would have us be in such situations.

Is God Still in Control at the Point of Suicide?

The fifth question: *Is God still in control at the point of suicide?* The answer is yes—God is still in control. God is in control of *all*, or God is not in control *at all*. If there is one exception, God is not sovereign. God was in control of the tragic event that transpired on Thursday. We may be tempted to say, "God was loving enough, but God was not powerful enough to stop that tragedy." Or we may be tempted to say, "God was powerful enough, but God was not loving enough to stop that tragedy." No, we must affirm *both* the love and the power of an all-wise God. God is loving—he's kind; he's tender; he's merciful; he's compassionate; he's powerful; he's mighty; he's sovereign—and

5. Westminster Shorter Catechism, answer 37.

Bryce's death was an awful, horrible, terrible tragedy. We affirm both the reality of a great God *and* the reality of a terrible tragedy, but beyond that we affirm that the great God was in control of the terrible tragedy.

Do we have questions? Of course! We want to ask a thousand whys, don't we? Why did God allow it to happen? Why did he not stop it? We want to know why God allowed sin to come into the world in the first place, don't we? God has answers for our thousand questions. He may give us an answer, or he may not give us an answer, but that does not alter the fact that God knows the answer. God knows what he is doing.

At age thirty-two, the great hymn writer William Cowper became so depressed that he determined to take his life. He ordered a horse-drawn cab to pick him up at his home and transport him to the London Bridge, where he planned to jump to his death. It was a foggy night. The cabbie got lost, and Cowper got frustrated. He told the man to stop, got out of the cab, paid his fare, and turned around to discover that he was right back at his own doorstep. He went inside, still bent on his evil intention. He drank poison, but it made him sick, and he threw it up. Then he determined to fall on a knife, but the knife blade broke. Finally, he made a crude attempt at hanging himself, but he was discovered, unconscious yet still alive, and he was cut down. In the days that followed, as he contemplated these events, he wrote:

> God moves in a mysterious way His wonders to perform;
> He plants His footsteps in the sea and rides upon the storm.
>
> Ye fearful saints, fresh courage take; the clouds ye so much dread
> Are big with mercy and shall break in blessings on your head.
>
> Judge not the Lord by feeble sense, but trust Him for His grace;
> Behind a frowning providence He hides a smiling face.
>
> Blind unbelief is sure to err and scan His work in vain;
> God is His own interpreter and He will make it plain.[6]

In his own time, whether in this life or in the life to come, God will make his own plan plain. Until then we must say with Habakkuk, "The righteous will live by his faith," and, "The LORD is in His holy temple. Let all the earth be silent before him" (Habakkuk 2:4, 20 NASB).

---

6. William Cowper, "God Moves in a Mysterious Way" (1774).

Do God's Promises Still Apply to the Person Who Commits Suicide?

The sixth question: *Do God's promises still apply to the person who commits suicide?* And the answer is yes. All of God's promises still apply to the person who commits suicide, for don't you see that all of God's promises in Christ are "yes" and in him "Amen" (see 2 Corinthians 1:20). Suicide does not contravene the promises of God. Suicide does not place one outside the parameters of the promises of God. Suicide does not make null and void the promises of God.

Can the Twenty-third Psalm—"The LORD is my shepherd; I shall not want ... Yea, though I walk through the valley of the shadow of death, I will fear no evil"—can the Twenty-third Psalm honestly, with integrity, be read at Bryce Teller's funeral service? Yes, I hope it will be. Can John 14 with all of its promises of peace for the distraught, the great legacy of Jesus Christ—"Peace I leave with you"—can this passage be read? Yes. What about the promise of Romans 8:28 (KJV): "All things [even suicide] work together for good to them that love God." Yes, even *that* promise applies!

Robert Haldane, one of the great Puritan ministers, wrote:

> If all things work together for good, there is nothing within the compass of being that is not, in one way or other, advantageous to the children of God ... The creation of the world, the fall and the redemption of man, all the dispensations of providence, whether prosperous or adverse, all occurrences and events, all things whatsoever they be, work for their good ... They do not work thus of themselves; it is God that turns all things to the good of his children. The afflictions of believers, in a peculiar manner, contribute to this end ...
>
> [Now, listen carefully.] Even the sins of believers work for their good, not from the nature of sin, but by the goodness and power of him who brings light out of darkness. Every where in Scripture we read of the great evil of sin. Every where we receive the most solemn warning against its commission, and every where we hear also of the chastisements it brings, even upon those who are rescued from its finally condemning power. It is not sin, then, that works the good, but God who overrules its effects to his children.[7]

Good even for Bryce's family? Yes. Good for Bryce's church? Yes. Good for the kingdom of God at large? Yes. Remember the cross. Remember the

---

7. Robert Haldane, *Exposition of the Epistle to the Romans* (Edinburgh: Whyte, 1837), 339–41.

cross. Out of the greatest evil this world has ever known came forth the greatest good this world will ever know.

And What Should We Do?

The seventh question: *And what should we do?* How should we respond in the face of this teaching from God's Word? We should cry. We should cry out in *pain*. The Bible says to weep with those who weep (Romans 12:15). This is a tragedy that calls for tears. We ought to hurt with those who are hurting—Bryce's family and Bryce's church—as if that hurt were our very own.

We should cry out in pain, but we should also cry out in *prayer*. We do not pray for Bryce. He is beyond the need of our prayers. But we should pray for Bryce's family, and we should pray for his congregation, and we should pray for those who are bewildered and confused by his actions, and we should pray that God will somehow use all of this for his own honor and glory. And we should pray that he would even use this to bring people to faith in Jesus Christ. And we should pray for ourselves—that we may be more sensitive to the pain borne by those around us, more supportive, more encouraging, more prayerful.

We should cry out in pain, and we should cry out in prayer, and we should cry out in *praise*. While we do not pray to God for Bryce, we can praise God for Bryce. We can praise God for Bryce's life and for his ministry and for all of the wonderful ways in which God has used him. We can praise God for the evidence of his own divine love and mercy and grace that we saw in Bryce's life. But most of all, we can praise God for being God, for being the God he really is, for being the God whom we can trust even in the face of such tragedies. He is the God to whom we can turn with all of our questions and heartache and pain, and he is the God who has already triumphed for us in Jesus Christ.

A letter has been prepared by the pastoral staff at our mother church, and it is being read to the congregation in the services there this morning. Listen to what that letter says in part:

We do not know the reason our friend, Bryce, took his own life. It brings us confusion, grief, and even anger. The one we looked up to so highly has fallen, and it shakes us and distresses us to the core. What Bryce did was not right. It causes and will cause intense pain in his family, his friends, and his church. The Bible tells us that we must not kill.

Bryce killed himself. The good news is that when Jesus Christ died for our sins, he died for all of them—past, present, and future. During times of distress, even strong believers can become weak in faith and love and fall into the greatest of sins. But when we do, we sin as a child of God, not as an enemy of God. Because believers are chosen by God and God is eternally our Father in Christ, we cannot fall completely away from God.

Bryce repeatedly declared his faith in Jesus Christ and his belief that only through Jesus could he be made right with God. We believe that it is not his right living or his right dying but the righteousness of Jesus Christ that enables any man to enjoy the presence of God forever.

Are *You* Right With God through Faith in Jesus Christ?

And so the last question. It's the most important question of all, far more important than any question we have already considered. It's just this: *Are you right with God through faith in Jesus Christ?* If you are desperate or despondent, do not believe that your sadness disqualifies you from Jesus' love or dismays your Savior. Instead, recognize that he is the Savior of the disconsolate and loves to call the sorrowful to his embrace:

> Come, ye disconsolate, where'er ye languish,
> Come to the mercy seat, fervently kneel;
> Here bring your wounded hearts, here tell your anguish;
> Earth has no sorrows that heaven cannot heal.
>
> Joy of the desolate, Light of the straying,
> Hope of the penitent, fadeless and pure!
> Here speaks the Comforter, tenderly saying,
> "Earth has no sorrows that heaven cannot cure."
>
> Here see the bread of life; see waters flowing
> Forth from the throne of God, pure from above.
> Come to the feast of love; come, ever knowing
> Earth has no sorrows but heaven can remove.[8]

Amen.

---

8. Thomas Moore, "Come, Ye Disconsolate" (1816).

Chapter 23

SUICIDE OF
A FRIEND

SITUATION

Theologian, author, and preacher Michael Horton[1] was asked to deliver the funeral message for a long-time Christian friend who had committed suicide. The friend had encountered a number of family, career, and health difficulties that led to a deep depression. Although the friend was theologically articulate and a sincere believer, his faith faltered. In this message, Horton speaks not as the regular pastor to the family and congregation but as a friend invited to bring biblical comfort to both.

CONCERNS

With the integrity of a theologian and the compassion of a pastor, Horton is concerned to avoid speculation about questions that cannot be answered with biblical certainty, and to affirm the answers Scripture yet declares to our hardest questions. He turns to the book of Job to identify the folly of venturing beyond the counsel of God and to that same book to divulge the answers God has revealed. The willingness to leave some questions unanswered provides assurance to thoughtful Christians that their reticence to accept simplistic or sentimental answers about tragedy is acceptable to God—and not a betrayal of faith. The determination to provide answers Scripture gives to

---

1. Dr. Horton is the author/editor of many books including *The Christian Faith*, *Putting Amazing Back into Grace*, and *A Place for Weakness*. He is editor-in-chief of *Modern Reformation* magazine and president of White Horse Media, for which he co-hosts *White Horse Inn*, a nationally syndicated, weekly radio talk show exploring issues of Reformation theology in American Christianity. Horton is professor of systematic theology and apologetics at Westminster Seminary, California.

other questions provides assurance that there is hope beyond human explanation—hope that is the essence of true faith. The result is a humble (though articulate) confession of what cannot be answered, and a bold declaration of what must be said about the sovereign mercy of God that provides comfort beyond reason and triumph beyond tragedy.

APPROACH

Dr. Horton addresses a family that is intelligent and informed about matters of faith, so his references and analogies reflect his respect for their intellects. At the same time, he proceeds with wonderful pastoral instincts, asking and answering hard questions about the spiritual destiny of someone who commits suicide, describing the nature of grace in the face of personal failure, and offering hope so glorious that it eclipses the darkness of human despair. The message's power lies not so much in the intellectual rigor of its opening passages, but in the movement from theological reflection to personal empathy and, finally, to glorious triumph in our resurrection hope.

THE SERMON

OUR REDEEMER LIVES — AND SO SHALL WE

Michael Horton

[23]"Yet if there is an angel on his side
   as a mediator, one out of a thousand,
   to tell a man what is right for him,
[24]to be gracious to him and say,
   'Spare him from going down to the pit;
   I have found a ransom for him' —
[25]then his flesh is renewed like a child's;
   it is restored as in the days of youth.
[26]He prays to God and finds favor with him,
   he sees God's face and shouts for joy;
   he is restored by God to his righteous state.
[27]Then he comes to men and says,
   'I sinned, and perverted what was right,
   But I did not get what I deserved.
[28]He redeemed my soul from going down to the pit,
   and I will live to enjoy the light.'"

Job 33:23–28 NIV [1984 ed.][2]

In this passage, Job's friend, Elihu, begins to understand something of the comfort Job needs in the midst of his great loss and burden. But after Job's friends finish their sermons — and after Job finishes his own commentary on his situation, God finally speaks up and preaches for himself. Out of the whirlwind, he answers Job: "Who is this that darkens my counsel with words without knowledge? Brace yourself like a man; I will question you, and you shall answer me. Where were you when I laid the earth's foundation? Tell me, if you understand" (Job 38:2–4). After listing a litany of divine actions that

---

2. All Scripture quotations in this chapter, unless otherwise indicated, are taken from the New International Version (NIV [1984 ed.]).

illustrate his wisdom and power over the universe, God shuts the mouths of Job and his well-meaning friends. For they have all assumed that they had access to the divine filing cabinet. They all operated under the assumption that they could discern the mind of God.

How easily we attempt this when suffering strikes us or our loved ones! We immediately set out to discern the purpose behind it all. But God refuses to be figured out in these matters, and his counsel is hidden to mortals. God asks all the human commentators in the book of Job, "Can you make a pet of [me] like a bird or put [me] on a leash for your girls? ... Any hope of subduing [me] is false; the mere sight of [me] is overpowering ... Who then is able to stand against me? Who has a claim against me that I must pay? Everything under heaven belongs to me" (Job 41:5, 9, 10b – 11).

After God's defense of himself, Job is left without excuse. In spite of his superior theology, his experience had led him to question God's sovereignty and goodness. Because he could not comprehend how his pain could be reconciled with his view of God, he concluded that God had no answers for him. But God reminded him, as he reminds all of us, that just because we don't have all the answers does not mean that no answers exist.

Job's friends thought they had all the answers: Job's suffering was the effect of his sin or his failure to claim victory over his circumstances. Refusing to buy into their works righteousness and hollow platitudes, Job becomes an existentialist, preferring no answers to wrong answers. Much like Jean-Paul Sartre after the despair of two savage world wars, Job concluded that suicide might be preferable to enduring his suffering. Again and again he cries out to God for an end to his life.

For those who are tied to the high masts of suffering, there is often a fear that is greater than the fear of death. It is the fear of life. It is the fear of the next morning, and the morning after that. In the face of deep despair, the temptation is great to either turn away from God because the suffering is somehow credited to his wrath toward personal sins, or to turn toward him because one knows that he or she is at peace with God. This is why Job said he would be able to turn toward God in this situation if only he had a go-between, an advocate. Gradually, he comes to a greater confidence in this mediator: "Even now my witness is in heaven; my advocate is on high. My intercessor is my friend as my eyes pour out tears to God; on behalf of a man he pleads with God as a man pleads for his friend" (Job 16:19 – 21).

Whatever was wrong in Don's life, he had an unshakable conviction that his witness is in heaven. He knew that Jesus Christ was his intercessor, a friend to whom he could pour out tears to God. And he knew that Jesus Christ, his Elder Brother, was pleading on his behalf with God as a man pleads for his friend. Don knew the meaning of Paul's despair over his ongoing sinfulness in Romans 7, where the apostle laments, "For what I want to do I do not do, but what I hate I do ... What a wretched man I am! Who will rescue me from this body of death?" (verses 15, 24). But also like the apostle Paul, Don knew the answer to that question: "Thanks be to God — through Jesus Christ our Lord! ... Therefore, there is now no condemnation for those who are in Christ Jesus" (Romans 7:25 – 8:1).

So why didn't this confidence keep our brother from ending his life? We cannot answer that question any better perhaps than Job's friends could resolve the riddle of their friend's suffering. But I can say this: Even if we are too weak to hang on to Jesus, he is strong enough to hang on to us. Even though we may not be able to face tomorrow, Jesus has already passed through death to the other side and has taken away death's sting for us. Like Job, who knew that his Redeemer lives and that he would see him in the very body that was at present covered with bloody and painful sores, the apostle Paul declared, "If Christ has not been raised, our preaching is useless and so is your faith ... If only for this life we have hope in Christ, we are to be pitied more than all men" (1 Corinthians 15:14, 19).

Christianity is not true because it works. In many cases, it does not work. That is to say, it does not solve all of the problems that we think it should solve. Those who become Christians because they were told it would fix their marriages, only to find themselves in divorce court, might well give up on Christianity. Those who expected to be free of sinful habits and desires after a conversion in which "sudden victory" was promised may find themselves disillusioned with God altogether soon thereafter, when they realize that they are still sinners saved by grace. And there are, no doubt, many in this city and in other places who will say, "If Christianity didn't work for someone like Dr. Donald Brown, how can it work for me?" It is an honest question, an understandable question. But it assumes that Christianity fixes everything. It doesn't fix everything, at least not here and now. Christianity does promise that everything will be fixed at the end of history, but in this wilderness experience we are on a pilgrimage to the holy city. Some pilgrims will find the journey much more difficult than remaining back in Egypt, in unbelief.

Don was not one of those pilgrims who turned back to Egypt. Don and Aletha Brown were towers of strength to me in my own pilgrimage, as I watched them meet successive disasters by turning again and again to God and his gracious promise. But Don was a pilgrim for whom the hike to that eternal city had become so heavy that he looked for a way out. With Aletha, he was longing for a better city but was unwilling to wait.

We are not called here this afternoon to judge God. God didn't promise any of us health, wealth, and happiness. In fact, he tells us that we who expect to share in Christ's glory will also participate in his sufferings. Christianity is true, not because it works for people in that pragmatic, utilitarian way, but because nearly two thousand years ago, outside of the center city of Jerusalem, the Son of God was crucified for our sins and was raised for our justification. This historical event may not fix our marriages, our relationships, or our messed-up lives the way we would like and in the timing we would like, but it saves us from the wrath of God to come. And surely in view of this, all else pales not into insignificance but into secondary importance to that great issue. For "it is appointed for men to die once, but after this the judgment" (Hebrews 9:27 NKJV).

We are not here to judge God today. But neither are we here to judge Don Brown. No one can justify his action, but Don Brown is justified before God. You see, being accepted before God is not a matter of what we have done or left undone, or we would all be lost. It is a matter of trusting in that which Jesus Christ has done, for he has finished the work of our redemption. He has paid the ransom for our sins and satisfied the justice that our guilt required.

The perfect righteousness that God requires of us was possessed by only one man who ever lived, the Redeemer to whom Job and Paul and every other saint has looked for shelter from death and hell. The moment we trust in Christ and renounce our own claims to holiness and acceptability, stripping away the fig leaves of our own making, God clothes us in the robe of Christ's righteousness. Because of Christ's life of obedience, his sacrificial death, and his triumphant resurrection, we are accepted by the Father and made his heirs, given the Holy Spirit and promised the resurrection of our own mortal flesh. This means that it is safe to look up at God again. As Job said that if only he had an advocate, a mediator, he could lift his eyes up to God in his suffering, so all of us can cry on our Father's shoulder this afternoon because we have nothing to fear. It is not his wrath that has sent us pain and suffering if we belong to him, for he intercepts Satan's designs and fashions even sin and evil into messengers of grace.

With Job and Paul, Don knew that his Redeemer lived, even though he himself did not think he could go on living here below. With the Redeemer, there will be no death, no suffering, no pain, no disease or disappointment.

Even now, Don is awaiting his new, glorified body while his spirit is already enjoying the immediate presence of God. If God's grace is greater than all our sin—even than this sin of suicide—then surely every one of us is warmly invited by the risen Christ, "Come to me, all you who are weary and burdened, and I will give you rest" (Matthew 11:28). And with Job and Paul, Don will reign with Christ because his Redeemer lives. Because Christ's tomb is empty, Don's grave will also be empty on the last day. With Job, Don can say, "I will see him in my flesh," in the very body that, at eighteen years old, fell seventy-five feet while rock climbing, leaving him with a broken back and reconstructed feet; in that body that witnessed the death of his brother from leukemia and his father's death while Don was in college.

It is in that body that, together with Aletha, held children with severe learning disabilities as gifts from God, and in the body that just four months ago was injured in a train accident, that Don will see God. It will be a body reconstructed, not by the skillful hands of doctors below, but by the hand of his Creator, the Great Physician—and so Don's body will be perfectly mended and free of pain. On that day, Scripture assures us, God "will wipe every tear from their eyes. There will be no more death or mourning or crying or pain, for the old order of things has passed away" (Revelation 21:4).

Until then, Don is in God's presence without his body, awaiting that triumphal entry of God's liberated captives arriving in triumphant procession together through the gates of the eternal city after a long, hard winter through the wilderness. Indeed, Christianity does "work" after all, for all of us who believe, just where and when we needed it most. Perhaps some of you here, like Job, have thought, "Since I am already found guilty, why should I struggle in vain? ... He is not a man like me that ... we might confront each other in court. If only there were someone to arbitrate between us, to lay his hand upon us both, someone to remove God's rod from me, so that his terror would frighten me no more. Then I would speak up without fear of him" (Job 9:29, 32–35). Don would want to remind all of us that we have this arbitrator, this mediator, who has removed God's rod from us, so that his terror frightens us no more. Now we can speak up without fear of him because he calls us children instead of enemies.

To Aletha and the rest of the family, I know you have lost your husband, son, father, and brother. Although I myself have lost one of my closest friends, I cannot begin to know your suffering, but God knows what this is like. For he, too, lost a dear one, his one and only Son. God committed his Son to dreadful suffering and a cruel death because through it he could save people who hated him and make them his own sons and daughters. You can turn to him as your Father, not only because he knows how you feel, but because his loss secured your adoption into his family and made Don a co-heir with Christ. And for all of us here who are afraid of death, or of life, the good news is that this man is still at God's right hand, this Advocate who pleads our case. His name is Jesus Christ, and if your faith is in this Rock of Ages and in this Mighty Fortress, he will be your friend, in this world and in the world to come.

Chapter 24

SUICIDE AFTER PASTORAL SCANDAL

SITUATION

On the verge of being exposed after years of secret struggles with immorality, a beloved, long-term, unmarried pastor took his own life. Theologian Jerram Barrs[1] had worshiped in this man's church for a few years but had also known the pastor for decades in the L'Abri circles of Francis Schaeffer. The L'Abri Fellowship and this church had constantly emphasized the necessity of deep relationships and community bonds, making the pastor's secrecy and suicide all the more shocking. Professor Barrs knew that the church was feeling deep wounds of pain, confusion, anger, and doubt — all of which needed to be faced squarely in this message in order for the gospel to penetrate hearts as deeply as was needed.

CONCERNS

This sermon is unusual, not only because the circumstances are scandalous, but also because the comfort offered is directed to an entire congregation rather than to a specific family. Professor Barrs has to answer the hard ques-

---

1. For many years Jerram Barrs was Director of English L'Abri and pastor of the Presbyterian Church (IPC) in Greatham, England. A protégé of Francis Schaeffer, he has served for more than twenty years as Professor of Apologetics and Outreach at Covenant Seminary. Known for his intellectual acumen and gracious heart, Barrs's books include *On Being Human* (with Ranald MacAulay), *The Great Rescue*, *The Heart of Prayer*, *Learning Evangelism from Jesus*, and *Through His Eyes*. Many of Barrs's sermons and messages are available at http://worldwide-classroom.com.

tions that are always asked in the face of suicide and that are made more acute when the deceased is a pastor: Can he go to heaven? Can he be forgiven? Was his faith real? Are we in jeopardy because the faith of the one who taught us was so weak?

In addition, Professor Barrs deals with the questions that loved ones and parishioners ask when facing the suicide of a Christian leader: Did we fail to help enough? Did we heap on too much pressure or blame? Are we to blame for not seeing the signs?

Finally, he dares to ask the questions about going forward: How can we go forward? What's the use? If the gospel wasn't enough for our pastor, how can it help us?

APPROACH

Professor Barrs's approach is quite simple: he asks out loud the hard questions that everyone is thinking, and then he answers the questions with gospel truths. His answers are straightforward and form the structure of the message. He logically and compassionately develops his message according to the questions that others will ask rather than according to the pattern of a passage of Scripture. Biblical texts and truths are brought to bear to substantiate the answers to the questions, and provide proof that we are allowed to ask such hard questions since they appear in Scripture. There is also a beautiful description of the openness of relationships in the Trinity that provides the basis for encouraging the congregation to be open regarding their own feelings and struggles. The message gives people the right not only to grieve but also to ask honest questions and express honest doubts. What else would we expect from a community bred on the teachings of Francis Schaeffer?

THE GREATNESS OF GOD'S MERCY

Jerram Barrs

[1]I am the man who has seen affliction
    by the rod of the LORD's wrath.
[2]He has driven me away and made me walk
    in darkness rather than light;
[3]indeed, he has turned his hand against me
    again and again, all day long.

[4]He has made my skin and my flesh grow old
    and has broken my bones.
[5]He has besieged me and surrounded me
    with bitterness and hardship.
[6]He has made me dwell in darkness
    like those long dead.

[7]He has walled me in so I cannot escape;
    he has weighed me down with chains.
[8]Even when I call out or cry for help,
    he shuts out my prayer.
[9]He has barred my way with blocks of stone;
    he has made my paths crooked.

[10]Like a bear lying in wait,
    like a lion hiding,
[11]he dragged me from the path and mangled me
    and left me without help.
[12]He drew his bow
    and made me the target for his arrows.

[13]He pierced my heart
    with arrows from his quiver.
[14]I became the laughingstock of all my people;

they mock me in song all day long.
¹⁵He has filled me with bitter herbs
and given me gall to drink.

¹⁶He has broken my teeth with gravel;
he has trampled me in the dust.
¹⁷I have been deprived of peace;
I have forgotten what prosperity is.
¹⁸So I say, "My splendor is gone
and all that I had hoped from the LORD."

¹⁹I remember my affliction and my wandering,
the bitterness and the gall.
²⁰I well remember them,
and my soul is downcast within me.
²¹Yet this I call to mind
and therefore I have hope:

²²Because of the LORD's great love we are not consumed,
for his compassions never fail.
²³They are new every morning;
great is your faithfulness.
²⁴I say to myself, "The LORD is my portion;
therefore I will wait for him."

Lamentations 3:1–24

The Questions We Must Ask

All of us here who have known our pastor for so many years are overwhelmed. We feel like we are stumbling in darkness. I don't know about you, but I feel many years older, more tired, weak, stretched to the breaking point. With the bitterness of gall in our hearts we have all cried, "Lord, what is happening? Do you know what you are doing? What credit could this possibly bring to the gospel? What honor could this bring to your church or your name? Won't people mock you and your church? Lord, we all had such hopes for this friend of ours, for his ministry. We had such plans for the future, things we longed to accomplish with him. Lord, what are you doing?"

We wonder, "Is it worth going on?" What we had hoped for from the Lord has not come to pass. I know this is how many of you have felt over these past days, and this is how many of you feel now. For some of you, the shock, the unbearable pain, and the numbness have hardly begun to sink in. In the days to come, there are going to be more tears, and there certainly will be moments when such tears will come to you in an overwhelming way.

As you meet here, the members of this congregation, Sunday by Sunday, he won't be here. Every week, there will be this gap; you won't be hearing ever again in this world his sermons on the mercy and the grace of the gospel. In your Bible studies and in your prayer meetings there will be an empty place. There won't be any more wise words from him; there won't be any more fierce challenges from him or any more sudden smiles or embraces. For all of you who have come to him in your brokenness, he won't be here again to encourage you, to comfort you. The loss you feel today is only going to become more acute in the days to come. And as the days go by, some of you are going to feel other things as well.

Some of you are going to feel anger. You're going to say, "Why did he do this? Wasn't this selfish?" Some of you are saying that right now. Some of you will be angry with God. And you are going to say, "God what are you doing, why did this happen? Where is your love? Where is your power? Don't you care for your people?" Some of you are going to sense a betrayal. "How could we be let down in this way by our pastor and by God?"

Some of you, though, are going to feel guilty. I am sure many of you have thought about this over the past few days. You've said to yourself, as I have, "Why didn't I reach out to him more? Isn't there anything I could have done to have stopped this? Was my life so full that I couldn't make a little bit more room for him?" There are others of you who perhaps feel you were hard on him over these past few months. You are going to feel a different kind of guilt. You might say to yourself, "Was I the one who pushed him over the edge? If only I could take back those words that I said!" We need to let each other feel these things and express these things, and not rebuke another as we do so.

I doubt if any of us will find words that are more expressive than those I've read from Jeremiah's lament. He pours out his grief and pain, his bitterness, and even his anger toward God. These words are here in Scripture for our encouragement, to let us know that it is alright to say things like this. You don't want to add to your burdens by feeling guilty for the pain and distress, the betrayal and the anger, and all these other things that we feel. As you go through these next few weeks, let's not heal each others' wounds lightly. We are forbidden by Scripture to say, "Peace! Peace!" when we don't feel that there is any peace (Jeremiah 6:14).

The Burdens We Must Bear

Every one of us gathered here today is acutely aware at this time of our own brokenness and vulnerability. We need to weep with one another and to speak to one another and to bear one another's burdens. Like Jeremiah, we need to let our words out. God has made us for relationships — relationships both of giving and of receiving. This is how God has presented himself to us through all eternity: the Father, the Son, and the Spirit, sharing with each other, bearing one another's sorrow, embracing one another's joys, honoring one another, glorifying each other, loving each other. This is what God calls us to do.

Jesus, when he felt forsaken, when he was condemned, cried out to his Father, "Into your hands I commit my spirit" (Luke 23:46, quoting Psalm 31:5). We need to cry out to each other in the days to come. I beg you, for your own sake and for each other's sakes, to open yourselves up to each other. This is one thing our pastor was not very good at. Many of you were hurt by that. Many of you feel even more hurt by it now and feel rebuffed. You wanted him to open up, to share his burdens. He was so good at helping you. So many of you owe so much of your lives to him, because he bore your burdens, because he saw into your hearts, because you shared yourselves with him, and because he helped you carry the burdens you struggle with.

The apostle Paul was also prepared to open himself up before others. He writes for us that he felt so utterly and unbearably crushed that he almost despaired of life itself; indeed, he felt in his heart the sentence of death (see 1 Corinthians 1:8, for example). Even Jesus, the Son of God, our model of humanity, the perfect man, shared his burdens with people. In Gethsemane, he begged his disciples to stay awake to try to bear with him the pain that he felt, as he prayed for the cup of suffering to be taken from him. He asked them, "Couldn't you just pray with me? Couldn't you stay awake with me just for this brief time?" (see Matthew 26:36–46). If Jesus could make himself vulnerable to his disciples, who owed everything to him, how much more do we need to open ourselves up to each other in a time like this? This is God's call for us — to bear one another's burdens and so fulfill the law of Christ (Galatians 6:2).

As for our pastor himself, what words of comfort do we have for him and for us? Jeremiah says these beautiful words here in Lamentations 3: "This I call to mind and therefore I have hope: Because of the LORD's great love we are not consumed." Our pastor has not been consumed by the judgment of God. He is not being rejected even if he doubted, at the end, the love that he had preached so often and with which he had to comfort so many of us here. Though he may have forgotten for a brief moment the grace that he ministered to so many, he has been received most royally by the King. He is able, at last, to share himself completely, to open his heart, to bear his soul, to off-load his burdens onto someone else. He no longer wipes away the tears of others; his own tears are being wiped away. He is no longer comforting those who mourn; rather he is being comforted right now. He is no longer helping the bruised reed, but he himself is being made strong. He is no longer bringing words of tenderness and touches of encouragement to those who are broken in their bodies with disease or to those who are broken in their minds and hearts by the heavy weights of their lives. No, he himself is being embraced; he is hearing the words, "Come to me, all you who are weary and burdened, and I will give you rest." Christ is his portion fully. Christ's victory over death and over the grave is his already.

We know these things, but still we miss our pastor. He has been a friend for so many of us for so long. He has been a fixed point in the spiritual journey of so many of you here. For all of us, he has been a friend in one way or another. And for you, his family, who hurt more deeply than anyone else, I hope it will be some solace in the hard days to come that you might remember how many people he ministered to for so many years. It is a comfort to know that he is loved very deeply and that he loved so many other people so very deeply and that he was a servant for many years to so many people. For many he was father, brother, and friend—day after day, month after month, year after year—with great faithfulness.

All of us are such broken people. We all have burdens to bear, such hard things in our hearts. All of us have many sins in our lives. None of us should forget that we are here to celebrate God's forgiveness for sinners like our pastor and for sinners like you and me. We are here today because we know that God is merciful to us in Jesus Christ, and so let there be forgiveness and grace in our hearts toward our pastor and toward one another from this day on.

The Battle God Has Won

Now I have no doubt that Satan will try to sow doubt and distrust, lies and deceits and discouragement among us, particularly in this congregation. His purpose is to make us unbelieving. His purpose is to try to arrest the great work that has been accomplished in this church through the ministry of our beloved pastor and so many others. God has done very great things here.

268 · PREACHING AFTER SUICIDE

Satan has not liked that at all, and he desires to bring it to an end. Let this one *imagined* victory—because in the end it is *not* Satan's victory—let this one imagined victory be all that he will get; let there be no more. God calls us to stand together, to love one another, to support and encourage each other, in the days to come. Comfort one another with the confidence that God's work is going to continue and that the gates of hell will never prevail against it. That promise is not just true in the world in general; it is true right here in our church, in this city. God is going to continue to build this church.

Many of you know that just a few years ago we had the most shocking crime at the seminary where I serve, which is still unsolved. Satan saw what God was doing at the seminary, and he wanted to destroy it. But while what happened there was a terrible thing, God's work has gone on unabated; his work has gone from victory to victory. He is building his people. He is doing his work, no matter how the devil may rage. And this sure work of God is to be our confidence here in this congregation. What Satan has done is indeed a terrible thing; but God is the one whose Word will triumph. God is the one whose gospel will endure; God is the one who will build this church. Satan will *not* prevail.

The under-shepherd has been smitten, but the sheep do not need to be scattered. God calls you to shepherd one another, to entrust your cares, your needs, your broken hearts to each other and above all to him.

The Lord is my shepherd; the Lord is your shepherd. Sometimes he makes us to lie down in green and pleasant valleys. But sometimes he goes before us through the valley of the shadow of death; yet he is *always* our shepherd. His rod and his staff can comfort us, and his Word can lift us up. One lost sheep has been found and is home with that Great Shepherd. His compassions to us who remain will never fail. They will be new every morning for the rest of our lives and for eternity. Like Jeremiah, we may be overwhelmed with grief; we may be overwhelmed with sorrow, with anger, and even with bitterness, but God is faithful, and we can say to him with confidence, "The LORD is my portion, my inheritance; therefore I will wait for him."

Chapter 25

SUICIDE OF A TEEN

SITUATION

Dr. George Robertson[1] delivered this message after the suicide of a teenager in his church. The young man had gone through most of his angst without notice. Quiet by nature, he had few friends and did not stand out as being particularly troubled. His parents knew he was struggling but did not know the struggles were so deep. And perhaps the young man did not know either. He was sadly characteristic of those young believers who, in moments of disappointment or loneliness, make a life-altering decision without the perspective that more years, family, or faith could offer. Thankfully, despite this awful decision, the young man's earlier affirmations and life of faith seemed genuine and gave the pastor a strong basis for comforting the family.

CONCERNS

Pastor Robertson was concerned to address the questions that always accompany a suicide. Why was this choice made? Does the choice automatically deny this young man entry into heaven? How can we reconcile this awful event with the reality of faith or the sovereignty of God?

Robertson is concerned to answer what he can and not provide answers beyond his or any pastor's knowledge. He wants to comfort the family, whose grief was intense, and a measure of his pastoral prudence and care is the brev-

---

1. Dr. George Robertson has pastored churches in Missouri and Georgia. He now pastors First Presbyterian Church (PCA) in Augusta, Georgia. A frequent teacher of preachers in seminaries, he is the author of *Deuteronomy: More Grace, More Love*.

ity of the message. Not all great messages are long. This message of great wisdom also shows special care for a hurting family—feeling the scrutiny of others as well the agony of their loss—by being mercifully short as well as biblically true.

APPROACH

The passage chosen is remarkable for its aptness. The brief reference to an ancient king of Israel would seem to have little connection to a family grieving the suicide of a child. But this experienced pastor chooses a short verse from the account of Asa that clearly shows that human frailty does not annul divine mercy.

Robertson not only provides the benefits of his experience; he also provides empathy—sharing that his family has also experienced such a loss. The brief note is a caring gesture toward a family that must be feeling guilt as well as grief.

Finally, the concluding illustration is chosen with great pastoral wisdom and care. The well-known emotional struggles of the hymn writer William Cowper are aptly applied to the suicide of a teen. More apt and brilliantly worded are the final lines of the message that leave the family—and all who have experienced similar loss—looking up to heaven's mercy rather than down into death's darkness.

THE BREADTH OF GRACE

George Robertson

> Although he did not remove the high places, Asa's heart was fully
> committed to the LORD all his life.
>
> *—1 Kings 15:14*

I want to speak to you briefly this afternoon not so much as a minister as a
fellow sufferer. My wife and I lost a family member to the same kind of death
as Stephen's.[2] I know some of the questions you are asking and some of the
doubts you are having.

In our years of grief—and by the way, your grief will not be quickly
resolved—we have learned that the Bible never says not to grieve; it says to
Christians that we must not grieve *as those who have no hope.* So in our years
of grief we have found it not so helpful to focus on the spiritual condition or
failures of our loved one. We have found it much more helpful to focus on
the hope we have—the breadth of God's grace and the sovereignty of its
application.

The Bible makes it very clear that no one enters heaven without trusting
in Christ alone for salvation—trusting him for righteousness and not supposing in any way that one can contribute to one's own salvation. Jesus said,
"I am the way and the truth and the life. No one comes to the Father except
through me" (John 14:6).

But the Bible also makes it very clear that God is sovereign over the entire
Christian life. He brings us to himself when we want nothing to do with him.
Jesus said, "No one can come to me unless the Father who sent me draws
them" (John 6:44). And Paul assures that God will complete the process of
our sanctification: "He who began a good work in you will carry it on to

---

2. Individual names and some personal details have been changed as an expression of care for
the family.

completion until the day of Christ Jesus" (Philippians 1:6). In fact, Paul says that the glorification, the heavenly perfection, of those who have been saved is so sure that it is as if it has already occurred (Ephesians 2:6).

In my meditation on the breadth of the grace of God in regard to those who are sometimes *identified* in human estimation as spiritual failures, I have returned again and again to a rather obscure character of Scripture, Asa, king of Judah (2 Kings 15:8–24; 2 Chronicles 14–16). Asa did some good things in his reign over God's people. He removed some of the pagan idols and restored the worship of the true God. But more space is given in the Bible to his failures. He didn't remove *all* of the idols. He entered into a treaty with a pagan king because he didn't trust God. He brutally oppressed God's people. And when he was afflicted with a disease in his feet, he refused to turn to God for help.

But do you know what the Bible says about Asa? Do you know the epitaph that God writes over his life? "Although he did not remove the high places, Asa's heart was fully committed to the Lord all his life" (1 Kings 15:14). And lest you think this was just a slip of the pen, listen to the summary of King David's life given a few verses earlier. David, who stole a man's wife and then killed her husband to cover up his sin, is described this way: "For David had done what was right in the eyes of the Lord and had not failed to keep any of the Lord's commands all the days of his life — except in the case of Uriah the Hittite" (1 Kings 15:5).

I don't know all that we should conclude from these verses, but I can tell you the very least. We can conclude that God's grace is sovereign and very broad. His mercy is broader than ours and can save and embrace even the most notorious of sinners.

Each of you here in one way or another sought to express your love to Stephen. Many of you here pointed him to Jesus Christ for his salvation and help. You did it again and again. And on numerous occasions, he professed faith in Christ as his Savior. Your focus now must not be on the enduring quality of his profession but on the broad mercy of the Lord Christ who saves. And you must not be uneasy about what could not be repaired or communicated here. You must know that what could not be repaired or communicated here is in heaven.

Some years ago, Webster University gave a theatrical presentation of the life of William Cowper, the famous hymn writer. Though at times in his life, Cowper could write great hymns like "There Is a Fountain Filled with Blood" and "O for a Closer Walk with God," at other times he struggled to accept the fact that God's grace could save a sinner like himself. He was depressed much of his life and tried to take his life on several occasions. Eventually, his friend, John Newton, a pastor and the author of "Amazing Grace," took the fragile Cowper into the pastor's home. Newton could not convince Cowper that God's grace was sufficient. In the last scene of the play, Newton stands at the bedside of Cowper, trying to convince Cowper that God's grace will take him to heaven. In those final moments, Cowper won't believe it, and eventually he dies. Newton pauses for a time, then looks up to heaven, and says, "See, Cowper, I told you so."

What could not be communicated or repaired here will be there.

HELPS

FOR

HANDLING
TRAGEDIES

TEXTS FOR TRAGEDIES[*]

Helpful Texts for National or Community Disaster

Genesis 50:20 "You intended to harm me, but God intended it for good ..."

Psalm 27 "I will see the goodness of the LORD in the land of the living."

Psalm 42 "Put your hope in God ..."

Psalm 46 "God is our refuge and strength, an ever-present help in trouble."

Psalm 62 "Pour out your hearts to him, for God is our refuge."

Psalm 90 "LORD, you have been our dwelling place throughout all generations."

Psalm 91 "Whoever dwells in the shelter of the Most High will rest in the shadow of the Almighty."

Psalm 118 "The LORD is with me; I will not be afraid. What can mere mortals do to me?"

Psalm 121 "My help comes from the LORD, the Maker of heaven and earth."

Ecclesiastes 3:1 – 8 "There is a time for everything, and a season for every activity under the heavens."

Isaiah 41:10 "Do not fear, for I am with you ... I will strengthen you and help you; I will uphold you with my righteous right hand."

Isaiah 43:1 "Do not fear, for I have redeemed you. I have summoned you by name; you are mine."

Isaiah 61 "They will renew the ruined cities that have been devastated for generations."

Lamentations 3:22 – 26, 31 – 32 "Because of the LORD's great love we are not consumed, for his compassions never fail ... For no one is cast off by the LORD forever. Though he brings grief, he will show compassion, so great is his unfailing love."

---

[*] These text excerpts are meant to guide pastors to the passages where the subject is addressed more fully.

Luke 13:1–5 Those who died when the tower in Siloam fell on them were not more guilty than anyone else in Jerusalem.

John 11:17–44 The raising of Lazarus from the dead. "Jesus wept."

Romans 8:28–39 In all things God works for the good of those who love him; and nothing can separate us from the love of God that is in Christ Jesus our Lord.

Helpful Texts after the Loss of a Child

2 Samuel 12:18–23 David after the loss of his son: "I will go to him, but he will not return to me."

Psalm 8:2 "Through the praise of children and infants you have established a stronghold against your enemies."

Psalm 139:13–16 "You knit me together in my mother's womb."

Psalm 145:1–13 "One generation commends your works to another ... Your dominion endures through all generations."

Isaiah 49:15–16 "Can a mother forget the baby at her breast ...? I will not forget you!"

Jeremiah 1:5–8 "Before I formed you in the womb I knew you, before you were born I set you apart."

Matthew 18:1–5, 10 "Whoever takes the lowly position of this child is the greatest in the kingdom of heaven."

Mark 10:13–16 (see parallels Matthew 19:13–15; Luke 18:15–17) "Let the little children come to me, ... for the kingdom of God belongs to such as these."

Luke 1:41–50 "... the baby in my womb leaped for joy."

1 Corinthians 7:14 By a parent's faith children "are holy."

1 Thessalonians 4:13–18 "We who are still alive and are left will be caught up together with them ... And so we will be with the Lord forever."

James 4:14 "What is your life? You are a mist that appears for a little while and then vanishes."

Helpful Texts for Funerals

Job 19:23–27 "I know that my redeemer lives, and that in the end he will stand on the earth."

Psalm 23 "The LORD is my shepherd."

Psalm 46 "God is our refuge and strength, an ever-present help in trouble."

Psalm 62:5–8 "My salvation and my honor depend on God; he is my mighty rock, my refuge."

Psalm 90 "Our days may come to seventy years, or eighty, if our strength endures ... Teach us to number our days ..."

Psalm 91 "Whoever dwells in the shelter of the Most High will rest in the shadow of the Almighty."

Psalm 116:15 "Precious in the sight of the LORD is the death of his faithful servants."

Psalm 126:5 "Those who sow with tears will reap with songs of joy."

Psalm 139 "If I say, 'Surely the darkness will hide me ...,' even the darkness will not be dark to you."

Daniel 12:1–3 "Multitudes who sleep in the dust of the earth will awake ..."

Isaiah 55:6–13 "You will go out in joy and be led forth in peace ..."

Isaiah 61:1–3 "The Spirit of the Sovereign LORD is on me ... to bestow on them ... the oil of joy instead of mourning."

John 5:21–29 "For just as the Father raises the dead and gives them life ..."

John 11:17–27 "I am the resurrection and the life. The one who believes in me ... will never die."

John 14:1–7, 27 "My Father's house has many rooms; if that were not so, would I have told you that I am going there to prepare a place for you ... Peace I leave with you ..."

John 20:1–11 Jesus' resurrection.

Romans 8:37–39 Nothing can separate us from the love of God that is in Christ Jesus our Lord.

Romans 14:7–9 "Whether we live or die, we belong to the Lord."

1 Corinthians 15:20–26, 35–38, 42–44a, 51–58 Our resurrection described: "We will all be changed ... 'Where, O death, is your sting?'"

2 Corinthians 4:14–5:8 "We have a building from God, an eternal house in heaven, not built by human hands ..."

2 Corinthians 5:8 "... away from the body and at home with the Lord."

Philippians 1:21, 23 "For to me, to live is Christ and to die is gain ... I desire to depart and be with Christ, which is better by far."

Philippians 3:20–21 "The Lord Jesus Christ ... will transform our lowly bodies so that they will be like his glorious body."

1 Thessalonians 4:13–18 "The dead in Christ will rise first. After that, we who are still alive ..."

2 Timothy 2:8–13 "If we died with him, we will also live with him ..."

1 John 3:1–3 "We know that when Christ appears, we shall be like him ..."

Revelation 19:1–8 The wedding supper of the Lamb.

Revelation 20:4–6, 11–15 "Blessed and holy are those who share in the first resurrection. The second death has no power over them ..."

Revelation 21:1–7 A new heaven and a new earth: "He will wipe every tear from their eyes. There will be no more death ..."

Revelation 22:1–5 "The Lord God will give them light. And they will reign for ever and ever."

Helpful Texts after Suicide

Genesis 1:26 "Let us make mankind in our image ..."

1 Kings 15:14 "Although he did not remove the high places, Asa's heart was fully committed to the LORD ..."

Psalm 8 "You have made them [human beings] a little lower than the angels and crowned them with glory and honor."

Psalm 88 "Darkness is my closest friend."

Psalm 103:8–17 "He does not treat us as our sins deserve ... He remembers that we are dust."

Matthew 5:3 "Blessed are the poor in spirit, for theirs is the kingdom of heaven."

Luke 23:39–43 To the thief on the cross: "Today you will be with me in paradise."

John 6:35–40 "And this is the will of him who sent me, that I shall lose none of all those he has given me, but raise them up at the last day."

John 10:27–29 "My sheep listen to my voice ...; no one will snatch them out of my hand."

Ephesians 2:5–7, 8–9 "By grace you have been saved, through faith—... it is the gift of God—not by works ..."

Hebrews 10:14 "He has made perfect forever those who are being made holy."

Appendix Two

HELPS FOR CONDUCTING FUNERALS

I. Resources That Will Help You Know What to Do

Be sure to have on your bookshelf your denomination's book of worship or a standard minister's service manual. Every minister should possess a manual that includes service and text suggestions and standard formats for weddings, funerals, baptisms, building dedications, missionary commissionings, and so forth. These resources are available from church sources and several reliable publishers.

Blackwood, Andrew. *The Funeral*. Grand Rapids: Baker, 1972 (the classic text on this subject).

Blair, Robert. *The Funeral and Wedding Handbook*, 2nd ed. Lima, Ohio: CSS, 2002.

Chapell, Bryan. *Christ-centered Preaching: Redeeming the Expository Sermon*, 2nd ed. Grand Rapids: Baker, 2005 (esp. appendix 7: "Funeral Messages").

Engle, Paul, ed. *Baker's Funeral Handbook: Resources for Pastors*. Grand Rapids: Baker, 1996.

Fowler, Gene. *Caring through the Funeral: A Pastor's Guide*. St. Louis, Mo.: Chalice, 2004.

Lloyd, Dan S. *Leading Today's Funerals: A Pastoral Guide for Improving Bereavement Ministry*. Grand Rapids: Baker, 1997.

Malphurs, Aubrey and Keith Willhite, eds. *A Contemporary Handbook for Weddings and Funerals and Other Occasions*. Grand Rapids: Kregel, 2003.

II. What to Do upon News of a Death

A. Drop everything and go to the family immediately.

Almost nothing takes precedence over this. Of course, there are exceptions. No one expects you to forgo the Sunday sermon because you got the news five minutes before the worship service, but virtually all other meetings and appointments should be postponed in order to go to the family. Recognize that everyone who knows the situation will be uncomfortable participating with the minister in any meeting or activity knowing there is a grieving family in need of pastoral care.

The family may be:

- at the deceased's home if the person died there and the spouse or other immediate family members reside in the home. Even if the others do not live in the deceased home, loved ones may have gathered there, especially if the funeral director has not yet arrived to pick up the body.
- at the hospital if the person died there with family members present.
- at the nursing home if the person died there and family members are present.
- at the home of another family member if the home of the deceased is not where most of the family members live or gather.
- at other locations if the loss is due to accident, crime, or military service. In such situations, family members may be called to the city morgue, police station, funeral director's office, pastor's office, friend's home, transportation center (to receive a messenger or the transported remains), and so forth.

B. Help notify family if necessary.

If the death is the result of accident, crime, or military service, the pastor may be asked to help notify the family. Accompany appropriate authorities to the family residence at whatever time of day or night the notification must occur. Ordinarily you should not telephone such news but tell the family members directly. In order to give appropriate pastoral care, you want to be present when the news is given.

C. Offer counsel regarding disposition of the body if needed and requested.

If the death is that of an elderly or long-ill person in a hospital or nursing home, family members will probably already have indicated where the body should be taken in the event of death. If the death is unexpected, one of the family's first decisions may be which funeral home to use. If you are aware of a reputable place, you may offer this information *if asked*. Be aware that in many communities, families may have previous relationships with particular funeral homes and will not appreciate being steered toward others by the pastor.

D. Offer to help with notifications and arrangements if appropriate.

If any immediate family members are elderly, ill, or overcome with grief, the pastor may offer to help with some matters that require immediate attention.

- Help make notification calls (relatives, friends, organizations, and so forth). Often the pastor can help organize this process with gathered family members or friends so that weary or distraught next of kin do not have to think about or handle all the necessary notifications.
- Accompany family members to the funeral home to make arrangements (usually done within the first half day after the death of a loved one). Arrangements at the funeral home will be handled by the funeral director or other staff members. Despite cultural stereotypes of the funeral industry being full of callous and crooked persons, most funeral professionals are reputable and empathetic. They cannot stay in business without a good reputation in the community.

The family's interaction with the funeral home usually begins with a call to pick up the body of the deceased. After the body has been collected and a time set for the family to come to the funeral home to make arrangements, the next contact with the funeral home will be in the director's office. There the director will ask more questions than most people expect with regard to funeral service preferences and participants, media notifications, legal and government requirements, pension and Social Security notifications, military background, organization memberships, type and place of interment, style and cost of casket or urn, cemetery/mausoleum and marker preferences, and so forth. Typical arrangements made with the funeral home include such duties or decisions as:

- completion of forms detailing individual and family histories, medical and government requirements, pension plan notifications, and so forth.
- time and place of visitation (a set time for members of the community to come to visit with the family at the funeral home, church, or other setting to express sympathy prior to the formal service) and funeral (the formal service honoring the deceased prior to burial or other interment). Note that many funerals are in funeral homes these days, in part because employers often allow only close relatives time off for funerals. As a result, more persons tend to go to the visitation with the family during nonwork hours than to the actual funeral—which for an elderly person is often attended mostly by immediate family members and retirees. Believers may prefer that a funeral service honoring God's eternal care of his saints be held in a church, and pastors should accommodate this desire.
- manner and place of interment (for example, burial versus cremation, cemetery versus mausoleum, local versus out of town).
- service nature and sequence (for example, funeral service, memorial service, graveside service, public or family members only). Ordinarily there is a public funeral service (honoring the deceased), followed by a public graveside service (committing the body to the grave at the cemetery or mausoleum). However, there are many variations. For example, if the deceased was well-known and a cemetery could not accommodate a large crowd, then the family may prefer a private burial service prior to a public memorial service.
- service participants (for example, pall bearers, minister(s), musician(s), eulogizers, family members for family seating, military dignitaries, company or organization representatives, and so forth).
- service particulars (Scripture to be read or preached; what, if

any, eulogies — and by whom; music — content, style, and by whom; open or closed casket; placement of casket; placement of flowers or pictures; presence of recognitions or honors; and so forth).

- choice of cemetery, casket, vault type, plot location and size, mausoleum, niche, urn, and so forth.
- choices of clothing, jewelry, hairstyle, glasses, and so forth for the deceased.
- presence of flowers and envelopes for memorial gifts.
- military rites, fraternal organization participation, and so forth.

All of the above decisions can touch on *very* sensitive issues. Family disputes, resource limitations, and past indiscretions are but a few of the possible disclosures that may surface during the information gathering that must occur during funeral planning. Families and funeral directors may or may not want the minister navigating or even hearing about these issues.

Throughout the whole process, offer help where appropriate. Don't be offended if your presence is not desired. Exit gracefully. Try to help people not be taken advantage of in a vulnerable time (for example, reminding an elderly spouse with limited resources that the cost of the casket is not a measure of respect for the deceased), but do not impose your wishes on a family. The pastor should not take responsibility for any of these decisions. The decisions remain the family's — and everyone must know this. When out-of-town relatives question a funeral choice, no one in town should be able to respond, "Well, the pastor made us do it." The pastor is expected neither to know all the answers nor to choose for the family. The pastor's task is only to be available to help the family make these arrangements *if the family wants pastoral assistance.* Most often, all that is really desired is the pastor's silent supportive presence.

III. What to Do at the Visitation (sometimes called the laying out, the viewing, or the wake)

The visitation usually occurs the evening and/or afternoon before the funeral when the people of the community come to the funeral home to offer sympathy to the family. Typically the body of the deceased is "laid out for viewing," meaning that, if there has not been a disfiguring illness or disease, the casket is open in a parlor setting, and the immediate family members gather near it to receive those who come to pay their respects.

In most communities more persons will come to the visitation than to the funeral (unless the funeral is that of a young person or a person of some reputation), because the visitation can be attended briefly and during nonworking hours.

At the visitation, the responsibilities of the pastor include:

- arriving at the funeral home several minutes before the family arrives. The pastor has the responsibility to greet the family and help them prepare for the difficult hours of the grieving process. Not only must the family handle grief, but older members of the family may also find the physical strain of greeting the community exhausting. The pastor may well advise younger members to provide seating and space for older family members or a grieving spouse.
- greeting the family members as they arrive. Until all immediate family members have arrived, the funeral director will typically direct the family members to a waiting room where the deceased cannot be observed. When all have arrived, leading in a prayer for comfort and strength is appropriate.
- guiding the family members into the room where the deceased is laid out. This will be the immediate family's first sight of their loved one in a casket. Though there are difficult services and duties ahead for the family, this may well be the most difficult moment of the entire death and burial process. This is the most likely moment for family members to come emotionally unglued (though it happens much more frequently with unchurched families than with those who know the gospel well). The experienced pastor will often take the arm of the grieving spouse or nearest kin when the family members enter the room as an expression of both pastoral and physical support.
- staying with the family at least through the time that the first sympathizers arrive to express their condolences to the family. During the minutes before visitors arrive, the pastor should be available for support, prayer, and words of encouragement.

In these awkward moments, ministers do not need to carry the conversation, discourage tears, or fill the silence. The best pastoral care may simply be a silent, supportive presence as the family expresses its grief in its way. It is usually not helpful for the pastor to mouth clichés the family will hear many times over the next several hours (for example, "He is in a better place now"; "The Lord must have needed her more than we did"; "Didn't they do a good job?"—meaning the morticians have made the body look natural). Once visitors begin to arrive, the pastor may choose to leave or tend to other duties after assuring the family of continued availability. No one expects the pastor to stay for the entire evening unless there are complications or relationships that need additional attention.

This time of gathering and conversation may also provide the pastor opportunities to ask if there are any special items or thoughts the family would like to have included in the funeral service. By the time of the visitation, most out-of-town family members will have arrived, and they can consult with local family members about special requests or desires for the funeral service (for example, grandchildren participating in the eulogy, a daughter singing, a favorite Scripture being read).

Tactfully inquire if the family is planning anything special or unusual for the funeral (e.g., military rites, Masonic rites, unusual music, multiple eulogies, words from clergy of another faith). Families sometimes have ideas of what would be appropriate for a funeral that may be problematic for a pastor. For example, Masonic rites requested for funerals in certain parts of North America could be an example of such a surprise. Despite its charitable endeavors, Free Masonry has anti-Christian roots that many Masons and the general public are not aware of. The pastor's request to separate these rites from the "Christian service" (having the Masonic rites performed either after the minister says the funeral benediction or before the public arrives for the funeral) is usually honored without argument.

It is important for the pastor to guide family members in healthy directions, but remember that decisions are ultimately theirs, unless the church or the pastor is being asked to endorse what is clearly non-biblical. On those rare occasions, the pastor may have to inform family members that they will need to find someone else to do the service.

Such indications typically sever the relationship of the pastor with the family, so the spiritual consequences must be carefully weighed.

Try to avoid saying things that are not true in attempts to comfort. Do not assure a grieving family that a profligate is "in heaven now" if there is no Christian basis for doing so. It is much better to sympathize with a family's pain than to give spiritual assurances that you are not sure are true. For example, you can provide quality care in good conscience by simply telling family members that you are "sorry for their loss" and that you "grieve for their pain." Sympathize rather than say something you think may be untrue.

IV. What to Do on the Day of the Funeral

Do not be at all hesitant or ashamed to ask church members, senior clergy in the community, and, most especially, the funeral director what you need to do. Community and regional expectations vary greatly and it is not unprofessional to ask for advice when you are new in a church. The funeral director will not mind being asked (and, in fact, wants you to ask questions), since he or she is much more concerned than you are that things "go well." The livelihood of the director depends on the funeral being well run. No one will be concerned if you honestly acknowledge you are new to this community or this task and would like to ask some questions about how things are done.

Arrive at the place of the funeral prior to the family. At this time, it is often wise to see if flowers, clothing, casket, memorial arrangements, and so forth are as the family requested.

Greet the family as they arrive. Gather with them in a preparation room (if available) and pray, prior to entering the room where the funeral will be performed.

Lead the family into the room with the coffin or urn. (Note: Many of the following instructions assume a casket. Adjustments can easily be made for an urn or memorial service—where no casket or urn is present.) In some communities the family will not enter the room where the funeral occurs until after the casket has been rolled (or carried) into the room. If this is the case, those in the room will stand as the casket enters the room and the family will follow the casket, being led by the minister.

If the casket is already in the room where the funeral will be performed, then the minister typically takes the family into the room prior to the arrival of those attending the service. The family will greet those arriving for the funeral, until a few minutes prior to the service. Then, the funeral director will gather the family and usher them to an adjoining room to wait until the service begins.

In common—but not required—practice, the minister then goes to the adjoining room (or other secluded space), once attendees begin to arrive in order to collect thoughts for the message, make final arrangements with other service participants (e.g., other participating pastors or family members), and await the family who will be ushered out of the service room prior to the beginning of the funeral service.

Most of the time, it is helpful to pray with the family prior to the service. The most appropriate time will be after members have been led out of the service room by the funeral director prior to the beginning of the funeral service. Once the family has left the room, the casket is closed for the last time (closing the casket with the family present can be emotionally traumatic). The minister typically receives the family as the funeral director brings members into the adjoining room in order to offer a prayer, short Scripture reading, or word of encouragement to prepare the family for the difficult minutes ahead. (Note: On occasion, families will not want the casket closed during the funeral services. Pastors tend to discourage open caskets during the funeral itself, since looking at the deceased during the service can be very difficult for family and friends. Still, the family's wishes should be observed if the members cannot be readily dissuaded.) When the service is ready to begin, the funeral director will take the family into the service room and lead members to family seating at the front of the room.

Wait in the adjoining room until the funeral director indicates that it is time for the funeral service to begin. (Note: If the family is distraught, the minister may choose to enter with the family in order to support members who are most troubled.) Then the pastor usually enters and sits at the front of the room until the conclusion of the prelude—which is the pastor's cue to begin the service.

Conduct Scripture readings and prayers according to the format and sequence suggested in your minister's service manual, book of common worship, or denomination's directory for worship. For more information about the order and content of a funeral service, consult the resources at the beginning of this appendix.

Preach a message based on the final Scripture reading. Typically the minister ties a theme of the scriptural passage to significant features of the deceased's life or personality in order to make the promises of eternal life in Christ Jesus clear and comforting. Because of the emotional strain on the family, the message is usually brief. Experienced pastors will speak directly to the family about the comforts of the gospel — in essence, pastoring the family while allowing the rest of the congregation to "overhear" the comforts of the gospel. (Note: For the form and content of a funeral message, see Bryan Chapell, *Christ-centered Preaching: Redeeming the Expository Sermon*, 2nd ed. [Grand Rapids: Baker, 2005], appendix 7.)

If the deceased is not known as a believer, the preacher should neither "preach the person into heaven" or "damn the person to hell." We look on the outward appearance; only God knows the heart (1 Samuel 16:7). The time-honored practice of experienced and Bible-believing pastors is "preach the person's facts and then the Lord's gospel." Say what is appropriate about the person's life and then remind everyone of the eternal promises the Lord makes to those who believe in him — without saying (or denying) that those promises apply to the deceased.

At the conclusion of the message, sit near the pulpit and wait for the funeral director to dismiss the congregation. Depending on the community, the funeral director may do one of the following:

- Dismiss the congregation row by row to go out a rear door.
- Dismiss the congregation row by row through a front door so that they pass by the casket and express sympathy to the family a final time.
- Take the family out first, then remove the casket before any of the congregation is dismissed.
- Invite the pall bearers or funeral assistants forward to remove the casket or urn. The pall bearers or assistants are followed by the family and then the congregation.
- Carry out other procedures that vary by region and tradition.

Walk in front of the casket or urn as it is taken from the room to the hearse and/or place of interment (i.e., the cemetery, mausoleum, etc.). If the casket or urn will be transported to a cemetery or mausoleum, lead the pall bearers or funeral assistants to the hearse. Then step aside as the casket or urn is placed inside. Regardless of the order of the family's and congregation's dismissal, the pastor's traditional task and place is to precede the casket or urn (four or five paces, if walking; or, in the funeral director's car ahead of the hearse, if driving) wherever it moves until it is placed in its final and permanent location (cemetery or mausoleum). As our society becomes less concerned for (and aware of) such traditions, these ministerial courtesies are not as important and should not take precedence over the care of families. For instance, it may be much more important for a pastor to ride with an elderly, grieving widow behind the hearse on the way to the cemetery, rather than ride in the car with the funeral director that is traditionally ahead of the hearse.

V. What to Do at the Graveside (also called a Gravesite or Committal Service)

Precede the casket or urn to the place of interment. When the funeral procession arrives at its destination, the pastor goes to the rear of the hearse. When the casket or urn is removed by pall bearers or funeral assistants, the minister again precedes the deceased's remains to the grave, crypt, or niche. In many regions, the congregation that has followed in cars will not advance beyond the hearse until the pall bearers have removed the casket and the family is advancing behind it to the grave site. In a cemetery setting, the grave is typically covered by an awning or tent with seating arranged for immediate family and with onlookers expected to stand outside the covering.

Once the casket has been placed over or beside the grave, stand at the head of the casket (usually the west side, since Christian cemeteries are traditionally laid out east to west — supposedly allowing the deceased to face in the direction of Christ's anticipated return). Often the design of a casket makes it quite difficult to determine which end is the head, so ministers commonly ask the funeral director where to stand.

Wait for the funeral director to indicate that you should begin the graveside service. The director will not signal you to start until *all* have gathered at the graveside, even if this seems to take a long time.

Conduct the committal service (i.e., a graveside service after a funeral service) as outlined in your minister's service manual or book of common worship. The committal service is usually brief. It involves words of committal—"Here we commit the body of our loved one and friend to the grave; the spirit has already gone to the Lord who gave it," a short Scripture reading, a prayer, and a benediction. If there is only a graveside service (i.e., no funeral) then a brief message may be given after the words of committal—but before the body is lowered into the ground, if that is part of the local tradition.

After the benediction, step forward and personally express your sympathy to the family, shaking the hands of all the immediate family. In most communities, no one considers the service over (and the funeral director will not dismiss those who have gathered at the grave) until the minister has shaken the hands of immediate family and stepped away from the graveside.

If there are military rites they will usually occur during the committal service. These usually involve taps, folding and giving of the flag, a gun salute, perhaps a short address by active or retired military personnel, or even a "missing man formation" fly-by. Taps and gun salutes are often quite shattering to a family. The pastor will want to draw very close to family members to offer a comforting touch or even physical support during these moments. Ministers, who do not know what military personnel will say or what the actions of an honor guard may be, usually choose to conclude the Christian service with a benediction before the military rites.

VI. What to Do after the Funeral

In many communities there will be a meal prepared at the church or the family home for relatives and friends. The pastor is usually expected to attend and pray for the family at the beginning of the meal.

In future days and weeks, the attention showered on the family at the time of death will quickly fade. The minister will need to take special care to continue pastoral support.

Scripture Index

Genesis

1:26 280
1:27 121
4:10 53
5:1–3 121
17 149
17:7–9 116
18:25 . . . . 105, 122
30:1 99
37 47
37:31–35 46
45:5, 8 13
50:20 . . . . . . 13, 55, 277

Exodus

20:6 116
20:13 244

Deuteronomy

1 123
1:35–38 123
1:39 123
4:37–40 116
29:29 105

1 Samuel

16:7 290
30:4 47

2 Samuel

11–12 150
12:18–23 278

12:23 . . . . .107, 122,
141, 150
20 47

1 Kings

15:5 272
15:14 . . . . . 271, 272, 280

2 Kings

15:8–24 272
22 47

2 Chronicles

14–16 272

Job

1:21 . . . . 126, 192
2:13 107
9:29, 32–35 259
16:19–21 256
19:23–27 278
33:23–28 255
38:2–4 255
41:5, 9, 10b–11 256

Psalms

8 280
8:2 . . . . 113, 278
22:9 116
22:16 15
23 . . . . 243, 249, 278
25:8 122
27 277

30:5 136
31:5 266
31:15 246
42 277
46 . . . . 277, 278
51:5 . . . . 116, 122
62 277
62:5–8 279
68:4, 33 16
71:6 116
88 . . . . 232, 280
90 . . . . 277, 279
90:4 93
91 . . . . 277, 279
100 180–81
100:5 116
102:28 116
103:8–17 280
103:17–18 116
107:1 122
116:15 . . . . 133, 279
118 277
119 47
119:136 47
121 277
126:5 279
135:3 122
135:6 192
139 . . . . 34, 192, 279
139:1–6 28
139:11–16 . . . . 21, 22

139:11–12 25
139:13–16 278
139:13 25
139:14 26
139:15–16 25
139:16 . . . . 25, 246
139:19–22 32
139:24 31
145:1–13 . . . . . . 91, 278
145:9–13 94
145:9 92
145:13 92

Proverbs
15:2 107
18:2 107

Ecclesiastes
3:1–8 277
3:4 48
3:7 106
9:1–3 13

Isaiah
6. . . . . 160, 165
6:1–8 161
6:5 165
40:10–11 . . . . . . 147, 148
41:10 277
43:1 277
43:6–7 124
44:3 116
45:7 13
47:11 13
49:15–16 278
53:4, 10 15
54:13 116
55:6–13 279
57:15 236
59:21 116
61. 277
61:1–3 279
63:9 193

65:23 116

Jeremiah
1:5–8 278
1:5 . . . . 26, 116, 124
4:8 47
6:14 265
9:10, 18 47
9:20 47
31:15 99
32:28–29 116
35:19 116

Lamentations
3. 266
3:1–24 263–64
3:22–26 277
3:31–33 136
3:31–32 277

Ezekiel
16. . . . . 139, 140
16:20 . . . . . 116, 140–41
30:2 47
37:25 116

Daniel
12:1–3 279

Amos
2:7 47

Habakkuk
2:3 85
2:4, 20 248

Zechariah
10:6–7 116

Matthew
5:1–3 230
5:3 280
5:4 47

5:21–22 245
5:27–28 245
6:12, 14–15 50
6:19–21 213
6:21 39
10:29–30 12
11:17 113
11:28 259
14:29–30 246
18:1–5, 10 278
19:13–15 . . . . . 110, 278
19:14 141
21:15–16 113
26:31 15
26:36–46 266

Mark
9:24 . . . . 237, 246
10:13–16 . . 110, 111, 278
10:14 114

Luke
1:41–50 278
1:41 116
1:44 122
2:25–32 199
13. 64
13:1–5 278
16:19–31 82
16:31 82
17:2 113
18:15–17 . . . . . 110, 278
23:39–43 280
23:43 195
23:46 266

John
5:21–29 279
6:35–40 280
6:44 271
10:27–29 . . . . . 151, 280
11. . . . . 204, 205

11:1–44 59–61
11:3 81
11:4 . . . . 75, 76
11:6 81
11:11 75
11:14–15 75
11:14 76
11:15 81
11:17–44 278
11:17–27 279
11:17 81
11:21 75
11:23 75
11:25–26 84
11:25 205
11:32 75
11:33 62
11:35 73
11:36 78
11:37 81
11:38 63
11:45–53 82
11:53 82
12:1, 12 83
14. 249
14:1–7 279
14:6 . . . . 80, 271
14:27 279
20:1–11 279

Acts

2:23 15
2:38 116
w9:1. 244
10:21 244
16:14–15 116
16:31 . . . . 116, 141
17:28 244
20. 47
26:11 244

Romans

1:19–21 123
2:4 238
3:28 124
5:1–9 177
5:1 178
5:2a 178
5:2b 179
5:3–4 180
5:3 180
5:4–5 180
5:4 180
5:5 181
5:6–9 178
5:12, 18–19 116
7. 257
7:15, 24 257
7:25–8:1 257
8. 131
8:1 244
8:7–8 122
8:18 129
8:28–39 278
8:28 . . . . 13, 249
8:37–39 . . . . . . 187, 279
8:38–39 239
8:39 238
12:15 . . . . 151, 250
14:7–9 279

1 Corinthians

1:8 266
1:28 96
2:9 133
7:4 128
7:14 . . . 94, 141, 149, 278
10:13 245
13:12 . . . . 92, 93
15. 134
15:14, 19 257
15:20–26, 35–38 279
15:42–44a 279

15:51–58 279
15:57 . . . . 165, 182

2 Corinthians

1:20 249
4:14–5:8 279
4:17 125
5:8 . . . . 93, 194, 246, 279
7:9–10 47
11. 129

Galatians

1:15 124
5:16–23 46
6:2 266

Ephesians

1:4 26
2:3 . . . . 116, 122
2:4–5 54
2:5–7 280
2:6 272
2:8–9 280
2:8 124
2:12 140
3:9 12
4:32 54
6:12 27

Philippians

1:6 . . . . 152, 271–72
1:21 279
1:23 . . . . .125, 194,
246, 279
3:20–21 279

Colossians

1:16–17 12
1:24 126

1 Thessalonians

4:13–18 . . . 170, 278, 279
4:13 46

5:18 54

2 Timothy
2:8–13 279

Titus
3:5 54

Hebrews
1:3 12
4:15 151
7:26 114
9:27 258
10:14 280
12:23 124

James
1:19 107
1:2–3 125
4:8–10 47
4:14 . . . . 125, 278
5:1 47

1 Peter
5:6–10 152

1 John
3:1–3 280
3:2 93
4:4 233

5. 139
5:1 144

Revelation
6:10 53
13:8 15
19:1–8 280
20:4–6, 11–15 280
21. . . . . 139, 140, 223
21:1–7 280
21:1–5 221
21:4 . . . . 92, 201, 259
22:1–5 280
22:16 185

Share Your Thoughts

With the Author: Your comments will be forwarded to the author when you send them to *zauthor@zondervan.com*.

With Zondervan: Submit your review of this book by writing to *zreview@zondervan.com*.

Free Online Resources at

www.zondervan.com

Zondervan AuthorTracker: Be notified whenever your favorite authors publish new books, go on tour, or post an update about what's happening in their lives at www.zondervan.com/ authortracker.

Daily Bible Verses and Devotions: Enrich your life with daily Bible verses or devotions that help you start every morning focused on God. Visit www.zondervan.com/newsletters.

Free Email Publications: Sign up for newsletters on Christian living, academic resources, church ministry, fiction, children's resources, and more. Visit www.zondervan.com/newsletters.

Zondervan Bible Search: Find and compare Bible passages in a variety of translations at www.zondervanbiblesearch.com.

Other Benefits: Register yourself to receive online benefits like coupons and special offers, or to participate in research.

ZONDERVAN.com/
AUTHOR**TRACKER**
follow your favorite authors